THE WORM
IN THE APPLE

Also by Peter Brimelow

The Wall Street Gurus:
How You Can Profit from Investment Newsletters

The Patriot Game:
Canada and the Canadian Question Revisited

Alien Nation:
Common Sense About America's Immigration Disaster

THE WORM
IN THE APPLE

How the Teacher Unions Are
Destroying American Education

Peter Brimelow

HarperCollins*Publishers*

HarperCollins books may be purchased for educational, business, or sales promotional use. For information, please write: Special Markets Department, HarperCollins Publishers Inc., 10 East 53rd Street, New York, NY 10022.

FIRST EDITION

DESIGNED BY SARAH MAYA GUBKIN

Printed on acid-free paper

Library of Congress Cataloging-in-Publication Data

Brimelow, Peter, date.
      The worm in the apple: how the teacher unions are destroying American education/ Peter Brimelow.—1st ed.
      p.   cm.
   Includes index.
   ISBN 0-06-009661-6
   1. Teachers' unions—United States.   2. Educational change—United States.   I. Title.

   LB2844.53.U6 B75   2003
   331.88'113711'00973—dc21   2002027586

03 04 05 06 07 NMSG/RRD 10 9 8 7 6 5 4 3 2 1

For
Hannah Claire Brimelow
Winner
Principal's Good Citizenship Award
Mrs. Leber's First-Grade Class
June 7, 2002

Light of My Life

ACKNOWLEDGMENTS

Although I have been writing about the economics of education since 1983, *The Worm in the Apple* still took—to my great horror—some seven years to complete. During this time it was delayed by a dizzying succession of contingencies, of which by far the happiest was the marriage of my original *Forbes* co-author, Leslie Spencer, to Dr. James Huffman, now dean of the Northwestern School of Law of Lewis and Clark College, and the birth, in stakhanovite succession, of Spencer, Claire, and Meg. To paraphrase Gibbon in his *Autobiography*, I grieved as a co-author, I rejoiced as a member of the human race. The fortunate reader will still detect, between the lines of the present work, her lovely face, and equally lovely mind.

I owe a great and continuing debt to James W. Michaels, editor of *Forbes* magazine until 1999, for his formative influence on my career, for his decision to run major stories on the teacher union and the economics of education, which provide the basis for important parts of this book, and for many other kindnesses. I would also like to take this opportunity to thank here my other friends at *Forbes,* including Steve Forbes, who once even took time off from a stump speech to praise my teacher union writings when I would have preferred him to concentrate on running for president.

Along with my entire family, I owe another great and continuing debt for many kindnesses to James and Nancy Upham, not forgetting Nancy's regular, gently stimulating inquiries about the progress of the manuscript.

At a critical point, I was greatly assisted by the knowledge, counsel, and professional skills of Michael Antonucci, proprietor of the Sacramento, California–based Educational Intelligence Agency (http://members.aol.com/educationintel/index.htm). Mike has emerged as the preeminent observer of the teacher unions, and his weekly e-mail communiqués are indispensable. His assistance to me extended to drafting, in whole or in part, a number of the chapters that are at the heart of this book, including chapter 10, part of which was originally published in somewhat different form by the Capital Research Center. Generally, anything that isn't footnoted comes from Mike's files. (All errors, omissions, and eccentricities in the final version are, of course, my own). Without Mike, *The Worm in the Apple* would not exist in its present—or quite possibly any—form. I am most grateful for his contribution. Mike will doubtless wish to join me in expressing our appreciation to the teacher union officials and members for tolerating our parasitical presence with as much grace as anyone could under the circumstances.

I am also especially grateful to the trustees of the William H. Donner Foundation and to the very patient Jim Capua and Bill Alpert of FIDES, LLC.

An earlier book of mine, *Alien Nation: Common Sense About America's Immigration Disaster,* was criticized for not featuring the usual warm anecdotage but instead relying on data and analysis—which, as a financial journalist, is naturally my idea of evidence. Needless to say, I viewed this complaint as an evasion by those who disliked the data and analysis and have ignored it here. For this book, the data and analysis have been largely provided by my dear friend and longtime colleague Edwin S. Rubenstein, now president of ESR Research in Indianapolis, whom I warmly recommend to anyone wanting data and analysis, or even anecdotage on the right subject.

Originally, *The Worm in the Apple* was to be edited at HarperCollins by Robert Jones, who had handled my afterword to the paperback edition of *Alien Nation.* Tragically, Robert died, to the sorrow of the entire industry, just as we were beginning work. I was fortunate to have Tim Duggan and his assistant, John Williams, take over; they have displayed heroic qualities.

A special thanks also to my colleagues, Edith Hakola, executive vice president of the Center for American Unity, a lawyer who might reasonably have thought she had finally escaped labor law, and James Fulford, a fellow editor of vdare.com and unrivaled Internet sleuth.

Many of the individuals and institutions helping me with this book and the work that lay behind it are quoted or cited in the text, albeit often inadequately. I take the slovenly course of thanking them collectively here.

Thanks also to David and Peggy Adair; Valerie Anderson; Louis R. Andrews; Gordon St. Angelo and Robert Enlow at the Friedman Foundation; Dale Ballou; George Borjas; Arnold Beichman; Ann M. Burton; Herb Berkowitz at the Heritage Foundation; Julian Betts; Kevin Cherry at Empower America; Martha Cote; Darienne L. Dennis; Douglas Dewey and Rick Hough of the Children's Scholarship Fund; Joseph E. Fallon; Gregory Fossedal at the Tocqueville Institution; Ezola Foster; Valerie Friedman; Marshall Fritz; Donna Garner; John and Jeanette Goodman of the National Center for Policy Analysis (which puts out another great free e-mail communiqué daily on education and many other issues); Arthur Hu; Jerry Jesness; Greg Kaza of the Arkansas Policy Foundation; Lisa Graham Keegan; Manny Klausner; Luisa Kroll; Jonathan Leaf; Isobel Lyman at www. homeschoolingrevolution.com; John and Dayle McBreairty; Rupert Murdoch; Sally Pipes, Lance Izumi, Cindy Sparks and other friends at the Pacific Research Institute; John Raisian, Tom Henriksen, Bill Evers and other friends at the Hoover Institution; Llewellyn H. Rockwell Jr. and other friends at the von Mises Institute; Pamela Rosa; Terrence Scanlon and Andrew Walke at Capital Research Center; Matthew and Crystal Seavey; Bob Simmons; Gaylord Swim; Phil and Karen Tannenholz; Kevin Teasley at the Greater Educational Opportunities Foundation; David Theroux and Robert Higgs at the Independent Institute; Rick Wood; Andrew Wylie, Sara Chalfant, Jin Auh, and other friends at the Wylie Agency.

I know from unfortunate experience that some acknowledgments will certainly be missed out, and apologize in advance, particularly to organizations that were thinking of helping promote the book.

The immediate cost of a book falls upon the author's family. My twin brother, John, is my most devoted reader, and his unwavering support has been fundamental to me. I am also most grateful to his wife, Ruth Streeter, and their children, Hope, Julia Grace, Constance, and Benjamin, for much practical assistance.

My own children, Alexander and Hannah Claire, have been equally unwavering in their objections to this project; I hope they will one day think it worthwhile but, more important, thank them for their unknowing but profound inspiration; and promise them makeup time now. (Thanks also to their teachers, my surreptitious case studies.)

Seventeen years ago, I ended the acknowledgments in my first book by thanking my dear wife, Maggy, for coming with me on the great journey of life. Her journey has turned out to be crueler than either of us could have anticipated. Ultimately, the pain of cancer cannot be shared. But the courage to face it can be; Maggy's generosity of spirit has held our family together day by uncertain day. I here once more record my thanks and fervently endorse, on her behalf, the transcendent hope expressed in perhaps the greatest of hymns from the Welsh Revival:

> *Open now the crystal fountain*
> *Whence the healing streams do flow.*
> *Let the fiery cloudy pillar*
> *Lead me all my journey through.*

CONTENTS

PREFACE

Introducing the NEA and Some Other Things

> *. . . a flea*
> *Hath smaller fleas that on him prey;*
> *And these have smaller fleas to bite 'em,*
> *And so proceed ad infinitum.*

—Jonathan Swift

Action and reaction are equal and opposite, at least according to Sir Isaac Newton, the famous English physicist known (or, all too possibly nowadays, not known) to every high school student.

Which is a comforting thought when contemplating the seemingly irresistible rise of the teacher unions. The 2.6 million-member, $1.25 billion-total-annual-revenues National Education Association (hereafter lovingly referred to as the NEA) has been around since 1857. But for most of that time it was a professional association, concerned with standards, ethics, educational technique, but not with bargaining on behalf of its members—what a more recent NEA executive director, Donald Cameron, once derided as a "tea and crumpets" organization. The NEA even included school administrators, which meant some of its members were apt to argue in favor of spending on books and buildings rather than maintaining a single-minded focus on teacher salaries and benefits. It only finally morphed into a labor union, shedding its administrator members, in the early 1960s.

The smaller, 1.1-million-member American Federation of Teachers (AFT), which was founded in 1916, has always aspired to be a labor union. It was an enthusiastic member of the American Federation of Labor and Congress of Industrial Organizations (AFL-CIO), the labor unions' umbrella organization, whereas the NEA was not (and is not). But the AFT just plain couldn't get to function like a labor union until the 1960s.

The reason: public school teachers were public sector employees. And even labor union advocates like longtime AFL-CIO president George Meany and President Franklin D. Roosevelt viewed unionization of the public sector as unthinkable. A public sector union would just have too much power. From an economic point of view, all labor unions are engaged in trying to monopolize the supply of labor in their particular industries—in order to increase its price in the form of wages. But a public sector union would be a monopoly on top of a monopoly: Education is a government-provided service. (Indeed, public education is in on top of a third monopoly, because compulsory attendance laws mean that parents have to accept this government service whether they like it or not.) So public sector unions were prohibited by law.

But this inhibition—like so many others—abruptly vanished in the 1960s. In return for labor union support, President John F. Kennedy issued an executive order allowing collective bargaining for federal employees. Similar developments occurred at the state level. Most prominently, the right of collective bargaining for New York City teachers was won after a bitter battle by the AFT under its legendary leader Al Shanker in 1961. (This was the period that won Shanker his fearsome reputation. They even made a movie about it: in *Sleeper,* Woody Allen awakes from 200-year sleep and discovers that the world has been destroyed. He asks what happened and is told "a man by the name of Albert Shanker got hold of a nuclear warhead." Shanker thought this was quite funny.)

The NEA began to lose potential members to the AFT. Pro-unionization militants inside the NEA—mostly from the labor union state of Michigan, like executive director Cameron and future NEA presidents Keith Geiger and Terry Herndon, hence known collectively as the "Michigan Mafia"—were able to seize control. They transformed the NEA into a full-fledged labor union. NEA official histories, however, tend to omit the embarrassing fact that it was the AFT that led the way.

(After years of rivalry, the leadership and officials of both unions now want to merge. This has not yet happened at the national level, because of unexpected opposition from grassroots NEA members, but there have been state-level mergers in Florida, Minnesota, and Montana. The idea of one big merged teacher union distresses some conservative observers. However, it probably makes little practical difference, since the labor union mentality now permeates them all—certainly including many of the opponents of merger, who tend to be focused on turf considerations).★

Forty years or so is a very short time in the life of an institution. It's not an unthinkably long time in the life of an individual. (At least, to refugees from the 1960s, it increasingly looks like a thinkably long time!) Thus

★Needless to say, no one would have welcomed NEA/AFT merger more than I, because it would have made my task in organizing this book so much easier. As the NEA grassroots membership has declined to oblige me, I have chosen to focus primarily on the NEA. NEA members outnumber AFT members by almost 5 to 1 outside of the AFT's stronghold of New York State. Even in the rest of the country, the AFT's membership is heavily concentrated in big cities like Boston, Chicago, Philadelphia, Dallas, and Detroit, which have distinctive big-city problems.

The AFT is much more decentralized than the NEA. The AFT's national headquarters is relatively small and its locals are relatively strong compared to its state level organizations. AFT local presidents run their unions like independent fiefdoms. Without term limits to bind them—unlike NEA elected officials—they often serve for twenty to thirty years. This explains why some AFT locals can be exceptionally progressive (the Cincinnati Federation of Teachers approved a merit pay system) or exceptionally hidebound (the contract for New York City teachers, enforced by the United Federation of Teachers, is widely considered to be a major cause of the problems in that school system). But whatever they are, their influence rarely extends outside city limits. By contrast, unless you control a particularly large NEA local, you rely on the state affiliate, and ultimately on the national organization, to supply you with expertise, bargaining assistance, political funding, and other kinds of aid—including, of course, helpful hints on toeing the union line.

Paradoxically, the AFT has been just as visible in the public eye and while lobbying Congress and the White House. This is partly a legacy of its forceful longtime president Al Shanker, whose occasional politically incorrect utterings also caused the union to be credited with being more moderate. Today, under the administration of Sandra Feldman, the AFT's policies are virtually indistinguishable from those of NEA.

Though the attempt to merge the two unions failed in 1998, they continue to cooperate, forming a "partnership" in 2001 to deal jointly with specific issues, such as tuition tax credits, health insurance, and non-union teacher organizations. I feel confident dealing with them collectively as the "Teacher Trust." But from time to time, I do take an individualized swipe.

teachers now just finishing their careers could easily have begun it in the old, tea-and-crumpets, NEA.

What this means is that, as is the case with other new public policy problems, many of today's politicians and pundits reached adulthood before the new reality of the teacher unions had reared its ugly bifocals. Politicians and pundits are human—despite reports to the contrary. They have the normal human tendency to stick with what they learned in their youth. So they have been very slow to notice that the teacher union problem exists at all.

And the teacher unions have helped them not to notice. Shortly after I began writing about the NEA in *Forbes* magazine, I was contacted by a producer for a major network television news show. The producer was planning to do a special on the NEA and wanted, as is the amiable habit of television, to pick a print source's brain. Then nothing happened. Much later, in conversation about another matter, I got the chance to ask about the NEA project.

"Oh," said the producer, "we changed our minds. It turned out there wasn't one big teacher union, there were *all these little local unions.*"

The hydra-headed nature of the NEA, and the fact that all the local heads do ultimately and emphatically belong to the same, fiercely militant Washington, D.C.–based body, is carefully explained in chapter 4.

Television rights are available from my agent, Andrew Wylie.

Despite the condition of public education, and despite the central role of the teacher unions in the propagation of that condition, the investigative cupboards are bare. For journalists, as *Education Week* once put it, the teacher unions are "Education's Dark Continent."

Academics don't study the teacher unions either. "Teacher unions are a popular topic for debate in political circles, but they rarely are subjected to scrutiny by academics," wrote Jeff Archer of *Education Week*.[1]

"Everyone has an opinion on teachers' organizations, but we really don't know very much about them," says Tom Loveless, a public policy professor at the John F. Kennedy School of Government. "There's very little empirical evidence as to what their impact on education really is."

Nevertheless, as in Sir Isaac Newton's physics, the action of the teacher unions' emergence is now provoking a reaction—if not, as yet, an equal and opposite reaction. The press, the public, and politicians are slowly becoming aware of the union problem. This book is a part of that process. A small number of professional journalists are finding themselves able to make teacher union–watching part of their careers. The NEA, basically, is a parasite upon the body educational. But as Dean Swift pointed out in the verse used as an epigraph to this preface, even fleas have smaller fleas. And here we all are, munching away.

Comparing yourself to a flea might seem to risk some rude retort. But I'm not worried. No one in the politically correct teacher union world will want to appear guilty of species-ism.

So you think I'm joking? Aha! In 1993, the NEA's California affiliate, the California Teachers Association, published on the cover of its monthly newsletter a cartoon showing three witches around a bubbling cauldron. This was to illustrate the CTA's typically no-holds-barred claim that all sorts of undesirables would open schools if state voters approved that year's initiative allowing "education vouchers" (the much-debated proposal that some tax monies earmarked for education should be sent directly to parents, who would then be able to spend it on the public or private school of their choice). The next month, the CTA published an apology . . . to a self-described witch. She complained that the cover was stereotypical.

As a financial journalist, I first tasted the education establishment's blood back in 1983. The National Commission on Excellence in Education's report, *A Nation at Risk,* a powerful indictment of public school failure, had attracted enormous attention and inflicted upon the NEA, which of course denied everything, its first really serious public relations defeat. My editors at *Fortune,* where I then worked, decided they wanted an article on education and ordered me, in their grand top-down style, to write it. I humbly suggested that this was a poor idea because (a) I hadn't attended an American public school; (b) I had no children at the time and consequently no firsthand experience; (c) it was summer, and all the schools were closed. The editors replied: "That will make you objective."

And guess what? They were right. I simply approached education as if it were any other industry. The important issues were input and output. The question of how the output is achieved is actually quite immaterial. When you write about the baked bean industry, you don't debate the best way to get baked beans into the can. You look at the profit and loss numbers, to see which firm is doing it most efficiently.

Seen in this perspective, the problem of public education immediately becomes clear: it's systemic. There is no market process that rewards success and punishes failure. Or that even holds down costs.

But looking at education as an industry is profoundly unnatural for professional educators—and for the great bulk of the journalists covering education, who have a marked and distressing tendency to go native. Thus in early 1987, the late Fred M. Hechinger, then perhaps the dean of education journalists, devoted his *New York Times* column to an attack on another of my education-industry magazine cover stories—this time in *Forbes* magazine, where I had by then come to rest. I had made the elementary point that the current taxpayer subsidy of children's education does not necessarily have to be delivered through a government-owned distribution system, namely the public school system. After all, Washington is in the food stamp business, not the supermarket business. Give parents the money directly, let them spend it on the school of their choice, and an efficient school industry will spring up to rival the supermarket industry. (This, of course, is the essential argument for education "vouchers.")

Impossible, huffed Hechinger: "The proposal seems to overlook the fact that annual tuition at good private schools approaches $6,000 [vs. the $3,600 average annual expenditure per public school student in 1987]."[2]

Thus Hechinger showed that he was quite unaware of one of the basic lessons of economic history: the Model T Ford effect—that capitalists are happier supplying masses of cheaper, no-frills products, making more money on volume, rather than being confined to small, high-priced Cadillac niches like much of the traditional private school sector today. *But the Model T effect can only work if the money is put in the hands of parents (or not taxed away from them).*

Hechinger's name is now commemorated in the Hechinger Institute on Education and the Media, a part of Columbia University's Teachers College. Its function seems to be to encourage yet more education reporters to go native. The economics of education do not figure prominently among its offerings.

Another editor must be blamed for getting me writing about the teacher unions: James W. Michaels, the longtime (1961–1998) editor of *Forbes* and the creator of the modern magazine. In his later years, Michaels ran the magazine by lobbing thunderbolts down from his farm, about one hundred miles from Manhattan. As a taxpayer in this rural community, he became interested in why his taxes were always going up and in who was spending his money. The answer was obvious, as usual: school spending is always the largest spending item in local government budgets, averaging up to 40 percent, sometimes much more. And the school budget was increasing because, according to Michaels's local paper, "the teachers" and "teachers' leaders" insisted they needed more.

That's *more*.

M–O–R–E!

Who exactly are these "teachers"? Michaels asked himself (or, more precisely, asked me and my very able cowriter Leslie Spencer). It materialized, of course, that the debate in this country area was being driven by a powerful and well-organized teacher unions local. Community political leaders were helpless, if not actually subservient, before it. The hometown newspaper accepted its word uncritically and even cloaked it in useful anonymity.

From the economist's perspective, viewing education as an industry, the teacher unions is immediately seen to be a comfortingly familiar problem: it's just a form of restraint on trade. It's the public sector equivalent of the monopolies or "trusts" that excited such public concern almost exactly a hundred years ago.

The "Teacher Trust" lives by extracting financial rewards from society as a whole by virtue of its privileged position. In doing so, it leaves society as a whole (and, ironically, quite probably many individuals among its own members) worse off. Economists have a word to describe the money extorted in this way: "rent." And they have a word for the process of extortion: "rent-seeking."

This book aims to be the public sector equivalent of Ida Minerva Tarbell's muckraking *The History of Standard Oil* (1904), which first dramatized the emergence of the national corporation and set the stage for the antitrust movement. Standard Oil, too, was a hydra-headed entity, with the relationship between its various subsidiaries in different states not widely understood.

Additional note to readers (1): Throughout this book, I refer to "government schools" rather than "public schools." I do this because I have been told to do so by Milton Friedman, the Nobel laureate who is generally agreed to be the greatest economist of the twentieth century.

Friedman's point is that the term "public schools" gives a fatally false impression of what is really going on. "Public schools" are not public in the sense of being something you can use without cost. You pay for them in taxes, and they are very expensive. Nor are "public schools" controlled by the public in any very meaningful way. They are locked away in a tower of government regulations—heavily guarded by teacher union patrols.

"Public" does not sufficiently define the character of the schools," Friedman e-mailed me while I was writing this chapter. After all, he went on,

> public utilities [such as power companies] are private entities. If the word public were used consistently, Catholic schools would be referred to as "public"—everybody recognizes that churches are public [i.e., open to the public] institutions. The so-called public schools are in fact government entities. "Government" describes them: "public" confuses.

Additional note to readers (2): In case you're wondering, I now have two children, Alexander and Hannah Claire, who do go, with varying degrees of protest, to their local public school—are its customers, as we like to think of it.

Additional note to readers (3): Some years ago, I published a book called *Alien Nation: Common Sense About America's Immigration Disaster.* It said that current U.S. immigration policy was, well, a disaster. Jerry Adler in *Newsweek* called it "one of the most discussed books of 1995." He might more precisely have said one of the most *denounced* books of 1995. I have not changed his mind about immigration policy and in fact now edit a webzine, www.vdare.com, dedicated to moaning about it. But nevertheless—readers will be delighted, or disappointed, to know—there is *no mention of immigration policy* in this book, the genesis of which actually predates my writing on immigration.

Additional note to readers (4): Periodically throughout this book, I use the term "Blob" to describe the enormous, interlocking educational establishment that has developed around the government school industry—not just administrators and school boards, but also schools of education, private foundations, and of course the Teacher Trust itself. There is a pervasive common culture in this establishment and great inertial momentum, although dissidents and countercurrents can be found if you look carefully.[3] The term "Blob" was invented by William J. Bennett, President Reagan's long-suffering but unusually vocal secretary of education.

Additional note to readers (5): I also regularly draw attention in this book to parallels between, on the one hand, the government school system in general and the Teacher Trust in particular, and, on the other hand, the Soviet Union in general, and its Communist Party leadership in particular. Even a decade after the collapse of Communism, this tends to make sensitive souls like publishers twitch unhappily. So I want to put on record that I make this comparison clinically and without prejudice, purely as a matter of economic analysis. I am *not* saying the Teacher Trust actually is Communist. I realize that any use of such a metaphor, no matter how appropriate, will enable the Teacher Trust's more unscrupulous defenders to portray me as an "extremist." But, hey, they do that to all their critics anyway—see Chapter 9.

THE WORM
IN THE APPLE

1

The NEA, Representatively Assembled

Alas, regardless of their doom
The little victims play!

— Thomas Gray,
"Ode on a Distant Prospect of Eton College"

They're extraordinarily *fat,* for a start.

Not all of them, of course. But as you stand looking out across the cavernous Orange County Convention Center, where the National Education Association is holding its 1999 annual meeting—which it calls its "Representative Assembly" and boasts is the largest democratic deliberative body in the world—you can't avoid the curious feeling that you've stumbled into a sort of indoor rally for human hot-air balloons. An alarming proportion of attendees wobble and waddle through the teeming crowds of teachers—there are reportedly nine thousand delegates and several thousand guests—with thighs like tree trunks, bellies billowing, jowls jiggling.

You don't want to be mean, of course. But you can't help thinking: what sort of classroom role model for America's schoolchildren can these teachers be?

Perhaps the NEA Assembly really is Representative. Although it often comes as news to national journalists isolated on both yuppiefied coasts, as Michael Fumento has pointed out, three-fourths of the U.S. population is overweight and at least a fifth is obese, to the point where Europeans can pick out Americans in crowds.[4] But it's somehow surprising, given the NEA's unmistakably teacherish air of perfection and its habit, deeply irritating to political conservatives, of demanding perfection from America and the world at large. Resolutions passed at recent Representative Assemblies include:

- "The Association also expresses concern that the practice of capital punishment in the United States impacts individuals disproportionately on the basis of social class, race, ethnicity, and gender." (*Gender?!*)

- "The Association strongly recommends pre-service preparation and staff development for education employees that present strategies for handwriting instruction of left-handed students. Such training should also address sensitizing instructional staff to the needs of left-handed students."

- "The Association also opposes the exploitation of women as mail-order brides."

Moral of this story: the NEA is human. It's fallible.

But still, it's also, well, large. You wouldn't want it sitting on you—the way it's sitting on America's government school system.

The NEA Representative Assembly is held over every Fourth of July weekend. But the atmosphere is not patriotic but partisan. In trusting private, speakers are blatantly political and unquestioningly liberal-Democratic. They routinely denounce the "Extreme Right" and the Republican Party, somehow not bothering to distinguish between the two. State delegations hold caucuses and are seated in separate sections with banners and insignia, just like a national political convention.

This year, the Florida delegation seems to be holding a competition for the most insulting poster punning on Governor Jeb Bush's name. (Bush has especially annoyed the union by signing into law a program that provides for the assigning of a letter grade to every government school in the state. Parents whose children attend schools with a grade of "F" are to receive a voucher for any school, government or private, they wish to choose.) The posters get very insulting indeed. Sometimes they are in dubious taste. The role-model question crosses your mind again.

When the NEA speaks, politicians listen. Every year, the NEA summons some prominent national political figure to be its guest keynote speaker. This year, it is Hillary Rodham Clinton. She is beginning what seems likely to be a bitter battle to be elected senator from New York. Her entrance is ecstatically hailed. Her exit is bid an ecstatic farewell. But the hail is no more ecstatic than the farewell, because Clinton's speech is artless, policy-wonkish and, frankly, mildly anti-climactic. It might almost have been written by an NEA committee—as it probably was. Much of it is a long, detailed list of somewhat trivial NEA objectives that she dutifully endorses ("Phase out emergency certification! . . . Don't give new teachers the toughest jobs!")

The crowd applauds each one until Clinton plods into a passage supporting charter schools, albeit only if they are staffed by NEA members. This is greeted with stricken silence. Charter schools are another fashionable reform idea in education: they are public but independent of local regulation, often with significant private input (see Chapter 11). The NEA has endorsed them reluctantly—and only if they are unionized, naturally. But they are still viewed with intense suspicion by the activist rank and file.

Clinton and her speechwriters have betrayed a tin ear. You begin to feel that she will not prevail in a contest against a ruthless counterpuncher like New York mayor Rudolph Giuliani, her presumed Republican opponent. (In the event, Giuliani withdraws from the race because of ill health and Clinton, with teacher unions support, handily beats the candidate put up by the Republican machine.)

The NEA's intense partisanship is actually even more surprising than it might appear. The union's own figures have shown that about a third of its members are Republicans. Almost half have voted for winning Republican presidential candidates like Ronald Reagan and George Bush. There is even an "NEA Republican Educators' Caucus," although cynics wonder who is supposed to be influencing whom. (Answer: the NEA/REC's literature on "Organizing a State Republican Educators' Caucus" says sternly, "Keep uppermost in your mind that the goal of our group is to support and perpetuate the cause of public [i.e., government] education . . .")

You do see a few of the thin-lipped, aggrieved-looking student-leftist types you've grown to know and love when you were attending college. Arguably in this category is the well-dressed, carefully coiffed figure of Robert Chanin, the NEA's longtime general counsel and partner in the Washington, D.C., labor law firm Bredhoff and Kaiser, viewed by many as the power behind the NEA throne. He prowls restlessly along the side of the auditorium and eventually leaves abruptly, muttering in disgust at one of the many procedural tangles.

But, quite clearly, many of the delegates, bouncing beach balls in the aisles as the conference grinds down into chaos on its last day, repeatedly having to be hushed from the podium (role model again!), are just fat *and* happy. They are simply having a good time. The sessions are long, but there are knowing jokes about how much time the delegates manage to spend at Disney World and Orlando's other attractions.

In a restaurant the evening after Hillary Clinton speaks, you even get talking to a pleasant delegate who cheerfully allows as how she liked Clinton and also the keynote speaker the previous year—Bob Dole!

Bob Dole? You are fairly certain that the NEA's politically-committed leadership would not—in fact, no way, never!—have invited Senator Dole (R.-Kansas), the GOP's presidential nominee in 1996. But she insists that they did: she saw him! Later you find out that she is confusing Dole with Vice President Al Gore, a distinctly different politician. Indeed, Gore was actually Number Two on the Democratic ticket that ran against and defeated Dole.

Close—but, well, no cigar.

Again, it is important to be fair to this woman. Amazing as it appears to journalists, normal people are simply not very interested in politics. To them, confusing two presidential candidates from a past election cycle would seem a perfectly natural mistake.

Still, the exchange does raise one of the unspoken realities of America's government school industry: its workforce is overwhelmingly female. About three-quarters of all government school teachers are women. Arguably, this influences the industry's values, such as its marked preference for cooperation over competition. There is a serious argument, made for example by Christina Hoff Sommers,[5] that this is part of a societal syndrome that has become a serious problem for little boys, who find competition exciting and hate sitting still.

But more particularly, almost three-quarters of the NEA's members are women. And this presents a paradox. Research over fifty years has clearly established that women, in every age group and at all educational levels, are systematically less interested in and knowledgeable about politics than are men.[6] (This is not, of course, to say women are interested in nothing. They tend to have a strong concern with concrete practical matters that affect them directly—like education.)

Yet this heavily female union is one of the most political. And so are its leaders. The NEA's officers are typically about a half to two-thirds male. There has been no female NEA president since Mary Futtrell, whose term ended in 1989. Ironically, the NEA parallels the pattern found on the management side of government schools: the rank-and-file teachers are women; the principals and, above them, superintendents, are men— increasingly so as you go up the organizational pyramid.

Critics argue that the NEA is a political science textbook case: it exemplifies the "iron law of oligarchy," the tendency of organizations with large memberships to degenerate from democracies into elite-driven groups, captured by their career staffs and serving the interests of their professional leaders.

It is at least possible that one reason this has happened, and why the NEA's policy stands are so left-wing, is that a lot of the membership just plain *doesn't care* what games the boys on the permanent staff are playing, out there in the political playground.

After Hillary Clinton leaves, so do the journalists. All of them —like chicks following the mother hen. The press section, a sort of chicken coop alarmingly placed right under the (fortunately indifferent) noses of the NEA delegates, who tower up in serried ranks to the distant ceiling, empties out completely. For long periods of time, the Educational Intelligence Agency's mustachioed Michael Antonucci is the only inhabitant, making voluminous notes and chuckling darkly to himself.

Mike Antonucci is a journalist who has also been a member of Local 3 of the International Brotherhood of Electrical Workers in New York City and an instructor-navigator in the U.S. Air Force—he says he was dismayed to find his students couldn't do simple mental arithmetic. He set up his Educational Intelligence Agency research firm (www.eiaonline.com) in Sacramento, California, in 1997. His signature product is a free weekly e-mail report on the world of government education and the teacher unions, now sent to thousands of readers.

EIA has found it tellingly easy to scoop both the major media and their local counterparts. For example, EIA first appeared on the national radar during the 1998 efforts of the National Education Association and the American Federation of Teachers to merge. Virtually every news outlet assumed the merger would occur in short order. After all, the union leaders told them so. But Antonucci reported that the merger was in serious doubt. For months he published updated lists of which NEA state affiliates would vote for or against merger. The week before the NEA vote, while NEA president Bob Chase was still predicting victory, Antonucci published an article on the *Wall Street Journal* editorial page (June 30, 1998) predicting defeat.

The merger needed a two-thirds majority to pass. It failed, with only 42 percent of the delegates' vote.

The defeat of the NEA/AFT merger gave Antonucci instant credibility. His bulletins are now disseminated not just to educators and interested policy people, but at the highest levels of both major teacher unions and their affiliates

This year, Antonucci has discovered that the press, i.e., in effect, Antonucci himself, has been forbidden to speak to delegates on the convention floor. He has responded by announcing in his daily e-mail conference communiqué that he will come in early each morning before the Assembly session begins, so that his many union readers can introduce themselves and chat. Later, he learns to his delight that delegates are downloading his communiqués in the center's computer center, copying them, and circulating them on the convention floor.

Antonucci has a market niche because, despite the NEA's power, and its very visible headquarters building in Washington, D.C.—conveniently placed between the White House and the former Soviet embassy—it receives virtually no attention from the huge national press corps. There have been no full-scale profiles in the major media of NEA presidents Keith Geiger (1990–1996) and Bob Chase (1996–2002), nor of executive director Donald Cameron (1983–2000) or his successor John Wilson. The NEA top brass seems to like it that way—they even refuse to appear in *Who's Who in America.*

Journalists don't like to admit it, but their business largely consists of the energetic use of stereotypes. This is not entirely a bad thing. The word "stereotype" itself derives from the standing blocks of type that printers used to keep handy so that they wouldn't have to waste time repeatedly setting phrases and sentences that recur frequently—such as "teacher union," "public education," and "must have more money!" The reason stereotypes worked for the printers is that the phrases did indeed recur frequently. Similarly, referring to the word's modern use, it's a common (if whispered) observation that "all stereotypes are true"—there's enough truth in them to make them credible.

But journalists have no stereotype to help them deal with the teacher unions. There is no familiar morality play for them to fall back on—nothing to compare with "Greedy Company Sells Dangerous Pharmaceuticals Harming Photogenic Children, Requiring Heroic Politicians To Pass Strict Laws." Or "Two Controversial Candidates Face Off In An Election To Be Held On A Date Certain, With [Usually] A Clear Result."

So off the journalists scuttle after Hillary, cheeping and flapping their wings importantly, following a story that they—and their editors—recognize as a story.

The story of the NEA moves on without them.

There are a few NEA-watchers left. One is Charlene K. Haar, a neat woman with elegant cheekbones and green-hazel eyes. She smiles enigmatically as she navigates through the milling crowds, inspecting the vast array of booths set up by exhibitors and NEA interest groups, as colorful as the hucksters and jugglers at any medieval fair, writing occasionally on a notepad. A former public school teacher from South Dakota, eligible to attend the conference because she is a paid-up member of NEA (Retired), Haar is president of the Washington, D.C.–based Education Policy Institute—and, in effect, a spy.

EPI is a small shoot in the vast proliferating jungle of education organizations. But it offers a rare market-based critique of the education industry and incisive criticism of the teacher unions movement, including Haar's own exposés of the way in which, unnoticed, it has captured the PTA. (Yes! Those nice ladies who hold bake sales. See Chapter 4).

Haar is currently engaged in one of her favorite conference pastimes. Studying the exhibitors tells her who is slipping money to the NEA. At one

point during the NEA-favoring Clinton administration, federal govern-
ment exhibitors included the Social Security Administration, the U.S.
Department of Education, the U.S. Environmental Protection Agency's
Office of Environmental Education, *and* the EPA's Office of Indoor Air *and*
the EPA's Office of Solid Waste *and* the EPA's Stratospheric Protection
Division . . . all of them, of course, paying for the privilege.

Haar is also interested in exactly what covens of cranks are trying to
recruit the teachers of *your* child. In the peculiar atmosphere of the NEA
Representative Assembly, they're barely noticed. There's the loony-Left
Peace and Justice Caucus, of course, third in size after the Women's Caucus
and the Black Caucus. But this is the NEA Representative Assembly, after
all. Out there in the real world, however, parents are shocked to hear that
the Gay/Lesbian Caucus is the NEA's next biggest and, according to some
measures, its most aggressive. (By the 2001 Representative Assembly in Los
Angeles, the Gay/Lesbian Caucus's efforts to influence school curriculums
had become a real public relations problem for the NEA, leading to picketing by Christian groups and counterpicketing by NEA delegates.)

Haar also notes, caustically, the paucity of textbook exhibitors . . . as
usual. Publishers have apparently learned from experience that—apart from
ensuring that textbooks take the politically correct line on racism, homo-
phobia, etc., etc.—no one at the Representative Assembly is actually interested in education.

Also still on the NEA trail is Haar's colleague Myron Lieberman, EPI's
chairman, a tall, athletic, balding, bespectacled bloodhound—still a regular
tennis player in his late seventies. Lieberman has an extraordinary history: a
former teacher-unions activist, narrowly defeated in 1962 for the American
Federation of Teachers' leadership by Al Shanker, life member of the NEA,
former expert witness for the NAACP Legal Defense and Education Fund
in school desegregation cases in the Deep South, labor negotiator for
school boards, finally converted to a leading free-market analyst of the education industry ("I'm a slow learner"), author of key books like *The Teacher
Unions* (1997) and *Public Education: An Autopsy* (1993).

Mike Lieberman is a tough guy. Glowingly treated by Leslie Spencer
and myself in one of our *Forbes* NEA cover stories (*"Public Education . . .* is
a classic and unanswerable application of economic concepts to education"), he rewarded us with a letter to the magazine's proprietor, Steve
Forbes, demanding that reporting on the teacher union be improved. This

year, when NEA president Bob Chase briefly converted Representative Assembly proceedings into a sort of secular memorial mass for the Columbine High School massacre victims—who *included an NEA member!*—and at his request everyone, including journalists, stood for a moment's silence, Lieberman did not. He just sat in the press coop unmoving, with his arms folded.

Congratulated afterward on this stern sit on principle, Lieberman was dismissive: "It's just like some corporation using Columbine in their advertisements."

And so the Assembly shambles on. Occasionally, there are eruptions of obscure acerbity. Hundreds of speakers want to address a proposal to forgive a $2.3 million loan to Education Minnesota, the new union resulting from a state-level merger between Minnesota's NEA and AFT affiliates. Opponents object that the merger had violated the previous year's agreement that there should be no state-level mergers until guidelines had been established. After a fierce two-hour debate and a roll-call vote, the loan forgiveness fails, by a mere 40 votes out of over 8,000 cast.

Obviously, the prospect of an NEA/AFT merger continues to generate bitter—and near-deadlocked—division. (Equally obviously, the NEA hierarchy still supports merger. The Education Minnesota loan forgiveness was simply brought up again at the next year's RA, and, late at night, narrowly passed.)

Other divisions do indeed represent the vast, multitudinous nature of America. Delegates from the hunting states of the West are clearly uneasy during a gun-control debate. But their concerns are brushed aside by the big-city battalions. A California delegate (Oakland's Bob Mandel, a perennial aggrieved leftist) speaks in favor of a resolution supporting black radical Mumia Abu-Jamal, jailed for the murder of a Philadelphia policeman—interestingly, it materializes that classes about his case are being taught in some government schools. But a Pennsylvania delegate complains that in his city this will inevitably lead to the newspaper headline: "NEA Supports Convicted Cop-Killer." The motion is referred to the Executive Committee, where it will be quietly buried. A Hawaiian delegate supports the anti-abortion motion and, to everyone's horror, reads an excruciating poem written from the point of view of an aborted fetus. The prospects for an anti-abortion motion at an NEA Representative Assembly make Bob Dole's chances of a speaking invitation seem positively golden, but it is nevertheless an annual event. A motion urging closing of the School of the Americas, a counterinsurgency training school, in Fort Benning, Georgia, is actually defeated after the intervention of an NEA delegate with military experience. (Really radical political motions have been somewhat out of fashion at recent Representative Assemblies, perhaps a measure of the pressure the NEA is feeling—and, this year, of the looming presidential election.)

A Connecticut delegate, Walter Domeika, proposes two motions about members' relations with UniServ staff—the full-time state-level union workers, largely financed by the NEA in Washington, who account for much of the NEA's famed discipline and electoral muscle (see Chapter 4). One of Domeika's motions calls for "a code of ethics for UniServ staff." It is defeated without debate. But the other, seeking "to reduce the interference by nonelected affiliate staff in policy-making and governance matters," passes in a close vote. Most support comes from the Connecticut, Wisconsin, Pennsylvania, and California delegations. Friction between UniServ staff and union members is a quiet but constant undercurrent in NEA life, audible to few ears other than Mike Antonucci's.

As the Assembly reaches its last day, its inherent unwieldiness becomes apparent. The final afternoon session lasts a marathon eight hours. No less than fifty "New Business Items" are disposed of. Any group of fifty delegates can propose a New Business Item at the Representative Assembly, which in a meeting swarming with liberal activists guarantees a lot of motions that will irritate conservatives out in the real world. But the motions look somewhat less meaningful when you see the increasingly frantic stampede in which they are debated.

Or not debated—as the evening wears on, delegates make repeated attempts to suspend the rules and limit discussion. A few are successful, but proceedings still don't move fast enough. The hall begins to empty and pizzas are ordered by some of the remaining delegates, who are quietly beginning to starve.

Finally, the rules are amended to allow for voting on items without debate—if there is no objection from the floor. But NEA vice president Reg Weaver,★ chairing the Assembly during one of President Chase's rare

★In July 2002, Reg Weaver was elected NEA President, succeeding Bob Chase.

absences from the podium, misunderstands the motion. Instead, he requires a majority vote to debate each item. This makes the threshold for debate much higher. Every debate vote fails. So each of the remaining items is voted up or down, without debate.

A large and vociferous group of delegates gets increasingly furious. A near riot breaks out. It has to be quelled by Bob Chase himself, presumably yanked back from a much-deserved drink.

But the majority still wants to finish up and go home. So, without debate, the Assembly commits NEA to a grab-bag of policies, such as documenting "the positive impact of higher salaries on the quality of education employees and the performance of their students" and—mysteriously— promoting "the true beginning of the twenty-first century and the third millennium as January 1, 2001." Two items calling for boycotts of Wal- Mart Corporation and "any company when its owners or its major stock- holders have taken a favorable school voucher position" are referred to the Executive Committee, in accordance with NEA rules. (Mike Antonucci confidently predicts they will be buried too. They are.)

Then the 1999 Representative Assembly is over. Everyone reels out into the steaming night.

Jaded eyes in the press coop have finally located a pretty woman, pack- ing up in the Puerto Rican delegation—tight slacks, long dark hair.

The Educational Policy Institute's Mike Lieberman, with combative instincts whetted in many union faction fights, argues that even a small group of conservative teachers could have a big impact at the Representa- tive Assembly. At least, they could ask embarrassing questions about issues the NEA staff doesn't want publicized, such as how much the staff is really being paid.

Maybe so. The NEA leadership does have great power, because Robert's Rules of Order invests great authority in the chair. Many dele- gates are liberal ideologues, who would no doubt react with their usual indignation at the sight of any opposition at all. But a lot of delegates, as we have seen, are not political. And a vast sprawling affair like the NEA's Representative Assembly is probably too chaotic to be truly under any- one's complete control.

On the other hand, challenging the RA status quo would probably be like punching a pillow—and in slow motion, because of parliamentary procedure. You would need real dedication to want to do something like that to an innocent July Fourth weekend.

The Orange County Convention Center's newspaper reports that the following week's conference is from a very different America: fifteen thousand members of the Christian Booksellers Association. They obviously are not impressed by the NEA's claim to numerical bragging rights for its Representative Assembly.

But then, the NEA—or at least its leadership—is certainly not impressed by the Christian Booksellers Association either.

2

Something Is Rotten
in the American Education Apple

"Either you're part of the solution or part of the problem."

—1960s slogan

Coincidentally, across the continent in California, while the NEA's Representative Assembly was in full shamble in Orlando, reporter Emily Gurnon of the *San Francisco Examiner* was spending her Independence Day in the local shopping malls, asking teenagers a simple question:

Identify the country from which America won its independence.

Here are a few of the answers she got:

- "Japan or something, China. Somewhere out there on the other side of the world. It's like Independence Day for the presidents, or some shit like that."

- "It wouldn't be Canada, would it?"

- "I don't know; I don't even, like, have a clue."

- "I want to say Korea. I'm tripping." (Of course, in the Bay Area, Korea may seem like a reasonable guess.)

"One student wondered aloud whether the Fourth of July was somehow related to Pearl Harbor," Gurnon wrote. "Another was not sure whether our independence came before or after the Vietnam War."[7]

How has America, victorious in the cold war, the world's richest country and its sole remaining superpower, been brought to the point where its very origins are unknown to its young adults? (A few months later, a survey showed that *a majority of seniors in the top fifty-five colleges and universities* could not identify Valley Forge, words from the Gettysburg Address—or even basic principles of the U.S. Constitution.)[8]

You're pretty well assured of horror stories like this whenever you talk to parents or trawl into the press. Thus, about the same time, Susan Reimer of the *Baltimore Sun* agonized in print over why her teenage son had never heard the word "predicate." "At 15," she wrote, "he cannot tell the difference among 'there,' 'their,' and 'they're,' and I fear for his future employment."[9]

Similarly, you're pretty well assured of finding horror stories, in some ways more disturbing, about teachers. Many parents have savored the experience—exquisite if they remember their own school days—of getting notes from teachers that contain spelling and grammar mistakes. Andrea Peyser of the *New York Post* found a particularly striking case. She published excerpts from a note that one Brooklyn elementary school teacher had written to a parent. The unnamed teacher described this parent's child as "*very high proactive . . . Why is he not learning or learning so but so little, with my* *help,*" the note continued. "*How comes his past teachers have been passing him from grade to grade without he advancing or progressing academically* [*sic*]. *I will like to know what is causing the mental blockage.*"

A sound sentiment. But still . . .

Peyser asked a representative of the local teacher union to comment on the note. "With some of the lowest wages in the state, we have difficulty attracting and retaining the best and brightest teachers," explained United Federation of Teachers spokesman Ron Davis.[10]

But at the time, the teacher pay scale in the Brooklyn government school system ran from $30,000 for starting teachers to $67,000. In other words, experienced teachers earned more than twice the average annual income in Brooklyn, which that year was $29,642.[11]

It gets better. For reasons that will become all too apparent, teacher candidates in forty-one states are now required to pass a competency test before receiving a teaching certificate. Despite low standards for passing and multiple opportunities allowed to make the grade, such tests remain controversial. A group of minority applicants who failed the California Basic Educational Skills Test (CBEST) sued the state, claiming the tests were racially discriminatory.

Their case was definitely not helped by the deposition of one plaintiff, Sara Boyd. Boyd was a former teacher and guidance counselor who was required to take the CBEST test to obtain a school administration credential. She had received many awards and accolades during her years in the government school system. But she could not pass the mathematics portion of the CBEST.

In a videotaped deposition, Boyd mentioned that 6 of 80 teachers at her school were black—1 or 2 percent by her estimation. Then she realized that 8 teachers were black.

"So, in fact, 10 percent of the faculty is African American," said the defense attorney.

"No," Boyd replied.

"What percent of 80 is 8?" the attorney asked.

For forty seconds, there was silence. Then Boyd asked, "Can you rephrase that? I'm drawing a blank here."

The attorney complied.

Boyd answered: "That's about 1 percent."[12]

Endless eructations about public education in the United States have joined death and taxes as inevitabilities of American life. As noted above, the publication of *A Nation at Risk* touched off one such furor in 1983. Its repercussions are still being felt. But there was another classic case twenty-five years earlier: the furor touched off by the Soviet Union's launch of the earth-orbiting Sputnik satellite in 1957. After that national trauma, authorities as diverse as nuclear submariner Admiral Hyman Rickover and the Rockefeller Brothers Fund put out books—urging "excellence" and improved scientific education—that could be reprinted today.

Significantly, the Sputnik-era reforms turned out to have a remarkable tendency to be things that the Educational Establishment wanted anyway. The New Math reflects its perennial progressive search for ways to finesse the distressingly unreconstructed grind of learning. The move to larger school districts and comprehensive high schools, advocated in a seminal 1959 report by former Harvard president James B. Conant, was a happy justification, in the language of managerial efficiency and national emergency, of a trend favored by Educrats and already well under way.

On current form, the next national panic about public education will strike in about, say, 2008. I helpfully provide a non-Educrat wish list of reforms in Chapter 14, so that, this time, parents and taxpayers can be ready.

How bad is America's government school system? I think it's important to distinguish two distinct problems. First, there is the much-celebrated *qualitative problem*—epitomized by the education level of seventeen-year-olds in their last year of high school (the "output," as I like to think of them) as measured by objective tests. But second, and much less discussed, there is the *quantitative problem*—what input of resources the system is consuming.

As I noted earlier, this economic way of thinking is profoundly unnatural for educators. They just think that education, and spending on education, is good and more education, and more spending on education, is better. So it's perhaps not surprising, given this mind-set, that the quick answer to the question: how bad is the government school system? is as follows:

● *qualitatively*—very mixed

● *quantitatively*—catastrophic

The most popular measure of public education's qualitative problem is the average scores on the Scholastic Aptitude Test, taken by college-bound seventeen-year-olds. Average SAT scores did start to deteriorate dramatically in the 1960s and 1970s. There was no obvious demographic or other reason for this. The test was being taken by a larger and more diverse group of students, but these changes were more or less complete by 1960. The conclusion was unavoidable: there really was a decline in the quality of education—a phenomenon that education commentators now call the "Great Decline." The mounting public distress that eventually provoked *A Nation at Risk* was indeed justified.

The NEA responded by calling for the abolition of standardized testing.

It is a very awkward fact for the NEA that the "Great Decline" occurred at exactly the time when teachers were becoming unionized.

There were essentially no teachers in collective bargaining units in 1962, when average SAT scores stood at their highest point, on the edge of the plateau they had traversed during the previous decade. Twenty years later, scores had slipped down, by about 10 percent or so. At least two-thirds of all teachers were in collective bargaining units. Average Math SAT scores have since recovered somewhat—back to 514 in 2001, as opposed to 516 in 1967—probably still below levels of the early 1960s, but test recentering has made comparisons prior to 1967 difficult. Average Verbal SATs in 2001 were 506, however, still decisively below the 543 average of 1967.[13] And about 70 percent of teachers are now in collective bargaining units.

Correlation is not cause, needless to say. A lot of other things happened in the 1960s and 1970s, as NEA leaders incessantly point out. But it is suggestive.

Of course, average SAT scores are not a perfect measure of the government school system's output quality. For one thing, the average SAT scores that are usually reported in the media include private school students— whose performance is significantly better. Separating out the private school effect over time is something else that has been made more difficult by test recentering. But since 1996, government schools alone have consistently averaged four or five points below the consolidated average for all schools. Thus in 2001 the government school system's verbal SAT average was 510 as opposed to 514 for all schools; its math SAT average was 502 as opposed to 506 for all schools. Quite probably this sort of shortfall has existed for many years.

And average SAT scores can certainly be distorted by the proportion of seventeen-year-olds taking the test. More students taking the SAT arguably means a lower average result, as the test reaches further down the barrel of academic ability. But average SAT scores, whatever their weaknesses, do have one indisputable virtue: They are the single best predictor of the college grades that the test-takers will eventually achieve. So, in production management terms, the semiprocessed material being fed into the higher education hopper has recovered somewhat from the "Great Decline"—but is still flawed.

A broader measure of education's output quality trend is provided by the Congressionally mandated National Assessment of Educational Progress (NAEP). It looks at the performance of the average—as opposed to college-bound—student, using a number of tests ("Reading," "Mathematics," "Science" etc.) Unfortunately, NAEP testing began only around 1970. By that time, much of the "Great Decline" had occurred. Generally, however, the NAEP data supports the more recent SAT story: early declines, some slight late improvements, basically sideways movement, ho hum.

Thus seventeen-year-olds' Reading scores averaged 285 in 1971 and 288 in 1999. Their Mathematics scores were 304 in 1973 and 308 in 1999. Their Science scores, however, did not recover—305 in 1970, declining noticeably to 295 in 1999.[14]

However, overall averages can be misleading in a society as diverse as the United States is becoming because of federal immigration policy. The NAEP racial subgroups appear to have a particularly interesting story to tell. It is a long-established phenomenon, for which the reasons are disputed, that black and Hispanic seventeen-year-olds systematically score below white seventeen-year-olds. However, in the 1970s and 1980s, both black and Hispanic seventeen-year-olds staged sharp rallies in achievement. But their progress seems to have stalled in more recent years.

In Reading, blacks rose from 239 in 1971 to 274 in 1988—and then fell back to 264 in 1999 (whites scored 295 in 1999). In Mathematics, blacks rose from 270 in 1973 to 289 in 1990—and then fell back to 283 in 1999 (whites scored 315 in 1999). In Science, blacks rose from 235 in 1982 to 260 in 1996—and then fell back to 254 in 1999, actually below the 258 they had scored as long ago as 1969 (whites scored 306 in 1999).

In Reading, Hispanics rose from 252 in 1975 to 275 in 1990—and then fell back to 263 in 1994, only partially recovering to 271 in 1999. In Mathematics, Hispanics rose from 277 in 1973 to 292 in 1992—but then effectively stalled, scoring 293 in 1999. In Science, Hispanics rose from 262 in 1977 to 276 in 1999, but even here there was a brief sagging back to 261 in 1994.

Just as the Vikings were driven from their settlements in Greenland by the medieval multicentury global cooling that has been called the "Little Ice Age," so in the 1990s American minority seventeen-year-olds seem to have been affected by what might be called (in homage to the old Dustin Hoffman movie) a "Little Great Decline." Significantly, we can find no particular discussion among educators and policymakers of this latest unfortunate development. The Blob assimilates bad news slowly.

Chester E. Finn is president of the Thomas B. Fordham Institute and a longtime member of the National Assessment Governing Board, which oversees NAEP. He summarizes its overall trend among seventeen-year-olds since the end of the "Great Decline" in one word: "flat." And, as author of *What Do Our 17-Year-Olds Know*, he points out that, regardless of the trend, the absolute achievement levels of seventeen-year-olds are low. Only about 30 percent of American seventeen-year-olds would be able to read a magazine like *Forbes*.

Which means that even fewer of them could read this book.

One way of judging American seventeen-year-olds' absolute level of achievement is to compare them with other countries. This is a story for which the media does have a handy stereotype. Over many years, international comparisons in mathematics and science achievement have regularly shown America students, on average, at or near the bottom of the league of industrialized countries.[15]

Even isolated outbreaks of good news, when examined closely, turn out to be deceptive. Thus in the summer of 1997, President Bill Clinton got a lot of publicity for claiming credit when American fourth-graders ranked second in the Third International Mathematics and Science Study, familiarly known as TIMSS. ("There are a lot of people who never believed that the U.S. would score in the top two in the world on any of these tests. Now they know they are wrong.") But Chicago psychologist and education writer Barbara Lerner pointed out at the time that American fourth-graders usually did about this well on international tests. Where American students do badly is where it really matters—as seventeen-year-olds, at the end of the K–12 educational process.

"Older children resist," said Lerner.[16]

The 1999 TIMSS science and mathematics assessments for eighth-graders, released in December 2000, seems to bear out Lerner's analysis. In science, American students were only just above average—but this was an average that included poverty-stricken Third World countries like South Africa, Morocco, and Tunisia. Comparable industrialized countries like Japan, the Netherlands, Australia, and England were all far ahead. The TIMSS mathematics assessment summarized its results starkly:

It has been argued, at least in the United States, that recent reforms in education had their greatest impact in the earlier grades, and that a second TIMSS assessment could show better results for the eighth grade in 1999 than in 1995. Despite a modest, nonstatistically significant gain at the eighth grade, however, the data show that the relative position of the U.S. at grade 8 was below the international average in 1999, just as it was in 1995.[17]

International comparisons are, of course, difficult to make. One problem is that the United States really is, indeed, diverse. Thus the 1999 TIMMS science assessment included data on eighth-graders in several individual American school districts. One—Naperville School District 203, in the "Silicon Prairie" of Illinois' Chicagoland—was top, outperforming even Taiwan and Singapore, the countries with the highest average scores. Another—Miami-Dade County P.S.—was near the bottom, below Indonesia, Turkey, and Tunisia.

Similarly, the 2000 Program for International Student Assessment organized by the Organization for Economic Cooperation and Development (OECD—basically a club of the world's leading industrialized countries) found that out of the thirty-one countries surveyed, U.S. fifteen-year-olds ranked, on average, fifteenth in Reading, eighteenth in Math, and fourteenth in Science. But—in reading for example—as large a proportion of American students scored at the highest levels as in the top-ranked countries. What brought the U.S. average down was that American students also scored disproportionately at the lowest levels.

The *New York Times* quoted an OECD official suggesting that the United States should direct more help to its lowest-performing students and the Bush administration education secretary Rod Paige intoning that "average is not good enough for American kids."[18]

But in fact, directing "more help" to the "lowest-performing students" has been the Educrat policy since the urban riots of the 1960s. In the mid-1990s, nearly three-quarters of all federal spending on elementary and secondary education went to the disadvantaged and the handicapped; the Department of Education report *National Excellence* found that state and local expenditures aimed at the gifted and talented amounted to two cents—that's 2 pennies, not 2 percent—out of every $100 spent.[19]

Still, this is a script in which all roles are comfortingly familiar. The taxpayers' role is to cough up.

Helpfully, there is another way to put the performance of the U.S. government school system in perspective: graduation rates.

Although NAEP scores are certainly a broader measure of the output than SAT scores, the news conveyed by them is still only a partial picture. The NAEP test is administered to seventeen-year-olds *who are in high school*. And a surprising number of them just aren't. Again, the 1990s made a small—but significant and, once again, sad—contribution to this story.

The assumption that everyone should graduate from high school is quite new. In the 1899–1900 school year, only 6.4 percent of America's seventeen-year-olds—i.e., potential seniors—got a high school diploma. After that, the proportion started increasing dramatically, but at the beginning of World War II it had only just exceeded 50 percent. However, the high school graduation rate continued to climb until 1968–1969, when it reached 77.1 percent. And there it appeared to run into a ceiling.

During the years of the "Great Decline" in test scores, there was actually a slight deterioration in the high school graduation rate. By 1979–1980, it had slipped back down to 71.4 percent. Then, perhaps responding to the reform efforts provoked by the *A Nation at Risk* controversy, the high school graduation rate recovered a little in the 1980s, struggling up to 73.8 percent by 1989–1990. In the 1990s, however, it deteriorated again, down to 69.3 percent in 1997–1998—the lowest level since 1961–1962. Again, we can find little discussion among education commentators of this further evidence of a mid-1990s "Little Great Decline."

Partly, this may be because the deterioration in the 1990s was masked by an increase in eighteen- to twenty-four-year-olds taking the General Educational Development (GED) certification. If you lump both together, you get a more respectable "high school completion rate" that's about ten percentage points higher. And this is indeed the happy number generally cited. Unfortunately, there is long-standing evidence that employers do not view a GED as the equal of a high school diploma.[20]

And the fact remains that for about one out of four children, America's government school system is completely failing to function as advertised. These children are not going to the Senior Prom, Graduation Day, etc., etc., according to the much-mythologized pattern of American teenagers' lives.

They are dropping out. And, despite successive waves of reform, the government school system has been failing in this way, with about a quarter of its students consistently dropping out, for nearly forty years.

The much-vaunted post–*Nation at Risk* reforms haven't helped the graduation rate at all. In fact, if anything, things have gotten worse. The high school graduation rate has *never* been above the 77.1 percent reached back in 1968–1969.

When you see a failure as profound and persistent as this, you have to ask if what is being attempted is, perhaps, impossible. At least you do if you're Charles Murray, coauthor with the late Richard J. Herrnstein of the controversial 1994 mega-bestseller *The Bell Curve: Intelligence and Class Structure in American Life* (and, like me, the father of two children who attend a local government school).

"Maybe this is the best we can expect," suggests Murray. His point: *if* you accept that people vary in intelligence *and* that intelligence matters in doing schoolwork, *then* you have to accept that eventually an irreducible core of students might be reached who just aren't capable of earning a high school degree. *Or* you have to accept that the high school course has been dumbed down to the point where even average students, let alone bright students, are bored rigid—so that maybe *they* start dropping out.

(This is actually what happened in the case of Dr. Alan Bonsteel, the emergency room physician who as president of California Parents for Educational Choice played a key role in forcing Educrats to admit that the dropout rate is far worse than the senior-year dropout number they usually report. But it would be unwise to assume that many dropouts are potential doctors.)[21]

In *The Bell Curve,* Murray and Herrnstein noted that essentially all whites in the top quarter of the intelligence range were completing high school. By contrast, only about three-fifths of whites in the bottom quarter of the intelligence range were completing high school. ("Completing" means GEDs are included. And note that Murray and Herrnstein focused here only on whites, as in fact they did through most of *The Bell Curve,* in the fond hope that they would thereby be able to isolate the consequences of intelligence and avoid the emotions triggered by any mention of race.)

Of course, it's distressing that so many of these students are dropping out, given that education makes such a difference in their ability to make a living.

But it's also thought-provoking to consider how many are *not* dropping out. Murray and Herrnstein estimated that over 60 percent of white teenagers with IQs below 90 were completing high school. And so were nearly half of those with IQs below 75—despite being at or below what is considered to be the threshold of retardation, according to its clinical definition.[22]

What does this say about the quality of a high school diploma?

(You don't accept that people vary in intelligence, intelligence matters in schoolwork, etc., etc? Fine. But, in that case, what's your explanation of the government school system graduation rate's apparently impenetrable ceiling?)

Note that I am here endorsing one of the defenses often mounted by the educational establishment. There has never been a Golden Age of American Education. The ideal that everyone should graduate from high school has never even been close to realization. And it is further than ever from realization today. Where I differ from the educational establishment, however, is that I think the universal high school ideal may simply be impossible—that it stretches too far the meaning of a common high school educational experience. And I wonder if it's worth the effort and the anguish. Let alone the cost.

Whatever way you look at it, however, it is impossible to avoid the message of that impenetrable graduation rate ceiling: America's government school system is either broke (*sic*) and needs fixing—or it is wrongly designed in the first place.

There is another way to put the government school system in perspective: the numbers of parents voting against it with their children—by putting their children in private schools.

The proportion of K–12 children in private schools at first appears to be eerily stable—and low. It was 11.3 percent of total involvement in 1998, the latest year for which figures are available and a virtually identical 11.2 percent in 1890, the earliest year for which we have data. There were actually a higher proportion of children in private schools in 1959 (13.9 percent) than there are today.

But a closer look shows two powerful trends that have masked each other. Enrollment in Roman Catholic schools has suddenly (if silently) slumped—from a peak of over 12.6 percent of total enrollment in 1960 to a recent 4.7 percent. Enrollment in other, non–Catholic private schools, however, has soared, from 1 percent of total enrollment in 1960 to a recent 6.5 percent.[23]

Catholic schools are—were—private schools for the poor. The move to the suburbs that began in the 1950s drew off their traditional clientele. And the decline suffered by all mainstream denominations reduced the numbers of nuns and priests available to teach cheaply. (In fact, the NEA has been making noises about organizing lay teachers in Catholic schools.) But by contrast, richer families led the move to private schools that began in the 1970s, a decade that saw the "Great Decline" in government schools' educational output. Their motive appears to be less religious and more educational—which must be seen as a more direct reproach to the government school system.

On top of this, the home schooling underground claims anywhere between 850,000, according to the U.S. Department of Education, to 1.6 to 2 million children in 2001–2002, according to Dr. Brian D. Ray of the National Home Education Research Institute.[24] (Many children, of course, go back and forth confusingly.) That could mean that homeschooled children amount to a staggering 1.6 to 4.1 percent of all school attendees. Even more staggering, Ray estimates that's up from only 12,000 children in 1970 and only 40,000 in 1980.

And a final way to put the government school system in perspective: how much America has to spend to clean up the mess it leaves behind. Public universities and colleges spend about $1 billion a year on "remedial education"—teaching students things they should have learned in high school. *All* community colleges, four out of five public four-year colleges, and even more than six out of ten private four-year colleges feel compelled to do this. (But note that the $1 billion doesn't include the private colleges' costs, for which I couldn't get a good estimate.)[25]

"You would have to look very far and very wide to find a college professor who, at least in private, doesn't think there's been a decline in the quality of students entering college," comments Professor Steven Goldberg, a sociologist at City University of New York's City College. Goldberg suspects that test scores don't fully capture the decline:

It may be that today's students are the equal of former students in vocabulary, ability to calculate, and the like, but possess far less of the knowledge that would have been assumed of a high school graduate of forty years ago (because, for example, their reading comprehension is satisfactory, but they don't use it nearly as much to actually read) . . .[26]

And these students are the ones who have done well enough in high school to go on to college. Major American corporations spend $1,100-plus a year per employee on training too—which, if it holds across the entire labor force, could be as much as $156 billion a year. Some portion of that should probably have been completed in the government schools.[27]

The American government school system is huge and complex. It embraces 5.4 million adults and 47 million children, nearly a fifth of the population. Its spending in 1999 amounted to $389 billion or 4.2 percent of economy's Gross Domestic Product—GDP, the standard measure of the economy's size—making it one of the country's largest industries, over three times larger, for example, than the entire auto, bus, and truck manufacturing industry ($115 billion or 1.2 percent of GDP). Big ships notoriously turn slowly. But this is more like a big fleet.

Because of this hugeness and complexity, I feel the need to be moderate in my answer to the question: So how bad is the American government school system (qualitative division)? The recovery from the "Great Decline" is incomplete at best. There are some worrying recent developments in scores and graduation rates, especially for minority children. Clearly, there is no decisive trend of improvement.

On the other hand, we respect Charles Murray and Richard Herrnstein's emphatic 1994 conclusion—itself perhaps surprisingly moderate if you haven't read the book—in *The Bell Curve*: "*According to every longitudinal measure that we have been able to find, there is no evidence that the preparation of the average American youth is worse in the 1990s than it has ever been* [emphasis added]."[28] (Note the word "average"—Murray and Herrnstein did think that the education of brighter children had suffered, basically because the curriculum has been dumbed down.)

But it must be remembered that the "average American youth" was not graduating from high school throughout much of the twentieth century. The "average youth" may have been no better off—but he was not costing the taxpayer anything. In fact, he was working and contributing the economy.

When I checked in with Charles Murray about his current impressions of the state of the government school system, he replied with one word: "Disaggregate." Some parts of the system work well (Naperville School District 203). Some are appalling (Miami-Dade County P.S.)

Conclusion: The system's results in terms of quality are, to put it moderately, mixed.

One reason I am comfortable with this moderate conclusion is that I think the government school system's qualitative problem is overshadowed by its quantitative problem—its hoggish consumption of ever-increasing resources to do, at best, the same job.

Annual current spending per pupil in the government school system has risen inexorably and relentlessly for more than a hundred years. ("Current spending" excludes capital spending—that's to say, it excludes special expenditures like the actual building of a school, rather than the costs of just running it. It's the more moderate measure.) Annual current spending per pupil was $275 in 1890 and $7,086 in 1999–2000—adjusted for inflation and expressed in year 2000 dollars. That's more than twenty-five fold, or an average increase of about 3 percent a year. By comparison, the U.S. inflation-adjusted Gross Domestic Product (GDP) has increased only about 8.2 times, or an average of 1.9 percent a year.

Note that in 1982, the year of A Nation at Risk, inflation-adjusted per-pupil spending was just $4,903. Whatever else the wave of education reform triggered by the report achieved—or, more to the point, did not achieve—it certainly does seem to have succeeded in increasing inflation-adjusted per-pupil spending, by a total of about 45 percent over the next two decades.*

---

*There is an unpleasant possibility that standard government school statistics understate per-pupil costs for a variety of reasons, possibly by as much as 25–30 percent. These reasons include: not appropriately accounting for underfunded teacher pension obligations; interest on school debt; ignoring private donations, education-related spending by noneducation government agencies; exaggerating school attendance. Mike Lieberman raised this issue in his *Public Education: An Autopsy* (Cambridge, Mass.: Harvard University Press, 1993), pp. 114–142 and it is the subject of his forthcoming book, coauthored with Charlene Haar, provisionally titled *The Real Costs of Public Education*.

Because people are so used to viewing the government school system as a sort of religion or charitable endeavor rather than as an industry, they really do assume that education spending is good and that more is better—as if education spending were prayer or good works. Naturally, their political leaders follow suit. I still remember the astonished look that came over poor George Deukmejian's face, when, as a fiscally conservative governor of California, he came to breakfast at *Forbes* and happily boasted that nevertheless he had increased school spending—only to be greeted with snarls from the editors who were fully indoctrinated on this subject because they had just gone to press with a story about it. No consumer would boast about spending more on a purchase than was absolutely necessary. Why is education different?

The U.S. government school system's per-pupil spending is quite exceptional in the world. According to the latest per-pupil spending league table prepared by the OECD, only Austria and Belgium spent more. Comparable countries like Australia, Great Britain, and Germany spent significantly less—from as much as one-quarter less to over one-third less per pupil.

And it should be noted that countries that do spend as much per pupil as the Americans tend to spend much less on their higher—college-level—educational systems. Thus, according to the OECD, Austria spent only 1.5 percent of its GDP on higher education and Belgium just 0.9 percent. By contrast, the U.S. spent (including private colleges) 2.3 percent of GDP—more than any other OECD country except South Korea (2.5 percent of GDP).[29]

No country has an ideal K–12 school system. By historical accident, all developed countries have school systems that are more or less government-dominated, just as governments always run the mail system, and for no better reason.

But most countries with expensive per-pupil government K–12 school systems do at least get graduates who can function satisfactorily in a modern, industrial economy without further processing by educators—or subsidies from taxpayers. The Americans, however, get to pay at both ends of their education system—K–12 and college.

Another measure of the government school system's hoggish consumption of resources is personnel. Ever more adults are sucked into the school system, just like matter and light are steadily sucked into the Black Holes that astronomers have detected in outer space.

Most dramatically—and quite contrary to the popular perception—the government school system employs ever more teachers compared to its number of students. This trend has been in place for as long as data has been collected, but it dramatically accelerated in the mid–twentieth century. For every single (heroic) teacher in the government school system in 1870, there were 37.6 students. In 1900, every teacher was facing 36.7 students. As late as 1930, for every teacher, there were still 30.5 students. But by 1970, there were only 22.6 students. By 1980, there were 18.7. By 1990, each teacher was facing just 17.2 students. And the decline has continued. In 1998, the last year for which numbers are available, the teacher–student ratio was 1:16.5.[30]

If, as a journalist, you note this trend in print, you are immediately inundated with angry letters from teachers complaining that they have thirty-five or forty children in their classes and how would *you* like to do their job? (Answer: no. That's why you worked so hard in school).

There is no doubt these letters are genuine. They reflect very real personal and professional distress. But the point is that *the resources are available*—they are already in the government school system. The system has indisputably hogged an ever-increasing number of teachers. If that increasing number of teachers is not translating into reduced class size, that can only mean the system is not deploying them effectively.

Why not? The thesis of this book is that the teacher union is a reason. Not the only reason, of course. But definitely one reason.

It is also true, although guaranteed to annoy teachers even more, that educational researchers have been able to demonstrate little or no consistent relationship between smaller class sizes and student achievement.[31] This finding is again shockingly contrary to what everybody thinks they know about education—largely because no one realizes how dramatically teacher-pupil ratios have been falling for the last hundred years. But the finding is well known, if not enthusiastically hailed, by education experts.

It's more understandable if you consider the effect on an average student of having a class reduced in size within any practical range—from, say, twenty-five to twenty. Might help, might not. Many teachers would hardly notice. We're not talking about one-on-one tutorials here. But, across the whole government school system, a reduction from twenty-five to twenty necessarily requires an enormous increase in resources devoted to education. Right off the bat, the bill for teacher salaries alone would increase by 20 percent—even apart from the extra classrooms and support personnel needed.

Much of this educational research has been done by economist Eric Hanushek, now of Stanford University's Hoover Institution. Hanushek is not dogmatic: he speculates that in certain special situations smaller class sizes might well help, although the effects are difficult to measure. In conversation with us, he added this:

> Teacher quality is much, much more important [than class size]. Variations in teacher quality across classrooms simply dominate everything. In other words, the choice between a good teacher in a large class and a mediocre teacher in a small class is pretty clear. Unfortunately, the two aspects tend to interact badly. In order to reduce class size, you have to hire new teachers. And nothing ensures that the new teachers are very good.[32]

This is not a theoretical issue. Beginning in 1996, California's Class Size Reduction (CSR) Initiative, actually did attempt to boost student achievement by reducing the size of K–3 classes from an average of thirty to a target of twenty or fewer students. With a price tag in its first year alone of over $1 billion, or $800 for every participating K–3 student, CSR was "by far the largest educational reform in the history of this, or any other, state"—in the words of the Class Size Reduction Research Consortium, which was commissioned to provide an evaluation of the program. The consortium consisted of educational establishment organizations like American Institutes for Research, RAND, Policy Analysis for California Education, WestED, and EdSource. Not a right-wing nut in the bunch. The consortium's conclusion in 2002:

> *The researchers found no relationship between statewide student achievement and statewide participation in class size reduction.*[33]

But not to worry. CSR did mean jobs for about sixty thousand more members of the California Teachers Association, the NEA's state affiliate. And that meant the CTA received about $25 million extra in annual dues. So CSR wasn't a total loss!

Sheer teacher numbers do not fully represent the increase in resources sucked into the government school system in recent years. Teacher quality (at least in terms of education and time served) rose too. Between 1976 and 1996, the proportion of government school teachers with graduate degrees rose from 38 to 56 percent. Median teaching experience rose from eight to fifteen years.[34]

It just doesn't seem to have done much good.

Teachers are not the only adults sucked into the Black Hole of the government school system. Non-teaching staff—administrators, supervisors, librarians, guidance counselors, secretaries—are being sucked in even faster. In 1949–1950, there were 2.36 teachers for every non-teacher; in 1969–1970 there were 1.5 teachers for every non-teacher; in 1998–1999 there were 1.09—almost parity. And remember, the teacher-pupil ratio had been falling throughout this period. So the number of students for each member of the educational staff, teachers and non-teachers together, has fallen even faster, from 19.3 students to 1 staff member, a.k.a. adult, in 1949 to 8.6 students to 1 staff member in 1998–1999.[35] In other words, there is now one adult for every eight or nine children in the government school system.

That's nationwide, of course. From state to state, there are striking— and suspicious—variations in school system staffing patterns. One recent look showed that teachers as a proportion of adults employed in government schools varied from 63.3 percent in Rhode Island to 45.2 percent in Michigan. No fewer than seven states succeeded in having more non-teachers than teachers in their education system staff. (Besides Michigan, they were Oklahoma, Indiana, Mississippi, Florida, New Mexico, Vermont.)

Of course, these crude statistical categories can't be taken as an index of virtue. For example, the District of Columbia had a relatively high (56.8 percent) proportion of teachers. But its per-pupil spending is exceptionally high (highest among all states) and its student scores exceptionally low (second lowest of all states).[36]

On the other hand, in last-ranked Michigan, not only were only 45.2 percent of the adults employed in the system actually teachers, but also no less than 40.2 percent of those adults were at the district level or what DOE statisticians called "other"—mostly in county and state offices. This meant that two out of every five Michigan "educators" were not in schools at all.

They did not have to see (or hear) any children in the course of their working day.[37]

Just teacher unions operatives—come to ask for more money. Perhaps not coincidentally, Michigan is a strong labor union state and the birthplace of the "Michigan Mafia"—the clique of activists who converted the National Education Association into a full-blown labor union after 1960. By their fruits, ye shall know them—to quote an authority no longer cited in American government schools.

Teachers, incidentally, don't *at all* mind you pointing this trend out in print. In fact, they are very quick to write letters in support. Quite clearly, teachers are intensely aware of the failings of administrators in particular and the educational bureaucracy in general. It's one of the curiosities of the education debate that this contradiction within the Educrat establishment so rarely surfaces in public.

However, regardless of whether everyone is right or wrong to believe that more teachers relative to the number of pupils must mean better education, from an economist's point of view more teachers relative to the number of pupils can only mean one thing: *declining productivity*. The most basic definition of productivity is output per employee ("labor productivity"). And, obviously, because the teacher-student ratio has been falling forever, labor productivity has been falling forever too.

Thus, as we have seen, in 1970—approximately when the government school system hit what appears to be its graduation rate ceiling—there was one teacher for every 22.6 students. By 1998, there was one teacher for every 16.5. This suggests a productivity decline of some 27 percent. If you assess productivity in terms of the total number of adults in the government school system over the same period, it's declined even more—by 37 percent. (And remember, this assumes that the quality of the output—graduated students—remained the same. As discussed above, that may very well not be the case.)

A more sophisticated measure of productivity looks at output per inflation-adjusted dollar spent ("total factor productivity"). A rising star in this uncharted area of the government school system's productivity is Caroline Hoxby, a young black Harvard economist whose father was a Carter administration official (and whose mother was a schoolteacher). In an elaborate calculation, she has estimated that the government school system's total productivity has fallen by roughly two-fifths (39.4 percent) just from 1970–1971 to 1998–1999. This means, she says, that if some way could be found merely to restore school productivity to its 1970–71 level, then the average student in the United States would be scoring at an advanced level where fewer than ten percent of students now score.[38]

Alternatively, if test levels remained the same, increased productivity would mean that per-pupil costs, a.k.a. taxes, would fall.

But the government school system's costs never fall. They only go up. There are apparently never *any* productivity gains in the education business, despite radio, television, photocopy machines, computers, videos (which your children spend more time watching at school than you might think, or fear), and all the technological advances of the last hundred years. There are only productivity declines.

This is a truly extraordinary, indeed unique, situation. In contrast, since 1970, labor productivity across the rest of the U.S. nonfarm economy has *increased* at an average rate of about 1.5 percent a year.[39]

I tried this on the American Federation of Teachers' Al Shanker during a debate sponsored by New York's Manhattan Institute some years ago. You had to watch Shanker, who was a formidable debater. He immediately broke my hold by retorting that education should properly be compared with service industries, like banking, where productivity growth was much poorer.

I was impressed. The banking industry was actually quite a good parallel to the education industry: highly regulated, relatively skilled, labor-intensive, ripe for computerization (ATM could stand for Automatic Teaching Machine).

But when I actually looked at the figures, I found that banking productivity had increased so much from 1970 through the 1990s—an era not just of computerization but of historic banking deregulation—that if the government school system's productivity had matched banking's after 1970, there would have been *no increase in inflation-adjusted per-pupil spending at all.*

Overall, labor productivity in the service sector has increased over the last three decades by about 1 percent a year—less than in the economy as whole, but still positive. But even if you take a service industry in which productivity has declined, such as the notoriously fragmented restaurant business, you still don't find a productivity catastrophe to match that of the government school system. Thus, if the school business had matched the restaurant business over the three decades from 1970 to 2000, annual per-pupil spending would have risen from $955 (worth $4,280 in today's dollars) to $5,841 in the 1999–2000 academic year. But in fact annual per-pupil spending rose to $8,177.

In other words, because school productivity did not keep pace with restaurant productivity, taxpayers in 2000 had to shell out—per pupil per year—an additional $2,300 or so.

That's a lot of hamburgers. Or even schoolbooks. And the gap is widening every year.

Like we saw—a catastrophe.

Why is the government school system's productivity so catastrophic? Al Shanker would certainly have thought of an ingenious excuse. But, alas, this lean, intense figure—with his shock of gray hair, his office window shelf overflowing with just-published books, and his little-known interest in fine wines—died tragically of cancer in 1997. The education industry is a duller place without him.

To an economist, however, the explanation for the government school system's productivity catastrophe is immediately obvious.

"You have an industry whose basic technology hasn't changed for hundreds of years," observes William A. Niskanen of the Washington, D.C.–based Cato Institute think tank, former acting chairman of the President's Council of Economic Advisers. "It's not allowed to change. Only competition can force it to."

"One of us frequently tells legislative groups that with the possible exception of prostitution, teaching is the only profession we know of that probably has no increase in labor productivity in the 2,400 years since Socrates was teaching the youth of Athens," wrote Richard K. Vedder and Joshua Hall recently in the *The Independent Review*.[40]

"Everyone laughs, but it is true," adds the irrepressible Vedder, an economist at Ohio State University (where correspondence, hate mail, etc. should be addressed). "Actually, productivity in prostitution has probably risen relative to teaching, simply because of advances in contraceptive and disease prevention technology."

Vedder advocates for-profit schools to change the system's incentives and has written a monograph, *Can Teachers Own Their Own Schools,* arguing that privatization could give teachers a personal financial stake in successful education reform.[41]

The government school system is simply the most prominent outbreak of socialism on the American scene. (Unemotionally defined, socialism is the government ownership of the means of production, distribution, and exchange.) And not surprisingly, after a hundred years or so, the government school system is displaying the classic symptoms of socialism—as they could be observed in the economy of the terminal Soviet Union. In fact, Americans' endless eructations about their government school system point unmistakably to the same problems that plagued the Soviets' collective farm system, which suffered some eighty years of alleged bad weather and turned Russia from an exporter into an importer of grain.

The symptoms of socialism, count them:

1) POLITICIZED ALLOCATION OF RESOURCES

Socialist economies are ones that "put politics in command," in the words of Chairman Mao Tse-Tung. Investment decisions are made on the basis of what the political leaders think will be best, not on the basis of what entrepreneurs think will be most profitable—and hence what is most efficient economically, as indicated by the price signals the economy sends out. Politics are in command of the U.S. government school system. The teacher union—along with other bits of the Blob, such as school board associations, and opportunistic politicians looking for popular causes—totally dominates the school funding decision process.

Thus the California Teachers Association was a key supporter of 1989's Proposition 98, which called for at least 40 percent of the state government's annual budget to be spent on K–12 education. From an economist's point of view, Californians might perhaps want to spend this much on "education" (a.k.a. teacher salaries) or they might not. The politicized allocation process, however, does not give them any choice.

Similarly, "Special Education"—the education of children with disabilities—is now virtually dictated from Washington, D.C., via a series of federal government "mandates." These mandates leave your local school district surprisingly little room for maneuver (at least if it wants federal money). (It does). The mandates have been worked out in the usual lovable Washington process of logrolling and back-scratching between interested parties. These include ideologues who make the highly debatable assumption that educating disabled children in special schools is the moral equivalent of racial segregation and that such children should be "mainstreamed," kept in the ordinary classroom regardless of the staggering expense. "Most people think it [special education] accounts for about 25 to 30 percent of the increase in costs since 1970," Caroline Hoxby says.[42]

Maybe that money could be spent more effectively. But again, you don't have the choice—unless you want to try some logrolling and back-scratching yourself. (Good luck!)

2) Proliferating Bureaucratic Overhead

See above, pages 30–31.

3) Chronic Mismatching of Supply and Demand

In the Soviet Union, mismatching took the form of factories producing too many left boots and not enough right boots, etc. Eventually, it resulted in arteriosclerosis and breakdown. In the U.S. government school system, mismatching takes the form of periodic scares about school overcrowding, not enough math and science teachers, not enough foreign language speakers, etc. The ultimate results are often felt at the college level, where there is overproduction of Ph.D.s in disciplines like pure mathematics and English. The most famous of such scares, of course: the Sputnik crisis.

4) Susceptibility to Top-Down Panaceas, Usually Requiring More Input

Just as the government school system is subject to periodic Sputnik-style panics, so it is prone to periodic one-size-fits-all Big Answers, usually advocated by interested parties. More money (M-O-R-E!) is the all-time favorite, of course. In the case of the Sputnik panic, as we have seen, larger school districts were one of the Big Answers. Frequently, however, the Big Answer is pedagogical, involving some new teaching fad: Open Classrooms, New Math, Whole Language Reading, Cooperative Learning, etc.

Big Answers can be liberal or conservative (e.g., more school days, more testing—or, most recently, charter schools).

From an economist's point of view, of course, technical solutions to education problems should be discovered through a market process that involves producers (schools) and consumers (parents). You don't find fashionable journalists and politicians conducting passionate debates about new methods of producing baked beans. But we do have cheap baked beans. The market produces them. A socialist economic system, however, must rely on these top-down solutions because it doesn't generate bottom-up solutions. It can't. It has no market process.

In exactly the same way, the Soviet Union's agricultural system was racked by panaceas like Nikita Khrushchev's "virgin lands" program (the plowing under of previously undeveloped steppes) or the massive use of chemical fertilizer (financed by detente-era loans from Western banks).

Plus, of course, the Soviet farm system in the final analysis was backed by coercion. Peasants were jailed and even shot if they didn't produce. There is a distinct danger that the politicians' current enthusiasm for mandatory testing of students, in an environment where the structure of incentives is simply all wrong for both students and teachers, will be the American government school system's equivalent of coercion.

What about charter schools? They are supposed to be free from some of the top-down direction. And they are supposed to compete for students. But they are still part the government school system, thus avoiding a direct challenge to its entrenched interest groups—but leaving them still subject to capture and control. Ominously, there is an exact parallel to charter schools in the Soviet economic experience: *perestroika,* the attempt made by Mikhail Gorbachev to introduce market features into the economy while keeping politics in command. It failed and the Soviet Union collapsed.

Similarly, we expect that charter schools, although in themselves praiseworthy—as indeed are many of these education reform Big Answers—will not by themselves solve the government school system's fundamental contradictions.

5) Qualitative and Quantitative Collapse

"The tariff is the mother of trusts," a Gilded Age's capitalist once famously observed.

What he meant was that an effective monopoly—like John D. Rockefeller's Standard Oil trust—could not emerge if consumers were able to import the equivalent goods cheaply from abroad. But the tariff—customs duties imposed on foreign goods by the government—meant that imports cost more. Therefore they could not compete in price and undermine the domestic monopoly.

The government school system is the mother of the Teacher Trust. It is because the government school system is so centralized and politicized that the teacher union, as it has emerged since 1960, has been able to acquire so much power, and to extract so much money ("rents") from Americans' continuing and desperate efforts to educate their children.

Researchers are only beginning to realize the effects of the Teacher Trust. Caroline Hoxby has looked at the effects of spreading unionization on the (already far from ideal) government school system from 1970 through 1992. She found that, in any given years, unionization raised inflation-adjusted per-pupil spending by 12.3 percent compared with non-union districts and also—intriguingly—that unionization increased dropout rates by some 2.3 percentage points. Hoxby found that union effects are largest in areas where competition from non-union schools is smallest. As she concludes, in careful academese:

> In summary, the results indicate that teacher unions succeeded in raising school budgets and school inputs but have an overall negative effect on student performance. . . . This is strong evidence that teacher unions serve, at least in part, a rent-seeking purpose. Teacher unions are, indeed, a potential answer to the puzzle of increasing school spending and stagnant student performance in the post-1960 period.[43]

How does the Teacher Trust do this? The Hoover Institution's Terry M. Moe provides this vivid insight into the teacher union effect on the running of government schools:

> There are rules, of course, about pay and fringe benefits. But there are also rules about hiring, firing, layoffs, and promotion. Rules about how teachers are to be evaluated, and how the evaluations can be used. Rules about the assignment of teachers to classrooms, and their (non) assignment to yard duty, lunch duty, hall duty, and after-school activities. Rules about how much time teachers can be required to work, and how much time they must get to prepare for

class. Rules about class schedules. Rules about how students are to be disciplined. Rules about homework. Rules about class size. Rules about the numbers and uses of teacher aides. Rules about the school calendar. Rules about the role of teachers in school policy decisions. Rules about how grievances are to be handled. Rules about staff development and time off for professional meetings. Rules about who has to join the union. Rules about whether their dues will be automatically deducted from their paychecks. Rules about union use of school facilities. And more . . .

Moe makes this further shrewd point (my emphasis):

> . . . the teacher unions' greatest power is not the ability to get what they want, but rather *the ability to block what they don't want*—and thus to stifle all education reforms that are somehow threatening to their interests.[44]

And "all" means ALL. The president of the California Teachers Association recently announced this ambition to his local leaders:

> If we are going to be held accountable, we should bargain curriculum, rather than have it forced down our throats by some curriculum deputy superintendent that [*sic*] doesn't have a clue. If we are to be held accountable, we should bargain textbook selection. We should bargain lesson plans, portfolios, etc. We should bargain grading students. We should bargain everything that relates to the classroom and teaching.[45]

The inmates are taking over the asylum.

The Teacher Trust, as it has evolved over the last forty years, is essentially a parasite. Its effect is to weaken and deform the government school system—which is already quite weak and deformed enough.

And it is in this sense that the teacher unions can be truly said to be the worm in the American education apple.

3

What the Worm Says About
the American Education Apple

*Periods of disequilibrium are a necessary and
important part of a healthy learning process.*[46]   ✎

—From the *MathLand Guidebook*

• California Teachers Association president Lois Tinson had a simple
answer for why test scores remain stagnant despite ever-increasing public
resources devoted to education. Today's low scores, she explained, *are evidence of the high quality of today's system.*

That's right.

Tinson compared the disappearance of high test scores to the disappearance of the .400 hitter in baseball.

"The so-called decline in test scores is just the opposite," she said.
"Instead of an elite five percent scoring 1100, we have 50 percent or more
scoring 900. And that is not decline, that is a spread of excellence. Further,
just as the extinction of the .400 hitter reflects greater excellence in other
aspects of the game of baseball, current test scores reflect the greater excellence of public education."[47]

Perhaps politicians should take this same approach with education funding ("It's not a pay cut, Lois, it's a spread of wealth.")

• Top Teacher Trust officials say constantly that high-quality education is a product of high-quality teaching. "We wouldn't allow a brain surgeon to learn on the job," said Day Higuchi, president of United Teachers Los Angeles. "Why is it OK to let someone who doesn't know what they're doing teach our kids?" Kentucky Education Association president Judith Gambill flatly told the Governor's Task Force on Teacher Quality that "research has shown that quality teaching is the key to improved student achievement."[48]

But turnabout is not (apparently) fair play. In the very same testimony, Gambill demonstrated why we have such a problem promoting teacher quality. "*Individual student achievement should not be a factor in teacher evaluation or compensation,*" she said (emphasis added).

Er . . . if improved student achievement is due to quality teaching, why can't we evaluate and compensate teachers based upon it?

• The Teacher Trust does have a solution for all our teacher-quality problems: higher salaries. Raise the pay to a level where academically gifted people will find it appealing and they will fill America's classrooms. "*There's no such thing as paying teachers too much,*" said Adam Urbanski, president of the Rochester Teachers Association (emphasis added).[49] "Nobody wants to work in the gulag," said California Teachers Association spokesman Bob Cherry when asked about shortages of qualified teachers in state classrooms.[50] "For all the discussions about schools adopting efficient business practices, why should people believe the laws of supply and demand end at the schoolhouse door?" asked NEA president Bob Chase.[51]

Answer: *because the government school system is not a market.* Using higher wages to improve the quality of workforce depends on being able to distinguish high-quality candidates from low-quality candidates. High salaries will also attract hordes of the unqualified. But the government school system has an abysmal record of filtering them out. The Teacher Trust opposes it. High wages could also be used to improve workforce quality by paying more for teachers of subjects that are hard and in demand, like math. The Teacher Trust opposes that too.

- Union officials will concede the presence of poor teachers (though they never identify them by name). Just as long as you don't want to *do* anything about it. In Florida in 1997, only 0.05 percent of teachers were removed involuntarily from their jobs. In the state economy as a whole, 7.9 percent of employees were.[52] In two large counties in Georgia, not a single tenured teacher was fired over a period more than five years.[53] The New York City Board of Education, with over seventy-two thousand teachers, sought to dismiss only three of them for incompetence over a period of two years. The teachers' contract requires them to receive two consecutive "unsatisfactory" evaluations before dismissal hearings can start. In 1999, only six hundred teachers received an "unsatisfactory" rating. And even after two "unsatisfactory" ratings, the process has only begun. It can take up to eighteen months or more to fire a teacher, should he decide to exhaust all appeals (down from three years!). In the meantime, the teacher must be kept on the payroll.

Reported Anemona Hartocollis in the *New York Times:*

> Every day, 300 New York City teachers accused of misconduct or incompetence—more than are employed in many suburban school systems—are paid to show up in district offices and do nothing while they wait for a long-standing system of disciplinary hearings to grind on, sometimes for years. Most of the teachers spend the day reading the newspaper.[54]

The Teacher Trust even resists efforts to rid schools of *criminals.* Teacher Christine Bradley, convicted of her third shoplifting offense, was paid a year's salary and benefits in exchange for her resignation in Saranac, Michigan. "To pay an employee for being a crook is nuts," said Donald Leslie, one of two school board members who opposed the settlement. Firing her outright would have cost $20,000 in legal fees plus her salary. "Your hands are somewhat tied," said superintendent Bruce Chadwick.[55]

Taalib Abdulmalik, a history teacher in New Haven, Connecticut, pleaded innocent to five counts of fourth-degree sexual assault of students. While his case was pending, he collected his full salary and benefits. When his case came to trial—a year later—he pleaded no contest.[56]

When legislators in Maine wanted to conduct a onetime background and fingerprint check on state teachers, the Maine Education Association called it a "witch-hunt."

"I sincerely believe that this is an invasion of my privacy. I believe it's an unreasonable search and seizure of my person," said Brewer Middle School teacher Suzanne Malis-Andersen of a process that has been instituted in some form in forty states.

As for parents who fear the presence of child abusers within Maine's teaching ranks, Malis-Andersen had this to say:

"Living in a free democratic society has its risks" (emphasis added).[57]

Teacher termination procedures are particularly onerous in California. The hearing is "a daunting, bone-crushing experience," says Santa Barbara attorney Mary Jo McGrath. "It is as detailed, as voluminous and painstaking as the O.J. trial."

Others agree. "It is easier to take away a doctor's license to practice medicine in California than it is to fire a teacher," said Frank Fekete, head of the Kern County Superintendent of Schools' Division of Schools Legal Service.

A tenured teacher in California can appeal a firing by having a termination hearing by the Commission of Professional Competence. If she insists, three people can hear the appeal: an administrative law judge, an educator chosen by the district, and an educator chosen by the *teacher.*

The union insists that such ironclad protections are necessary. "If a child fails, or a teacher gives a failing grade to a member of an athletic team, parents may engage in a vendetta," explained California Teachers Association chief counsel Beverly Tucker. Teachers need a representative on the termination panel because, according to Tucker, "neither the judge nor the administrator chosen by the district knows anything about *the conditions in public schools these days* [emphasis added]."[58]

This idea that the rest of us are not competent to judge what goes on in the public schools is an article of faith within the teacher unions. "We must work together with a display of unity that *we,* the professional educators, know what is best for our students; that *we* know what is best for our schools and colleges; and, yes, that *we* know what is best for ourselves," wrote Massachusetts Teachers Association president Stephen E. Gorrie, in an editorial to his members.[59]

Which has to be judged against this eyewitness account of "the conditions in public schools these days":

> [A high school social studies teacher] stands wordless in the middle of the classroom as students yell, throw candy wrappers, apply makeup and ignore the assignment they have just received: an open-book test with simple multiple-choice questions pertaining to the Industrial Revolution. . . . students of high school age who cannot read beyond the third-, fourth- and fifth-grade levels, who cannot write a coherent sentence, who cannot add two fractions or subtract one decimal from another.

The principal of this high school *requested* that teachers write daily objectives on the board. One of his teachers filed a grievance with her local union. A union spokesman called the school's leadership "Draconian zealots."[60]

Clearly the union spokesman was an educated man. The teacher stood a good chance of winning her grievance. But chances are good she never learned who Draco was or who the Zealots were. It's fairly certain that her high school students have no idea what being a "Draconian zealot" means. The vocabulary of the average American fourteen-year-old has reportedly decreased from 25,000 words to 10,000 words in the last fifty years.[61]

• Even a teacher who has gotten through education school and the competency tests is not guaranteed to have aptitude or knowledge. The Connetquot school district in New York received 758 applications for 35 teaching vacancies. In an effort to narrow the applicant field, they administered a short version of a multiple-choice reading comprehension test taken from the state's old eleventh-grade Regents English exams. Just 202 applicants correctly answered at least 40 of the 50 questions.[62]

• Silver Lining Department: But the union will help getting rid of *some* teachers. There was one teacher in California who was regarded as an interfering fanatic. He violated rules of the contract. He reported teachers who were selling real estate in the teachers' lounge or calling in sick to extend their weekends. He was so hated by union officials that they circulated a celebratory note when he left the district. "We got him out!" it read.

The teacher's name: Jaime Escalante—whose achievements in teaching calculus to inner-city Hispanic students led Hollywood to produce a film about him, *Stand and Deliver.*[63]

• District officials in Franklin, New Hampshire, thought it would be professional for male teachers to wear neckties, and for female teachers to wear skirts, dresses, or slacks, i.e., no jeans. The union disagreed. "Wearing a tie doesn't get respect from the students. Coming to class prepared to teach earns respect. This is reactionary, not constitutional and not part of the bargaining [agreement]," said Franklin Education Association co-president Dennis Perreault.[64]

When a Los Angeles middle school set a dress code for teachers, CTA president Wayne Johnson was livid. "What have we got, an educational Taliban here? Are they gonna require *burqas* soon?" he asked.[65]

• Teacher John Anagbo stopped by the senior prom to wish his students well—during a labor dispute in which a New Jersey union had instituted a "work-to-rule" (teachers go home at the final bell, with no extra work grading papers, counseling students, meeting with parents, etc.). When union officials learned of Anagbo's "infraction," they sent him a letter of reprimand. "You must not realize that by your action you betrayed 649 colleagues," the letter read. "So do not be surprised, John, that your colleagues have lost respect for you."[66]

• In Connecticut, the Waterbury Teachers Association filed a grievance demanding pay for the additional two minutes a week the union claimed teachers worked that year.[67]

• At Port Huron Northern High School in Michigan, teachers took to posting a "Teachers Not Available" sign outside their classroom doors during their work-to-rule effort. Students responded by wearing buttons that read, "Students Not Available." One of the button-wearers, Janal Little, explained: "Although we support the teachers, we are just showing our disapproval of the steps the teachers are taking. I think they are using the students to try to get what they want."[68]

• When Florida's Citrus High School was forced to cut a drama teaching position, Judy Poplawski, the director of a local community playhouse, stepped forward to teach drama as a volunteer. Parents and students applauded. But not the local teacher union. Citrus County Education Association president Pam Pate claimed Poplawski was in a position to solicit business from students.[69]

This complaint was so transparent it prompted the local theater critic to lambaste the union. "The union's concerns do not seem to me to be those of well-meaning people working for the benefit of students and parents. They seem more like maneuvering in the never-ending game of education politics," wrote Jorge Sanchez of the *St. Petersburg Times*. He added: "It's time to fetch the hook and yank this thinly plotted sham from the stage."[70]

• In Vermont, former Air Force Lt. Col. Bill Corrow taught a course as a volunteer called "Conflict in the Twentieth Century." The Vermont NEA filed a grievance, saying it would allow Corrow to continue teaching only under supervision—and only if no credit were allowed for his course. The union insisted that if Corrow was going to teach, his working conditions, compensation, and benefits should "conform to the terms of the master agreement."[71]

• In California, the Fremont Education Association won a contract that "restricts the district's ability to hoard money in its reserves and forces administrators to share its surplus with teachers." Said FEA president George Gredassoff: "They can't create another reserve category for any purpose, unless the union agrees to it or it's mandated by law."[72]

In New York City, principal Alexander Cornbluth ran out of lockers for his students. He came up with a simple solution: assign them lockers in the back of classrooms. The union balked, saying the idea would require teachers to act as administrators rather than teachers for the periods when students were using the lockers. After five weeks of negotiations, it was agreed that assistant principals, deans, and security officers would monitor the rooms between classes. "For better or worse, New York City school principals are bound by a series of obdurate rules that prevent them from executing even the simplest decisions in an instant," opined the *New York Times*.[73]

• In perhaps the classic example of extreme interpretations of the teacher contract, the Jim Thorpe Education Association in Pennsylvania filed a grievance against the school district because coffee and doughnuts were not provided during a teacher training day. "It's simply a courtesy and a convenience," explained Pennsylvania State Education Association field representative Bob Whitehead. "Why stop now? And if you're going to stop, at least teachers have a right to anticipate it." After days of bad publicity, rank-and-file teachers forced the union to drop the grievance.[74]

• The principal of New York City's School for the Deaf wanted to replace thirty-five teachers who were not proficient in American Sign Language. The local union prevented him from doing so.[75]

• Former Washington, D.C., superintendent Arlene Ackerman wanted to alter starting times for the district's schools in order to improve bus service for special education students. The Washington teacher union shot down her proposal. "We have teachers living in Maryland, and they have their own children," said union president Barbara Bullock. "They drop them off in school. They have day-care problems."[76]

• Virtually every district in the country sets aside several days each year for teachers to receive continuation training. Pay schedules are designed to reward teachers financially when they reach specified levels of college credit. But usually there is little oversight of this training. The Ringwood, New Jersey, school board put a stop to what passed for professional development after discovering that teachers were being awarded graduate-level credits for bird watching and, according to the board, "attending the Passaic County Education Association dinner."

The local union vowed to fight the ruling. "I think it's kind of offensive from a professional point of view that people who work extremely hard should not receive some sort of recognition for that," said Ringwood Education Association president Mary Kunert.[77]

• The Kansas Association of American Educators, a non-union teachers group, wanted to distribute information about its services through the school mailboxes of teachers in the Olathe School District. The local NEA affiliate blocked the attempt, as its contract with the district gives the union the exclusive right to use the mailboxes.[78]

• Garbage In Department: First stop in the teacher pipeline: schools of education, or teachers colleges. The Teacher Trust has been working hard to capture these, which would give it control over the supply of teachers in the profession. It has been working rather less hard on improving what these schools actually teach.

"Schools of education are cash cows to universities," said Dean Edwin J. Delattre of Boston University School of Education. "They admit and graduate students who have low levels of intellectual accomplishment, and these people are in turn visited on schoolchildren. They are well-intentioned, decent, nice people who by and large don't know what they're doing."[79]

One look at what instruction is taking place and it's little wonder that new teachers are struggling. John Leo of *U.S. News & World Report* listed education courses offered by the University of Massachusetts-Amherst. They included:

> Leadership in Changing Times
> Social Diversity in Education (four different courses)
> Embracing Diversity
> Diversity and Change
> Oppression and Education
> Introduction to Multicultural Education
> Black Identity
> Classism
> Racism
> Sexism
> Jewish Oppression
> Lesbian/Gay/Bisexual Oppression
> Oppression of the Disabled
> Erroneous Beliefs.[80]

City Journal writer Heather MacDonald visited City College in New York to see how their education school operated. She found a professor talking about "building a community, rich of talk" and how prospective teachers should "develop the subtext of what they are doing." Each student wrote for seven minutes on "What excites me about teaching," "What concerns me about teaching," and "What was it like to do this writing?"

> After the students read aloud their predictable reflections on teaching, Professor Nelson asks: "What are you hearing?" A young man states the obvious: "Everyone seems to be reflecting on what their anxieties are." This is too straightforward an answer. Professor Nelson translates into Ed-speak: "So writing gave you permission to think on paper about what's there."[81]

What Heather MacDonald calls Ed-speak is really quite different from English as understood by parents and taxpayers. Take the example of Mathland, an elementary grade math curriculum cited as "promising" by the U.S. Department of Education. "The only rules in Mathland are the ones students invent for themselves," the guidebook tells teachers. It goes on to give them advice such as:

- *"Don't worry if the students' graphs are not exactly accurate."*

- *"Trial-and-error is a valid solution technique, allowing all students to approach the problems at some level."*

- *"Division in MathLand is not a separate operation to master, but rather a combination of successive approximations, multiplication, adding up, and subtracting back, all held together by students' own number sense."*

- *"This student solves the problem using a guess-and-check multiplication strategy."*

- *"Let the final conclusion about which answer is right come from the class, through discourse, not from you."*

- *"Do not feel that you must know the answers to every problem before class begins to discuss them. In fact, not knowing the answers ahead of time can be an advantage as you facilitate the discussion. Let the class debate the solution alternatives and through this debate convince themselves (and you) of the best choices."*

Here are some rough translations from the Edspeak: "A guess-and-check multiplication strategy" = "guessing." "Not knowing the answers ahead of time" = ignorance.

Experiencing this process at close range may be enough to turn even the most promising and dedicated candidate into a blithering idiot. But there is an inexorable drive, encouraged by the unions, to make an ed-school degree compulsory for everyone teaching in the government school system.

• Garbage (not to be crude about it) In Department: But how many teacher candidates entering ed schools are, in fact, promising and dedicated? Embarrassing questions have been asked about this for some time.

Early in 1999, ACT, Inc. and the Educational Testing Service, both major nonprofit institutions engaged in educational testing and research, released a report on teacher quality. The press release contained the headline

"Teachers' Academic Skills Higher Than Many Think, New Study Says."

The press release went on to claim that "the conventional wisdom that education students have lower standardized test scores than other college graduates is inaccurate for large numbers of individuals, especially those seeking licenses to teach in specific subjects, such as mathematics, science or English."

This is the sort of news that the Education Blob very much wants to hear. NEA president Bob Chase evidently read the press release. Barely able to contain his glee, he banged out one of his own on the very same day:

> It has become the biggest hoax since the Loch Ness Monster that teachers are low scorers on standardized tests. We applaud ETS and ACT for joining forces and putting an end to this myth. The report released today confirms that SAT and ACT scores and college grade point averages for prospective teachers seeking certification are as high, if not higher than, their college peers.

Which just goes to show that you can't trust press releases. Because, unfortunately for Chase, the actual report itself led to a quite different conclusion. Teacher candidates seeking licensure in math, science, English, and foreign languages did outscore their peers. But teacher candidates seeking elementary education credentials scored an abysmal 1012. And, according to the report, teachers with an elementary education license make up more than half of the teaching population.

Overall, teacher licensure candidates had an average combined SAT score of 1029, significantly *lower* than the combined score of 1085 averaged by all college graduates.

The report concluded flatly:

> In the career selection process that takes place during college, the group of students who choose teaching as a career, taken as a whole, are not as high achieving as their college peers with respect to SAT scores.[82]

Look out, worm! That's a Loch Ness Monster on your tail.

4

The National Extortion Association

Quit talking about letting kids escape.

—Keith Geiger, president of the National Education Association, denouncing the idea that tax monies now spent on education should instead be given directly to students to be spent in the public or private school of their choice; on the *Larry King Show,* November 10, 1992

As president of the National Education Association (1990–1996), Keith Geiger's style got a lot more polished than it had been when—as an up-and-coming leader of the NEA's militant Michigan Education Association affiliate—he astonished Walsh College economics professor Harry C. Veryser by gesticulating obscenely at him during an in-studio debate on the Detroit-area radio station WXYT.★

"He flipped me the finger when school choice came up," remembers Veryser. As an economist familiar with the concept of rent-seeking, Veryser is the author of a joke now famous among education reformers: He quipped

★Much of the material in this chapter is adapted from "The National Extortion Association," by Peter Brimelow and Leslie Spencer, *Forbes* magazine.

that the union's ruthless and insatiable drive for power and perquisites should earn it a new name—the National Extortion Association.

(Typically, when Leslie Spencer and I reported this little anecdote in *Forbes,* the NEA issued a denial. But in fact the show's host, the late Kevin Joyce, confirmed Veryser's account.)

This most powerful labor union plays very rough. Thus, in October 1981, Geiger was reported blaming "Reaganomics" as the Alpena, Michigan, school system shut down—apparently the first school shutdown for budgetary reasons since the Great Depression—after voters had repeatedly refused to increase local property taxes. (The blackmail worked: Alpena capitulated, along with several other Michigan districts threatened with shutdown.)

And in March 1993, Geiger was still at it: As NEA president, he appeared in person at a rally in another northern Michigan town, Kalkaska, as it ended its school year two months early, again after voters had repeatedly rejected tax hikes.

The Kalkaska shutdown got nationwide publicity. But the unreported truth is that it was little more than a union-orchestrated stunt. Kalkaska's school budget was not out of line with that of other districts in the region. Its main problem, since teachers' compensation makes up about two-thirds of all school budgets: a contract calling for 6 percent annual salary increases three years running. This in a poor rural area (average income about $22,000), where teachers (average income about $32,000) were already among the top earners.

And the school system could easily have made cuts, for example, in support staff or busing. Or it could have followed established procedures for going into deficit. The shutdown expenses amounted to $1.1 million. The teachers' retirement scheme, for instance, had to be fully funded. (The teachers themselves, of course, were eligible for unemployment benefits.)

"We coordinated the whole thing when the [shutdown] decision was made," boasted Allan Short, chief lobbyist for the Michigan Education Association. "We rented a [television] transmission dish and set it up there."

So complete was the union capture of Kalkaska's school board that an editorial writer from the *Detroit News,* which had watched critically while the NEA displaced the United Auto Workers as the principal power in Michigan politics, found his phone call asking for the board's viewpoint referred to the local MEA office.

Shutting down a school—with the inevitable accompanying TV shots of sobbing students and persecuted parents—is a classic example of the so-called Washington Monument strategy. A government bureaucracy that wants more money can often get it by punishing the public, for example, by curtailing a popular service like visiting hours at the Washington Monument. But the NEA had also made its point for other parent-taxpayers, and their elected officials, who might be tempted to trifle with it. Keith Geiger's implicit message to the voters: Never mind the nonsense about teaching as a public trust; pay up or we'll shut you down.

Interviewed in the NEA's breathtakingly palatial Washington, D.C., headquarters, Geiger said bluntly that other Michigan school districts also faced shutdowns—if their voters didn't cough up on cue. This is why the NEA fights all voucher and choice proposals that might allow students to "escape"—as Geiger put it in the quote used as this chapter's epigraph—to a private or non-union school. The children are needed as hostages.

With the economic slowdown of 2001–2002, teacher layoffs are once again in the news.

Watch for school shutdowns to start putting in their roughly decennial appearance soon.

"After the post office, schools are the most unionized activity in America," says Lamar Alexander ruefully. As U.S. secretary of education, and earlier as governor of Tennessee, Alexander found his reform proposals repeatedly blocked by the NEA and its Tennessee affiliate. "They collect a lot of money in dues, they are often the largest lobby in the state, they are very, very powerful. . . . Only a very determined governor has the influence to marshal enough power to overcome [NEA affiliate] opposition."

The NEA's intense commitment to partisan politics, which is both ideological and also its chosen method of getting what it wants, has been frankly described as "axiomatic" by longtime NEA executive director Don Cameron. William J. Bennett, another former secretary of education, says that, in contemplating the NEA, "you're looking at the absolute heart and center of the Democratic Party." (In Bennett's lexicon, this is not a compliment.)

Indeed, in some states the NEA affiliate seems virtually to have *become* the Democratic Party. Thus, in 1990 in Alabama, at a time when some 40 percent of the legislature were teachers, ex-teachers, or teachers' spouses, state Education Association executive secretary-treasurer Paul Hubbert won the Democratic gubernatorial nomination, while his staff was asked to raise $20 per member to finance his unsuccessful general election campaign. He ran again in 1994 but was defeated. (In fact, Republican Fob James won partly by capitalizing on education system difficulties.) Nevertheless, in January 2002, Gary Palmer of the free-market Alabama Policy Institute, which has a pretty good idea who its enemies are, wrote that

> there is no bigger mule in Montgomery than Paul Hubbert, head of the AEA. Hubbert's influence over the [Democratic governor Don] Siegelman administration has been so strong that a *Birmingham News* editorial referred to him as "Gov. Hubbert" during one of the special sessions last fall. And because there are as many as 40 or more legislators who are current or retired education employees, Hubbert has tremendous power, especially in the Alabama House of Representatives.[84]

On the federal level, the NEA endorsed its first presidential candidate only in 1976—Jimmy Carter, who in return promised to create the federal Department of Education, and did. But since then, the NEA has endorsed every Democratic presidential candidate. The quid pro quo was expressed with unusual directness by Bill Clinton when he appeared before the NEA candidate screening panel in December 1991: "If I become President, you'll be my partners. I won't forget who brought me to the White House." Typically, as many as one in eight delegates to the Democratic National Convention are NEA members—making it the largest single bloc, the union claims, at every Democratic convention since 1976.

In January 1993 the NEA celebrated its victory by sending posters entitled "Bill Clinton's and Al Gore's Most Excellent Inaugural" to more than twenty-six thousand junior high and middle schools. In January 2001, NEA had budgeted $200,000 for its inaugural celebration. But George W. Bush won, so it frugally spent less than $36,000.

It should be noted, though, that the NEA has shown itself quietly adept at influencing the Republican Party when necessary. Thus, in an early and highly symbolic test of strength after the 1994 Republican congressional sweep, a proposal to end NEA headquarters' District of Columbia property tax exemption—a privilege unique among labor unions, a relic of the

NEA's origin as a federally chartered Red Cross–type charitable organization that saved it some $2 million a year—was defeated because of key defections among Republicans from labor-union states. (Significantly, the NEA began making a "voluntary" contribution to the D.C. government, indicative of the pressure it feels itself to be under. Finally, it began to pay the tax.)

The NEA is generally prepared to be opportunistic in politics when the ideological price is not high. For example, in 1998 the NEA Illinois affiliate endorsed George Ryan, a moderate Republican candidate. It was rewarded by commission appointments and other considerations after the election.

But, significantly, the NEA will also pay an ideological price to defend what it considers its vital interests. Although the 1993 New Jersey gubernatorial election was widely viewed as a classic contest between a tax-raising Democrat incumbent (James Florio) and a tax-cutting Republican challenger (Christie Whitman), the NEA's New Jersey affiliate was officially neutral—i.e., objectively pro-Whitman—because of a dispute with Florio over pension funding. Not coincidentally, Whitman subsequently proved a great disappointment to education reformers. For example, she undercut Jersey City mayor Brett Schundler's attempt to introduce vouchers into local schools. And in her 1997 reelection race, the teacher unions was once again "neutral." (Whitman subsequently joined the Bush administration as head of the Environmental Protection Agency.)

Thus, in the final analysis, the teacher unions forms alliances with parties and can dominate them. But it has its own agenda. It might well be best considered as a political actor in its own right.

The NEA's persistent streak of left-wing loonyism is perhaps less obvious with the end of the cold war. Unlike in the 1980s, no nuclear freeze campaign operates from its Washington, D.C., headquarters. But the NEA remains committed to the radical premise that sweeping social reform must precede any real education reform. Blame society, not the school system. Thus NEA executive director Don Cameron was "chair" of the Center for Policy Alternatives, the liberal think-tank that virtually invented the hot new idea for picking the public's pocket: "economically targeted investing" (ETI), the use by pension funds of their members' money for politically targeted subsidies to various liberal-favored enterprises—and their indemnification by taxpayers for the inevitable losses.

And the NEA's zealotry still shows occasionally. Thus, immediately after President Clinton's inauguration in 1992, the NEA demanded and got the instant firing of Tom Tancredo, a former high school teacher and Bush Department of Education Denver regional office head, in revenge for his outspoken public support for educational choice in Colorado, and also possibly for his cutting DOE local staff by two-thirds.

(This may not have worked out quite the way the union wanted. Tancredo went on to head the Golden, Colorado–based Independence Institute, a vocal critic of the state's government school system. In 1998, running as a Republican in a Denver suburban district, he was elected to the U.S. Congress, where he has introduced legislation providing for federal tuition tax credits.)

In 1992 the NEA-affiliated California Teachers Association used unprecedented tactics to disrupt the effort to place a school choice initiative on the ballot—including blocking would-be signers access to the petition in shopping malls, allegedly sabotaging the petition with fake names and offering a signature-collecting firm $400,000 to decline the account. The justification offered at the 1992 NEA convention by CTA president D. A. Weber was frankly totalitarian:

> There are some proposals that are so evil that they should never even be presented to the voters. We do not believe, for example, that we should hold an election on "empowering" the Ku Klux Klan. And we would not think it's "undemocratic" to oppose voting on legalizing child prostitution.*

---

*The CTA succeeded in winning a delay, but Proposition 174, a plan to offer tuition vouchers to be spent by parents at the school of their choice, did get on the California ballot in 1993. The union had to impose a $57 special levy on its 225,000 members to defeat it. Other characteristic CTA capers: organizing high school students into a mass letter-writing campaign to protest Governor Peter Wilson's proposed school budget cuts, despite case law prohibiting school funds to support partisan activities; publishing in its newsletter the home telephone number of *San Francisco Chronicle* columnist Debra Saunders, urging its members to tell her in person what they thought of her *Los Angeles Daily News* article revealing that some teachers earned $90,000-plus salaries. "The CTA is the most brazen of all the NEA affiliates," says Milton Chapelle, a hardened observer of union goonery from his battle station at the National Right to Work Legal Defense Foundation in Springfield, Virginia.

The NEA is newer, bigger, more centralized, more politically influential, and in key respects nastier than is generally realized. And even more than traditional labor unions, the NEA is critically dependent on legal privileges and favorable public policy. The result is a weird institutional mutant: part labor union, part insurance conglomerate (of all things), and part self-perpetuating staff oligarchy. And part political party—as Edwin Vieira, a former constitutional law professor and key legal strategist for the National Right to Work Foundation, argued in a celebrated 1978 *DePaul Law Review* article.[84]

Through its collective bargaining power, this mutant has claimed privileged access to public policymaking. In the 1960s rush to recognize public sector unions, what legal scholars regard as a serious constitutional objection was never answered. Most public sector unions inevitably end up bargaining policy with government. Other concerned groups are ignored—such parties as students, parents, and taxpayers. This is arguably quite alien to American constitutional principles of equal protection and republican government.

Far more than other unions, the NEA saturates most of the country. Its power is felt almost everywhere. It has fifty-one affiliates in every state and some thirteen thousand local-level affiliates. In each community these may appear autonomous. But in fact the NEA plays a powerful centralizing role. "Keith [Geiger] personally contacts all local presidents who are on strike," Beverly Wolkow, hired by Geiger to be Michigan Education Association executive director, said at the time of the Kalkaska shutdown.

And, unusually for a labor union, the organization divides authority between quickly rotated elected teachers and school employees, such as the presidents, vice presidents, etc., and the permanent professional staff, such as executive directors, who critics say tend to control it.

Any teacher joining a local "education association," the level at which salaries are mostly bargained, also involuntarily joins a state affiliate and the national organization, which together consume most of the strikingly high membership dues. (Average: about $500 a year—more than twice what independent teacher organizations charge.) Imposing a single "unified dues" payment, thus extracting that state and national tribute automatically, was top priority for the 1960s union-builders. It was achieved in 1971 after bitter controversy: The NEA's Missouri affiliate, the Missouri State Teachers Association, eventually seceded from the national union over the issue.

Regardless of its needs, the teacher union's dues are a fixed proportion of the average teacher's salary. Thus, just as real estate agents have a vested interest in rising property prices, so does the union have a direct institutional interest in teacher salary increases. In 2002–2003, the NEA in Washington, D.C., will get $130 per member. But its projected dues income of about $300 million is only a fraction of the total dues collected at state and local levels throughout the union structure. Our estimate for the union's unified total: an impressive $1.25 billion.

The NEA's centralizing power is further enhanced by its partial financial support and effective control of the about fifteen hundred UniServ professionals, at least one in every congressional district. Their official function: to assist union locals with collective bargaining. But they also constitute what has been called the largest field army of paid political organizers and lobbyists in the United States, dwarfing the forces of the Republican and Democratic national committees combined.

In theory the NEA has internal democracy. But in practice it is controlled fairly effectively by its leadership, albeit tempered periodically by chaos. The union seems to have all the trappings of democracy. It has elected officers and representatives at several levels. Resolutions and business items are brought before these governing bodies. Elected representatives can be voted out of office—and they are subject to term limits (unlike the permanent staff).

But the *flow* is in the opposite direction. The NEA and its affiliates maintain all of the forms of representative democracy but none of the substance. In fact, the NEA has achieved a nearly perfect reverse democracy, where representation is stood on its head.

NEA members elect site representatives in the school where they work, representatives to the state council or assembly, and delegates to the annual Representative Assembly. In each case, the elected representatives are supposed to act as the voice of their constituents. In practice, however, very little meaningful representation takes place.

There are many reasons for this, but the most important is that teachers are simply too busy to spend much time worrying about what their union is up to. The vast majority are concerned with their classrooms and their schools. Unless union activities can be shown to make a difference in their daily work, most teachers ignore them. This indifference is not unique to union activities. Teachers show similar indifference to school board activities, district programs, and state legislation—never mind federal activities and pronouncements.

The NEA has had such success in equating itself with "the teachers" in the public mind that even union critics fail to differentiate between the views of the NEA headquarters, its affiliates, their staffs, their locals, and their rank-and-file members. Union propaganda, and countervailing criticism from education reform organizations, assumes that whatever comes out of union headquarters must reflect the feelings of classroom teachers themselves. But in fact EIA's Mike Antonucci says that it's not at all unusual for teachers to be uncertain to which of the two major unions they belong.

Apathy begets oligarchy. Sometimes, a conscientious union representative will spend time learning the views of his colleagues. (Or of her colleagues—but union activists tend to be men, especially as you go up the hierarchy.) Most, however, don't worry about it. The representative's opportunities for regular meetings or communications with his "constituents" are quite rare. The representative has plenty of opportunity, however, to meet with other reps and union superiors at regional meetings, conferences, or assemblies. Since these people are well versed in union issues, the body becomes cliquish and insular.

The local representative has entered the union's magic circle. He rapidly falls under its spell.

Example: the actions of the California Teachers Association during the Proposition 226 "Paycheck Protection" campaign of 1998. This measure—long advocated by conservative groups—would have required labor unions in the state to get annual written permission from their members before using funds for political purposes. Unions find this irritating and quite probably have a healthy suspicion that their members wouldn't cough up, if given the chance. In January, the 660 members of the CTA State Council voted unanimously to oppose the initiative. That's right—unanimously. CTA even sent out a press release boasting of its unanimity.

But at a union conference in March, where officials thought only union ears were listening, a speaker from the NEA told the assembled activists that internal polls showed CTA member *support* for the initiative at 70 percent. David Sanchez, now secretary-treasurer of the CTA, remarked from the back of the room that the figure was down from 76 percent support.[85]

So, while three-quarters of the membership supported Paycheck Protection, their "representatives" were voting unanimously not just to oppose it, but also to *spend the dues of these same members to oppose it.*

But that wasn't the ultimate irony. The State Council also voted to spend $500,000 on an "internal campaign." That is, the council voted to spend a half-million dollars in dues to *convince its own constituents—with their own money—that they were wrong to support the initiative.*

And this "internal campaign" worked. Exit polls indicated that CTA had managed to swing about 40 percent of the member vote from support to opposition. (But note that about three out of ten CTA members still voted for Paycheck Protection.)

This is far from the sole example. In March 1999, the CTA State Council agreed to support a ballot initiative that a union task force had drafted, and appropriated $1.5 million to spend on the campaign, without a single council member having read the text of the measure. Nor did the CTA leadership feel compelled to disseminate copies of the initiative prior to the vote.

Who were the "representatives" actually representing? Simple. They were representing the people who would advance them up the union ladder.

California is typical. CTA members elect the State Council directly, but the State Council elects the twenty-four-member board of directors, the president, vice president, and secretary-treasurer. Thus the NEA state councils and delegate assemblies elect the union's highest officials, just as U.S. senators used to be elected "indirectly," by state legislatures. But, unlike state legislatures, most NEA state councils and delegate assemblies meet no more than four times a year, and only for a few days at a time. Some, modeled after the NEA Representative Assembly, meet only once a year. Boards of directors may meet monthly, sometimes less often. Consequently, their authority over the day-to-day running of the union is limited. And the overwhelming tendency is to rubber-stamp the decisions of higher-ups.

Each member of an NEA affiliate's state board of directors represents a large geographic region. But since they are not elected directly by union members, their connection with their constituents becomes tenuous. As the union officer moves from the Representative Assembly to the board of directors, he becomes more absorbed by the status quo and less likely to cause trouble.

It's a living. An NEA affiliate's state board member receives a cash stipend from the union, extended periods of release time for union duties—up to seventy-two days in California—and a host of fringe benefits. A state board member receives opportunities to act as a spokesperson for the organization, to work with the staff, and to get noticed by the executives. A "team player" can score enough points to work his way into a run for higher office.

Having been elected to higher office, the union activist becomes a de facto union employee. He receives a generous salary and a dizzying array of perks. More important, he becomes part of the inner circle—the ruling politburo, as it were—consisting of the three executive officers (president, vice president, and secretary-treasurer), the permanent executive director or chief of staff, and the most powerful department heads. These are the people who set the day-to-day policies, allocate the resources, and assign the staff. The president of an NEA state affiliate becomes a powerful player (a "big mule" in Alabama terms) in the education policy and the politics of state government. His personal relationships with the governor, key legislative leaders, and other members of the state's educational establishment have a profound effect on whether budgets are passed, bills make it out of committee, and regulations are enforced.

Election to the presidency of the NEA or a state affiliate more closely resembles the inner workings of the Vatican's College of Cardinals than democracy in the free-for-all American tradition. Once you're in, you're in. For example, in California in 1999, CTA vice president Wayne Johnson was elected president. Secretary-treasurer Barbara Kerr was elected vice president. David Sanchez, who held a seat on the CTA Board of Directors, was elected secretary-treasurer. The same pattern occurred in Connecticut and Pennsylvania. In Illinois, the secretary-treasurer defeated the vice president for the presidency—a big upset! In North Carolina, the president and vice president ran for each other's jobs. They both won.

Of the forty-three state affiliate presidents whose previous positions could be determined in 1999, twenty-six (60.5 percent) were sitting vice presidents of the affiliate when they ran for and won the presidency. Another four were sitting secretary-treasurers. Five others were on the

NEA Board of Directors. Only eight presidents won their jobs from out-side state headquarters—and they were usually already a member of the state board or the president of a large local.

NEA president Bob Chase is the model union man. He won the pres-idency after eight years as NEA vice president. He succeeded Keith Geiger, who was also NEA vice president before his accession. Chase's opponent was Marilyn Monahan, then the sitting NEA secretary-treasurer.

Before becoming NEA vice president, Chase had climbed up the union ladder via these rungs (given in descending order):

- member of the NEA Executive Committee

- member of the NEA Board of Directors

- president of the Connecticut Education Association

- vice president of the Connecticut Education Associa-tion

- member of the CEA Board of Directors

- president of NEA Danbury

- vice president of NEA Danbury

- NEA Danbury grievance chairman

- site rep at Rogers Park Middle School

Chase has said he became site rep in his second year as a teacher. Once he became president of NEA Danbury, he started to get extensive release time from the classroom. The Educational Intelligence Agency's Mike Antonucci says derisively he has taught class more recently than Chase has.

But how does this elective monarchy exert control over such a large group? Sure, the representative bodies meet infrequently. Still, they do meet. Can't they reject decisions made by their leaders?

Technically, they can. And sometimes they do. But NEA's governance structure is designed for consensus, not confrontation. As we have seen, almost 10,000 delegates attend the annual NEA Representative Assembly. Anyone can run for delegate, but in practice it is the people who already hold union office who tend to run and win. With such a gigantic group, and such a limited period of time, meaningful debate is impossible. It's ironic that the NEA insists smaller classes are necessary for good education, then puts 10,000 people in one room for four days and claims they can democratically decide the detailed course of the union for the next year.

As unwieldy as the Representative Assembly is, it is less than two-thirds the size it could be. According to the NEA constitution, one state delegate is allowed for every 1,000 active members, and one local delegate for every 150 active members. Theoretically, the RA could have over 17,000 delegates.

But even the RA's current size is difficult to maintain. In 1999, the Michigan Education Association elected 619 delegates to the RA. But only 468 actually attended. Across the country, 967 elected delegates were no-shows.

And the delegates attending the RA may not actually, well, *attend*. Thus the Kentucky Education Association has approved a policy that would withhold 20 percent of a delegate's expense money if he or she was not present at the conclusion of the RA. Furthermore, the person's name would be published in the union's newsletter.

Who were the no-shows and semi-shows representing? Who ended up speaking in the name of their members? More than 90 percent of motions are decided by voice vote. Only one vote of several hundred at the 1999 RA required a roll call. Thus there are very few instances where rank-and-file union members can tell how their individual representatives voted—or even how their state caucuses voted.

State caucuses meet prior to each day's debates to decide their positions. On the RA floor, most states assign a delegate to hold up a sign before each vote that tells the delegation, whether the caucus and/or leadership recommend an "aye" or "nay." Tolerance for opposing the caucus leadership varies from state to state. But one thing is certain: no one has ever suffered repercussions for voting *with* his or her caucus.

State representative assemblies are smaller than NEA's RA, but they are still unwieldy. As the 1999 NEA RA demonstrated, neither teachers nor their union representatives are necessarily skilled parliamentarians. The results have significant consequences for union policies and can be comical.

In April 1999, the North Carolina Association of Educators (NCAE) voted on whether it should include education support personnel as members. Because such a move would require amending the union's constitution, it required a two-thirds majority of NCAE's representative assembly.

The union leadership was very much in favor of the constitutional amendment. So was NEA headquarters—it provided funds to lobby representatives in support. NCAE publications admitted to "intensive lobbying by NCAE leaders" and listed the locals and districts that supported the amendment. The day of the vote, banners, fliers, and buttons reading "ESP Yes!" were seen everywhere in the convention hall. A long debate was held. Then 1,304 delegates voted.

The final result: 869 in favor, 435 against. The measure was pronounced "passed."

It took two hours after the canvassing committee announced the totals, but amendment opponents (evidently led by math teachers) challenged the result. They pointed out that it was one vote short of a two-thirds majority. Unfortunately for them, an election challenge can only be upheld with a majority vote of the delegates. Since they only had slightly more than one-third support, the opponents lost this vote. Thus the definition of "two-thirds" succumbed to the will of the majority. Education support personnel are now full voting (and dues-paying) members of NCAE.[86]

Efforts by rank-and-file union members to gain a greater voice in decision-making are usually unsuccessful. In April 1998, the Montana Education Association's delegate assembly voted 245–54 to merge with the Montana Federation of Teachers. Then, after an hour-long debate, the assembly voted down a proposal (166–153) to allow rank-and-file union members to have the final say.

"To me, it's extremely disappointing that the association doesn't recognize the right of our members to give their views on such a historic occasion," said Scott T. McCulloch, president of the Billings Education Association."[87]

The Hawaii State Teachers Association (HSTA) had a similar controversy the same year. The state had a close race for governor that year, between the Democrat incumbent Ben Cayetano and the Republican mayor of Maui, Linda Lingle. HSTA conducted two surveys of the membership, both of which reportedly showed majority support for Lingle. The union refused to release the survey results. It ultimately endorsed Cayetano (who won reelection).

"The polls are confidential," union spokeswoman Danielle Lum said. "To say someone won is a bad word; it is a snapshot of where people are at the moment."

Not surprisingly, dissidents get discouraged by occurrences such as these. When their efforts are stymied again and again, they either quit in frustration, or recognize the folly of fighting city hall and fall into line. This leaves a large number of union representative bodies without any kind of loyal opposition—members willing to stand up for unpopular issues.

Inevitable result: in January 1999, the California Teachers Association divided its State Council into seventy-seven focus groups to evaluate its policies and future direction. Unsurprisingly, the pollsters concluded: "Most agreed that CTA is on the right course. . . ."

The NEA would like you to believe that it is run like Congress. That is, there are constituents, representatives, and votes reflecting that relationship. As with many other things, the union is telling only part of the truth. The NEA is run like Congress is run *internally*. The party leadership has a great deal of clout in how individual members vote. Committee assignments, promotions, and support for higher office are all tied to positive relationships between representatives and the party. The NEA is the party. And the Representative Assembly is the party convention. Its role is to sanction the decisions that have already been made.

The analogy is not exact. The American electorate is detached, but they are much more involved with government than teachers are with their union. The two-party system may lack diversity of thought, but there is only one party in the NEA "democracy."

The NEA's weak elected officials are further compromised by an exceptionally strong permanent staff. At the national level, and each of the NEA state affiliates, an executive director heads the staff. In most cases, the executive director is more powerful, and better paid, than the president of the union. While the maximum terms for elected officers differ from state to state, there is no such restriction on executive directors. They can hold the position for decades. For example, Don Cameron, who retired as NEA executive director in 2000, had been in place for seventeen years. By contrast, NEA presidents are limited to two three-year terms. (The AFT does not have term limits—one reason its elected officials, like Al Shanker, become so much better known.)

With top officials coming and going on a regular basis, and representative bodies that are huge and anonymous, the permanent staff is what holds the NEA together. And the commissars of this American Red Army, enforcing discipline throughout the union, are the men and women of the little-known NEA Unified Staff Service Program—UniServ.

Each NEA state affiliate employs a number of these UniServ directors, although they are subsidized by NEA headquarters. They are experts in union organizing, contract bargaining, political action, district finances, public relations, and just about any other darned activity the union might call for.

The Nebraska State Education Association (NSEA) has published the best synopsis of UniServ duties. These are the headings—the whole thing is exhaustive and exhausting:

> *Member Rights:* . . . advice in preparing responses to evaluation, grievance assistance, representation at probationary-teacher hearings, general counseling of individual teachers, responses to reprimands, intervention with administrators and school boards, and member rights training.

> *Collective Bargaining:* . . .

> *Legislation and Political Action:* . . . assisting locals in electing recommended candidates.

> *Instructional Advocacy:* UniServ help is available to aid in the understanding of teacher evaluation. [apparently a major concern].

> *Communications:* . . . developing such communications areas as local newsletters, American Education Week messages [one of about a dozen national PR events for government schools] helping access NEA publications, NEA/NSEA Member Benefits, and news releases.

> *Membership:* . . . recruiting members, targeting traditional non-joiners.[88]

The NEA requires that each state affiliate divide itself into regions and that each UniServ director be assigned to identified locals. This is an enormous advantage for the union. School boards have constant turnover. The labor negotiation specialists they hire change over time—and certainly have other business to take care of between contracts. But the UniServ director, on the other hand, is full-time on the spot. He may have negotiated the last contract—and the one before that—and the one before that.

The board's negotiator may be able to call upon his own expertise or that of partners. The local UniServ director can do that, plus call upon the state affiliate, plus the NEA, plus UniServ directors in other states who may have experienced similar negotiations.

UniServ directors are usually former teachers—but only those who have been very active in the union. In fact, UniServ is quite often where elected union officials go when they die—er, are term-limited out. These officials often seem to find a return to the classroom not quite as appealing as it might once have been. Funny thing.

Thus John Ryor, a former NEA president, became the executive director of the Florida Education Association. Craig R. Christiansen, former Nebraska State Education Association president, was hired by the union as a UniServ director in the Metro South area immediately on completing his final term.[89] Gary Obermeyer, who sat on the NEA Executive Committee from 1980 to 1986, was hired as a networking consultant for NEA's National Center for Innovation.

According to union mouthpiece *NEA Today,* in an article celebrating the twenty-fifth anniversary of the program:

> In 1970, UniServ was intended "to build strong local Associations, capable of defending their members' interests in every regard and capable of promoting their members' interests in every matter." In 1995, that still rings true. But the definition of "members' interests" has expanded.[90]

That is, as is often in union propaganda, the definition of "members' interests" has "expanded" to mean the opposite of what it apparently was. Rather than promoting strong, independent locals, UniServ has had a powerful centralizing effect in at least two ways. It has brought the full weight of the national and state organizations to bear even in the smallest, most

remote districts. And it has tended to unify all levels of the teacher unions—national, state, and local—behind a single agenda for the government school system.

The UniServ grant application puts it bluntly: "The local association shall actively support state and national program priorities in political action, legislative support, professional development, and affirmative action."

Furthermore, "full-time and part-time staff funded under the UniServ program shall provide whatever assistance is deemed necessary by elected local, state and national leadership."

What this means is that NEA HQ can redeploy any UniServ director to carry out tasks in any other part of the state—or of the United States. Thus, just prior to a union representation election in Puerto Rico, the NEA commandeered Spanish-speaking UniServ directors from across the country to aid in the organizing effort.[91] (But the AFT won, and now has monopoly bargaining rights in Puerto Rico.) Most NEA members are quite unaware that their local UniServ director, supposedly dedicated to see to their particular needs, is in fact subject to a Higher Power.

This also strengthens the NEA leadership against potential dissidents: Cause NEA HQ a problem, and your funding may be cut off. Or, more subtly, you may find your region's UniServ director in Puerto Rico when you most need him.

NEA elected officials often complain about the permanent staff's reluctance to carry out orders and of its interference in governance matters. The permanent staff can easily ride out the wave until any reforming elected official is term-limited out, and then return to their normal habits.

Needless to say, the NEA permanent staff has quite a different view of its relationship with their elected officials. Staffers see themselves as more in touch with the real world, since they work with those in the union trenches, and they see elected officials grandstanding and sending out directives like armchair generals. As professionals who are trained—and depended on—to be innovative and think on their feet, permanent staffers react very badly to the "because I say so" approach.

This conflict was one factor in the unexpected collapse of the NEA/AFT merger. The NEA permanent staff was known to be less than enthusiastic (although the merger proposal did preserve all staff jobs). This

provoked a threatening growl from executive director Don Cameron. In May 1998, Cameron *sent* an e-mail memo to all NEA staffers about the merger, informing them: "NEA is NOT neutral on this issue. Therefore, neither is NEA staff. NEA strongly supports, and is actively advocating for, the approval of the Principles of Unity by the delegates to the 1998 NEA Representative Assembly. So, therefore, is the staff. . . . [The staff must] use available opportunities to advance NEA's unity position and policy."

Cameron's growl was mostly ignored.

More openly, in the fall of 1998, the California Teachers Association began some tentative contacts with charter school advocates and officials from the Edison Project, a for-profit business that contracts to manage public schools. But in November 1998, CTA's staff met and pledged to "resign from any CTA task force, committee, or work group which may endorse collaboration with, or advocate for, the Edison Project."

Soon after, CTA let its fledgling effort peter out.

Elected union officials can be equally direct in expressing their resentment of the permanent staff. In April 1999, all five union-backed candidates in the Milwaukee school board elections were defeated. When asked about what had gone wrong, Milwaukee Teachers Education Association president Paulette Copeland said, "I wasn't consulted as far as what we should do. I was just informed of what the staff did."[92]

Sometimes the criticism is not even that subtle. *Education Week* reporter Ann Bradley has described how "some leaders within the NEA are expressing displeasure with the union's longtime staff structure, complaining that the association has built an entrenched internal bureaucracy." She quoted John Grossman, president of the Columbus Education Association, on the UniServ program:

> I'm not sure this is a process or organization that has promoted the NEA and its affiliates to be innovative. Quite the opposite. It has promoted the status quo, and in many cases, the status quo internally. It's not conducive for the organization being in the place it needs to be, in an era when public education is endangered.

"I think that even the staff is beginning to realize that they have to be willing to look at change," former NEA president Keith Geiger told Bradley. "But they'll be one of the last to do it. The smart ones are saying, 'This is not 1972.' "[93]

Why 1972? Geiger's choice of the date has a certain poignancy. It was the year after unified dues were achieved, when Geiger and the rest of the Michigan Mafia were riding high and the National Education Association was being transformed into a union amid much solidarity-forever rhetoric. Everything must have looked so simple. Now things are complicated, and the union is being forced to find a new rhetoric—the "New Unionism" dissected lovingly in Chapter 12.

But, having chosen to metastasize into the National Extortion Association, the NEA staff and elected officials may find that adjusting their rhetoric is not enough.

The NEA has hidden dimensions that further reinforce its power. Thus it is not only a labor monopoly; it also endeavors to be a monopsony—a monopoly of buyers. Exactly like the organization formerly known as the American Association of Retired Persons (AARP),[94] it is an affinity group and political lobby that also, quietly but importantly, profits from marketing insurance and other services to its own members. But, unlike the AARP, the teacher unions can also sometimes suppress competition.

Federal government filings have shown that the NEA has received as much as a quarter of its income from its share of the premium that members pay for NEA marketed life insurance and for selling other services. The NEA nonprofit subsidiary involved in all this has built up substantial net assets.

The NEA has also had a close relationship with Horace Mann Educators Corporation, a property/casualty and life insurer named after a nineteenth-century advocate of government schooling, which specializes in marketing to educators. According to former NEA executive director Terry Herndon—who subsequently moved on (surprise!) to run the Wisconsin NEA affiliate's insurance arm—the early leadership of Horace Mann came from the executive of several NEA state affiliates. Some affiliates and individuals associated with them owned Horace Mann stock. At one point the NEA itself held stock options. But, Herndon told *Forbes's* Leslie Spencer, he let them lapse because he considered it a conflict of interest. This relationship is obviously mutually profitable, although the details have not always been clear. At one point, the NEA reported in its annual filing to the Department of Labor that Horace Mann had paid it

$400,000 in a "fixed fee" agreement in return for "sponsoring" products to its members. Horace Mann simultaneously reported to the Securities and Exchange Commission that it did "not pay NEA or any affiliated associations any consideration in exchange for sponsorship," although it acknowledged buying advertising in NEA publications.

Horace Mann is one of the companies that have at various times provided the NEA with the professional liability insurance it offers its members. Liability is a real concern for teachers because of the increasing threat of litigation from parents backed by hungry tort lawyers. But the NEA insurance program, included in member dues, is not designed merely to help teachers; it also further strengthens the union's grip on them. Significantly, teachers in collective bargaining states who exercise their option of not joining the union but instead paying their alleged "fair share" of bargaining costs—the so-called agency fee—are denied access to liability insurance, although the premiums are included in union dues.

That the union consciously views the provision of insurance as a means of disciplining its members became embarrassingly clear in Tennessee when Governor Lamar Alexander, later secretary of education, proposed that liability insurance be provided by the state. To his astonishment, the Tennessee Education Association, the state NEA affiliate, opposed him.

"They were busy spending member money keeping the state from paying for liability insurance. They called what I was doing union busting," Alexander said later. "They consistently advocate proposals that are against the interest of their members."

Insurance-monopsonizing may have been imported from Michigan, along with Herndon and the rest of the "Michigan Mafia" who fought to convert the NEA into a labor union. The state is the home of the granddaddy monopsony of teacher unions insurance: the Michigan Education Special Services Association (MESSA), a subsidiary of the Michigan Education Association (MEA).

When Leslie Spencer looked into MESSA as part of a *Forbes* cover story on the NEA, she found a $370-million-revenue, 200-plus-staff organization whose sale of Blue Cross/Blue Shield teacher health insurance was bargained into contracts with school districts under threat of strikes. "We just aim to break even," MEA's Beverly Wolkow told Leslie Spencer, but in fact MESSA had reported an $87 million surplus. Its insurance was expensive—some $1,000 a year more per head than the state employee health plan. But the cost was just imposed on the school boards, which passed it on to taxpayers.

MESSA subsidized the union in many ways: paying a fee, buying services from a for-profit union company, carrying MESSA workers on its payroll, and even sharing the same switchboard. And it strengthened the MEA's grip on Michigan's teachers.

"You take members that don't believe in collective bargaining, that don't believe in our political ends, but you talk to them about MESSA, they'll stand in the middle of a highway to defend it," said MEA lobbyist Al Short. "That's the tie." Michigan school boards knew that any threat to the MESSA relationship was a strike issue for the MEA.

But MESSA's privileged position was significantly weakened in 1994, when school boards were legally prohibited from bargaining it into the contract, part of a titanic struggle over education reform between the MEA and Governor John Engler. "I attribute this change directly to the increased public awareness caused by the June 1993 *Forbes* article," says David Denholm, president of the Vienna, Virginia–based Public Service Research Foundation and a close student of the union.[95]

(Engler also survived an enraged MEA's effort to take vengeance at the polls. It can be done!)

The NEA's hidden insurance-monopsony dimension explains some of its more obscure activities. For example, in 1992, on the recommendation of an NEA-influenced employee committee, the school board in the Washington, D.C., suburban area of Fairfax County, Virginia, transferred teacher health insurance business from Blue Cross/Blue Shield of the National Capital Area to Prudential Insurance. Critics claimed the coverage was inferior and more expensive. They alleged a number of motives, including the fact that the Prudential Foundation had made $300,000 in donations to an NEA foundation.

NEA president Keith Geiger felt obliged to respond to the criticism in an open letter to school employees. Mysteriously, despite the grant and the fact that the NEA was marketing Prudential life insurance, he claimed that "NEA receives no money or other financial benefit—in the form of an exclusivity fee or otherwise—from the Prudential Insurance Company."

Prudential Insurance, which coincidentally at the time owned some 13 percent of Horace Mann common stock, has a history of being remarkably sensitive to labor unions. The National Right to Work Committee says that during the construction of its Virginia headquarters, Prudential—the financier—removed its name from the usual work-in-progress sign, apparently intimidated by union protests.

The NEA's hidden dimension includes important institutional alliances. One of the most important is with the AARP. With 35 million members and $580 million total revenues in 2000 (only a quarter from dues—much of the rest from "royalties" and health insurance premiums). The AARP is more than half as big as the U.S. Catholic Church. Like the NEA, it is notorious in Washington for its commitment to liberal policy goals, far to the left of its membership in the country at large.[96]

Less well known is the AARP's intimate interlock with the Teacher Trust. AARP was originally founded by a teacher. Many of its presidents and directors have been former educators, including at least one ex-president of an NEA affiliate. Many AARP staffers "come out of the education world," according to an internal source, sometimes directly from the teacher union. Not surprisingly, the AARP and the Teacher Trust are regularly to be found lobbying and agitating in harmony.

A more obvious Teacher Trust ally (or, more accurately, handmaiden): the National Congress of Parents and Teachers, universally known as the PTA, the fifth biggest voluntary organization in the country. Despite its bake-sale image, in many parts of the country and especially at the national level, the PTA has degenerated into little more than a Teacher Trust front. It was perhaps inevitable that, once the PTA's teacher members became unionized, they would rapidly dominate the less-organized parents. As early as 1968, teacher pressure forced the PTA to direct that its affiliates should be "neutral" in teacher strikes. But the PTA has long been in the NEA's pocket quite literally: It rented space from the NEA for years before World War II, and its "government relations" staff worked out of the NEA's Washington headquarters until 1990.

But the PTA is not at all neutral when it comes to the Teacher Trust's legislative agenda. For example, it hates any sort of vouchers. Yet, given that voucher proposals invariably poll well before the union starts spending millions on negative advertising, many parents, and PTA members, must be at least interested in them.

"You were the voice of California children!" Pat Dingsdale, president of the California PTA, told its convention to great applause in 1994. "PTA volunteers defeated Proposition 174 [the tuition voucher proposal]; all the California Teachers Association did was put up the money."

At least, that's what Dingsdale said according to notes kept by Charlene K. Haar, author of *The Politics of the PTA*. Dingsdale herself later vehemently denied that she made the statement. But she flatly refused to release the convention video. In fact, however, it was perfectly clear from leaked documents that the PTA slavishly followed the teacher union's lead on the school choice initiative. The PTA even joined in the controversial effort to keep the measure off the ballot altogether by harassing its supporters as they tried to gather petition signatures.[97]

So committed is the PTA to union positions that it has been prepared to alienate its own constituency. For example, it has been willing to alienate Catholic parents, who can't see why their tax dollars should not be used in Catholic schools. This has contributed to the PTA's continuing membership slump, from over 12 million in the early 1960s to the 6.5 million claimed recently.

Dingsdale was sensitive about her slip of the tongue because, like the NEA itself, the PTA presents a very different local face. Most PTA members do spend their time on bake sales and volunteering in their children's schools. Many might be shocked to find that $1.75 of their dues that is quietly diverted to the national bureaucracy actually finances an auxiliary in the NEA's partisan crusade.

The IRS might be shocked, too. Under the murky law governing tax-exempt 501(c)(3) organizations, the PTA is supposedly barred from all but "insubstantial" lobbying on issues like Proposition 174.

"They attribute almost nothing to lobbying expense, but virtually every [PTA] session I attended is about their legislative agenda," says Haar. Presumably this is why PTA officials have sometimes asked Haar to remove herself from PTA conventions, despite her press credentials.

And why does an organization supposedly focused on local schools and financed with tax-deductible money need "government relations" staff in Washington, D.C., anyway?

The Teacher Trust's attitude to the PTA was frankly expressed at a conference in 1995 by Kim Moran of the AFT—yet another unwary victim of Charlene Haar's notepad:

The PTA has credibility, [and] that is why we always use the PTA as a front. They are also the most disorganized [among volunteers]. They have no money and they must be educated, so we support them in a thousand different ways.[98]

Just as the NEA is more accurately described as the National Extortion Association, maybe the PTA should change its name—to Poodle-Teachers Association.

5

No Bargain

I don't see why unions are deciding when the school bell rings."

—Mary McIntosh, parent in Worcester, Massachusetts

"We slipped Agency Shop [legislation compelling non-union teachers to pay union fees anyway] through in the early 1970s," Michigan Education Association lobbyist Al Short says casually.

But for retired Swartz Creek teacher Kay Jackson, who didn't want to join any union, it was anything but casual. It meant over a decade of litigation and ostracism—even, she believed, dead cats thrown at her house and the murder of her pet German shepherd. Talking to *Forbes* magazine's Leslie Spencer at the age of seventy-eight, some twenty-four years after it all began, she burst into tears at the memory.

The NEA is a creature of legal privilege, such as "Agency Shop." But those privileges come with a price—often paid by individual teachers.

The extraordinary economic and political power of the NEA did not occur in a vacuum. It's the result of one of those curious institutional accidents that occasionally happen in a dynamic but structured economy like the United States. Occasionally, the framework of checks and balances that normally restrains an organized interest group gets broken. The organized interest group gets a chance to hold the rest of society to ransom. It does.

Other recent examples: stockbrokers in the 1960s, who were able to make institutional investors like banks and insurance companies pay full commission rates when they bought or sold stocks because stock exchange rules forbade volume discounts. Airline pilots in the 1970s, whose powerful unions extorted stratospheric salaries out of an industry straitjacketed by regulation. Trial lawyers today, enriched by the interaction of contingency fees and the arbitrary judicial relaxation of liability law.

From an economic point of view, of course, all unions are legally sanctioned efforts to monopolize a particular labor supply. But the Teacher Trust is in an exceptional position: the near-monopoly supplier to a government-enforced monopoly consumer. Parents are legally compelled to send their children to school. Most parents have no alternative but to send their children to the government school that they have been taxed to support—partly because they *have* been taxed to support it. After paying taxes, they just don't have the money for private school fees.

"Unlike consumers in the private sector," says labor attorney LaRae Munk, director of legal services for the Association of American Educators, "taxpayers cannot easily vote with their feet to choose a better service provider."[100]

In short, this typical 1960s experiment, of overthrowing traditional restraints and allowing public sector unionization, has (not for the only time) had an Unanticipated Consequence. It has left the Teacher Trust with a legally protected monopoly, rather like a cable TV franchise—but with none of the countervailing regulations, price controls, or service requirements.

Every state in the United States now permits government school teachers to join a union. But that's just the beginning of the legal privileges that a strong union wants—and must have. The bedrock of the Teacher Trust's power is the public-sector collective-bargaining legal regime, as it exists in each state.

Collective bargaining law gets very complicated. But these are the key questions to ask. (To see how YOUR state's government school system stacks up, see Appendix A).

1) DOES THE STATE PERMIT COLLECTIVE A.K.A. MONOPOLY BARGAINING?

A state with a collective bargaining law compels the school board to deal with the union if a majority of teachers in the bargaining unit vote to have the union represent them. (Because some teachers don't bother to vote, the number actually supporting the union can be less than half the total of teachers employed.) In the United States, as a practical matter, only one union gets to deal with management—hence collective bargaining is accurately described as "monopoly bargaining," although unions prefer the gentler term "exclusive representation." Currently, there are collective bargaining laws in thirty-four states.

2) DOES THE STATE REQUIRE NON-UNION MEMBERS TO PAY FEES ("AGENCY SHOP")?

After bitter dispute, the U.S. Supreme Court has established the constitutional principle that Americans cannot be forced to join a union to get a job—or to keep a job. That is, the Court has prohibited "closed shops" and "union shops," respectively.

But monopoly bargaining means that the Teacher Trust in effect speaks for non-union teachers, whether they like it or not. And in twenty-one states, the Teacher Trust can bargain to have these non-union teachers forced to contribute fees to the union, on the theory that they would otherwise be "free riders," benefiting from but not paying for the union's heroic efforts on their behalf. (In fact, these teachers could well be suffering from the union's attentions, especially if they teach a subject like math that is in demand, but for which the union won't allow preferential pay.)

This forced contribution is the "Agency Shop" provision that the Michigan Education Association's Al Short was boasting about at the beginning of this chapter. In California, New York, and Rhode Island, the Teacher Trust has succeeded in persuading state legislatures to impose Agency Shop as a matter of state law.

Ingeniously, the union has awarded itself an enforcement mechanism unavailable to other private entities. If you refuse to pay your health insurance premium, that's between you and your HMO. But if a teacher refuses to pay her union fee, the union-bargained contract with the local government school board obligates the district to garnish her pay.

This provision from the San Francisco contract is typical:

> In the event that a unit member shall not pay such fee directly to the Union, or authorized payment through payroll deduction as provided in Section 5.16.2, the Union shall so inform the District and the District shall immediately begin automatic payroll deduction. . . . *There shall be no charge to the Union for such mandatory agency fee deductions.* [Emphasis added].

Agency Shop strengthens the union significantly. It gets money from every teacher in the bargaining unit. And teachers who might otherwise stay out decide to join anyway, figuring that if they have to pay, they might as well play.

In addition, Agency Shop greatly increases the union's incentive to be aggressive about organizing more bargaining units. Every time the union succeeds in getting certified as a unit's exclusive, a.k.a. monopoly, representative—which may only take a majority of those voting in the certification election, perhaps only a third or less of the teachers—it gets to extract fees from everyone in the bargaining unit.

But Agency Shop has come with a certain cost to the union movement. Its encroachment looked like the last nail in the coffin to beleaguered businessmen and martyred managers in the years after World War II, when unions were riding high with allies throughout the executive, legislative, and judicial branches of the government and with generally uncritical support from the Depression-scarred American public. For several decades, however, resisting Agency Shop has been the rallying cry of the National Right to Work Committee, and its litigating arm, the National Right to Work Foundation.

Under its longtime head Reed Larson, operating from its headquarters high-rise right on (but—as he likes to point out—*just outside* of) Washington's Beltway, the National Right To Work Committee has become a refuge for a variety of union critics. It has lobbied for legislation securing non-union workers the right to opt out of paying union tribute, both at the federal (unsuccessful—up until now) and state levels (successful in many states). In the case of the government school teachers, Agency Fees are effectively prohibited in thirty states.

Next question: How much union tribute does the non-union teacher have to pay? The U.S. Supreme Court ruled that non-union teachers could be forced to pay Agency Shop tribute in a decision called *Abood v. Detroit Board of Education* (1977). But at the same time, it also ruled that non-union teachers only had to pay their "fair share" of the bargaining costs—i.e., not any of the union's political spending.

Result: continuing hand-to-hand combat between the Teacher Trust and litigants backed by the indefatigable National Right to Work Legal Defense Foundation about how much union activity is, in fact, collective bargaining—and how much political. One horrifying precedent: the "fair share" determined in the case of one private-sector union, the Communications Workers of America, was just 21 percent.

Generally, however, the "fair share" has recently been running at between 70 and 90 percent of full union dues, arguably because the union has gotten better at burying its political activity.

It's a gray area, because in one sense any attempt to influence an elected body like a school board is "political." A public sector union is inevitably involved in politics—politics is, as NEA executive director Don Cameron said, "axiomatic" to the Teacher Trust.

This is why Rutgers economist Leo Troy argued in his 1995 book *The New Unionism in the New Society: Public Sector Unions in the Redistributive State,* these "new unions" are fundamentally different from the "old," private sector unions. Their primary weapon is political, not economic, power. They use it to redistribute income toward government, a process Troy calls the "new socialism," and to insulate themselves from the key factor in private sector union decline: competition, from the service sector and from overseas.[101]

There is a fundamental asymmetry about collective bargaining in the government school sector. Monopoly bargaining means that not just non-members of the teacher unions, but also members of the public, are excluded from the making of public policy. It's decided by the school board and the union in conclave.

Theoretically, the public gets a say on education policy when it votes on taxes, or for the legislators who impose taxes. And the public elects school board trustees to oversee the hiring and paying of teachers. However, the school board trustees usually don't bargain either; they hire a professional negotiator to represent the district's interests. In concert with a negotiating team, usually appointed by district officials, the negotiator is the one who bargains. The public is at least two steps removed from process. It rarely even knows what's going on.

In fact, the quickest way to raise the ire of a local teacher unions is to make public the details of ongoing contract negotiations. Thus in 2000, when the Manalapan-Englishtown Regional School District in New Jersey alerted parents to the details of its latest offer and to the possibility of work stoppages—illegal in the state—by sending a note home with the children, its usual method of communication, union vice president Marguerite Schroeder denounced it:

> The association is appalled and disgusted that the board has chosen
> to use the children to disseminate negotiation information. We are
> in the process of checking the legality of that, but quite frankly, the
> use of the children as pawns in the negotiations is something that
> is totally reprehensible. The board is trying to undermine the
> whole process of negotiations.[102]

The union negotiators' incentives are powerful. In most cases, the income of the teacher union is directly tied to the salaries of the teachers it represents. If the average teacher gets a 4 percent raise, the union gets a 4 percent raise in dues. But many unions also have contracts with their own staffs that limit raises to the increases in the union's income. (Note: the union's—not the teachers'). Therefore, union negotiators benefit personally when they bargain higher salaries for teachers—and when they succeed in imposing Agency Shop on non-union teachers.

By contrast, the school board's incentives are weak. There is little countervailing reason for it to save taxpayer money or to safeguard management prerogatives. Surrendering gets the school board labor peace. School board trustees can be voted out of office for giving too much away—but the union is often the largest monetary contributor to school board campaigns and will support its friends. And if a school board trustee is philosophically aligned with the union, he may positively enjoy giving away the store.

Thus the teacher/school board conclave effectively excludes other interested parties, such as parents or taxpayers. And, because what is being decided is public policy, Edwin Vieira, the National Right to Work Foundation strategist, has argued before the U.S. Supreme Court that it is a violation of the equal protection clause of the Constitution. But the Supreme Court, still notoriously reluctant to challenge labor unions, disagreed.

Silver lining: collective bargaining doesn't always work out the way the union wants. Teachers in the Warner Unified School District in Warner Springs, San Diego County, voted to decertify the California Teachers Association in 1999. The union brought this on itself by throwing its weight around at a point when contract negotiations were getting contentious.

"All [Warner Unified] teachers [whether union or non-union] used to make decisions by getting together in a room and all voting on what to do," according to Doris Burke, a fourth grade teacher who led the decertification drive. Then the union decided to exclude non-union teachers, a common Teacher Trust trick. "We had a majority of teachers who wanted to act on their own behalf," Burke concluded. "They wanted their votes to count and they wanted it to be a democratic process."[103]

This is a particularly fascinating story because it shows that the professional and collegial ethic is still alive among government school teachers—despite being in a strong labor union state and despite nearly forty years of Solidarity-Forever rhetoric.

On the other hand, it's significant that Warner Springs is a small—fewer than 500 students—and very intimate district.

Pamela A. Riley, associate director of the Pacific Research Institute's Center for School Reform and author of *Contract for Failure,* a major survey of the impact of monopoly bargaining in on California government schools in which the Warner Springs story appeared, predicts more decertifications ("particularly in smaller districts"). The reason: California's new mandatory agency fee law, which became operative in 2001.

Non-union teachers can vote to decertify completely, but they can't hide—or at least they can't avoid paying dues—any longer. So their incentive to show up and vote in certification elections has been sharply increased.

Two enlightened states, Virginia and North Carolina, actually ban collective bargaining by government school teachers outright. This creates a very

interesting situation about which the first thing to be said is that the union
doesn't go away. It functions like any other special interest group, albeit an
unusually well organized one. It can still lobby school officials and participate
in school board meetings. Critically, it can still finance and campaign for candidates in school board and other elections. Plus the Virginia and North Carolina government schools remain socialist systems, with all their inherent
problems and perverse incentives for teachers and managements.

But Virginia and North Carolina government schools do seem relatively efficient socialist systems. Comparing scores and costs between states
is dauntingly difficult because of vast differences in their demographics and
living standards. No one seems to have done it properly in this case. But
one back-of-the-envelope comparison in 1997 did find that students in
Virginia and North Carolina had average NAEP scores slightly higher than
New York's, while consuming annually just over half as much per pupil.
Perhaps more pointedly, Virginia outscored neighboring Maryland, a strong
union state, while spending nearly $1,000 less a year.[104]

"People in Virginia complain that the teacher unions is too powerful,"
says David Denholm, president of Public Service Research Foundation.
"It's because they've no idea how bad the situation is in other states!"

If the public-sector collective-bargaining legal regime in each state is
the bedrock of the union's power, The Contract is the castle it builds upon
it—complete with dungeons.

Bargaining for the contract is supposed to be local. But the NEA and
its state affiliates are heavily involved, providing support, training, and
expertise in even the smallest school districts. The NEA provides technical
assistance in states that have public sector bargaining laws, and helps to
develop bargaining programs in states that don't. State affiliates hold collective bargaining training for local union teams.

Typical is an Indiana State Teachers Association workshop for locals
with training on

> Negotiations Methodology
> School Finance
> Organizing for Settlement (with an emphasis on
>   internal communications between the union and
>   the members)

Grievance Processing
How to Handle Discussion
How to Bargain Insurance and Other Fringe Benefits

The ISTA also provides materials for locals, such as sample contract language, the full context of the collective bargaining law, a grievance training manual, a negotiation methodology training manual, salary schedules of every district in the state, expected lifetime earnings according to each contract, a list of salary settlements, the total cost to the district of any chosen salary schedule, contract analysis, insurance data.

Similarly, the national and state union develops and coordinates strategy for locals. In an untitled 1996 pamphlet, the California Teachers Association listed these as bargaining goals:

- *Organize to avoid leaving money on the table* [emphasis added].

- Present bargaining proposals that are CTA-data driven.

- Achieve on schedule salary settlements better than ongoing base revenue limit received from the state.

- Coordinate bargaining.

- Secure fully paid benefit plans for all bargaining unit members and dependents.

- Avoid multiyear agreements without binding arbitration and agency fee.

- Achieve improvements in noneconomic areas of the contract including academic freedom, just cause, evaluation, and areas of concern.

- *Increase the Association's role in educational decision-making* [emphasis added].

In collective bargaining states, the contract effectively controls the school. In Milwaukee, one study noted that only a handful of "largely anonymous management and union staff" are knowledgeable about the

174-page (!) contract and the *2,000 pages* (!!) of accompanying grievance-arbitration rulings, memoranda of understanding, and state declaratory rulings.

The study concluded that the collective bargaining's "cumulative effect has made one question a common refrain when board members and administrators consider administrative and policy decisions: *Will the contract allow it?*"

"When you get through talking about all this reform, the reality is that there's this document sitting there that in large part—and in some instances almost exclusively—determines whether or not anything happens. Somehow, people have to grasp that," the study's coauthor, former Milwaukee school superintendent Howard L. Fuller, commented.[105]

In 2002, Pam Riley's study *Contract for Failure,* which took the austere position that "curriculum, assessment, pedagogy and instruction materials should not be part of the bargaining process," found that almost three-quarters of the several hundred California school districts surveyed did in fact yield too much power in these areas:

> In a kind of silent coup, union power has steadily colonized the system to the point that this influence is now so pervasive that by 1999, California's nonpartisan Legislative Analyst's Office (LAO) could calmly describe the process as business as usual: "Districts that enter into collective bargaining *share* power with unions over a wide range of decisions that affect district educational policies and the distribution of district resources." [Riley's emphasis][106]

Significantly, in the Teacher Trust's contract castles, it's not always at all clear who are the guards and who are the prisoners. There are literally dozens of stories of teacher unions taking action against a school principal or district for giving teachers more money or better benefits.

Here's one: the Evergreen Teachers Association in California negotiated a contract that granted teachers "personal necessity days," allowing them to take days off for personal reasons rather than using sick days. The union discovered some teachers were asking principals if they could use their personal necessity days to attend weddings and parties. Some principals were granting permission even though the contract didn't allow it. The union told teachers to stop asking.

"By asking, teachers are weakening the contract and encouraging the district to make capricious decisions that treats [sic] membership unequally," the union explained in a notice to members. "The integrity of laws and contracts can only be measured by the fairness and quality of their enforcement."[107]

The all-or-nothing approach to teacher pay is the hallmark of the union contract. After eighteen years of teaching and high praise from parents and administrators alike, Arizona teacher Andrew Creighton-Harank went to the Kyrene School District governing board and asked for a raise. Sounds straightforward enough? But this is exactly what monopoly bargaining is designed to prevent. Only the union can represent the teachers—and the union wants all teachers paid the union rate.

The board was sympathetic to Creighton-Harank. But it explained that giving a raise to one teacher would be a violation of . . . The Contract.

Creighton-Harank resigned.

"People felt like he shouldn't be out for himself," said Kyrene Education Association president Debbie Dinyes.[108]

Why can't the union allow individual teachers to make more? The answer was revealed in a labor dispute in New York. The Port Jefferson Office Staff Association filed an unfair-labor complaint after the school district paid an internal auditor a stipend of $3,000 a year. The state Public Employees Relations Board (PERB) upheld the complaint. In its decision, PERB wrote:

> The provision of benefits that are more than what is called for in a collective bargaining agreement is inherently destructive of a union's representation rights. *It can be construed to give a message that unit employees would do better if they abandoned their union* [emphasis added].[109]

Well, we can't have that!

Keeping teachers in the Teacher Trust dungeon is the reason that the NEA has opposed the "merit pay" so hard and so long. Merit pay is an attempt to improve the incentives faced by the classroom teacher. If she taught successfully, she could be rewarded directly for it.

This idea upsets unions profoundly. A "position paper on merit pay" put together by the California Teachers Association in the early 1990s revealed an institutionalized anti-market prejudice:

> one of the oldest and most persistent myths in our society is the belief that people are paid according to the value of the work they perform and the amount of effort they give. Few things are more arbitrary and capricious than the distribution of monetary awards.

The paper also noted that "no objective, clearly defined, and generally accepted standard exists for evaluating the quality of teaching."

Of course, this is also true for evaluating the quality of food, medical care, housing, legal services, or thousands of other endeavors in a capitalist system. But the market does make a judgment, through the price system.

It's not, it should be emphasized, a moral judgment. All sorts of worthy things go on outside of the cash nexus. But it is a practical judgment.

Besides, each year at its annual Representative Assembly, the NEA honors the national "Teacher of the Year." Was this teacher chosen at random—or by some agreed-upon standard that could be replicated in a compensation system?

"Basing teacher pay on student performance is no answer—it's a thinly disguised assault on us," wrote NEA official Lynette Tanaka in 1996. "Every day, we educators do the best we can, often under horrific conditions, with the best of intentions. No single determining factor—least of all student achievement—should dictate who among us will be paid more than others."[110]

Least of all student achievement?

The Teacher Trust's practical, as opposed to ideological, objection to merit pay is that differentiating between teachers, whatever the purpose or the standard used, is contrary to its raison d'être. The union requires that all teachers can and must be treated equally—so they can be mobilized equally, under the union's leadership.

Paradoxically, the union has repeatedly endorsed the market argument that paying teachers more will attract people into the profession. But it vigorously opposes spending that money *only* on attractive candidates. In order to attract a good teacher, you must raise the pay of all teachers, including the bad ones.

The union will only allow differentiation in teacher pay on the basis of the numerically indisputable: years on the job and college credits earned. This is entirely contrary to a market approach.

• In Florida, the Florida School Recognition Program rewards schools with cash for high or improved test scores. Lawyers for the Florida Teaching Profession–NEA threatened a legal challenge, arguing that the teacher bonuses are unconstitutional and an unfair labor practice.[111] (One of the NEA's favorite arguments is that merit pay destroys the "collegial atmosphere" in schools by precipitating cutthroat competition between teachers. A few merit pay programs have sought to circumvent this problem by offering merit pay to entire schools, rather than individuals. The union remains opposed.)

• In Washington State, the Washington Education Association won a complaint against Central Washington University after the institution boosted starting salaries. The union claimed that using this method to attract new faculty was "unfair to veteran employees."[112]

• In the District of Columbia, superintendent Arlene Ackerman wanted to raise starting teacher salaries by 11 percent, to $30,000 annually, in order to attract better candidates during a teacher shortage. The union shot it down. "I would love for them to have the $30,000," said Washington teacher union president Barbara Bullock. "But it's not fair for the teachers who have been here, paying their dues, working hard, not to get more money also."[113]

• In Richmond, Virginia, district officials proposed a $5,000 "signing bonus" bonus for new teachers. Richmond Education Association president Roger Gray said it "sends a signal that the inexperienced teachers are more valuable than teachers who have committed to this system."[114]

• In Maryland, an effort to award bonuses to new teachers was called an assault on collective bargaining by the Maryland State Teachers Association. (State delegate Daniel Riley, a teacher supported by the MSTA, had an unusual reason for opposing the measure. "We're going down the wrong track," he said. "We can't just throw money at the problem.")[115]

• In Texas, education commissioner Mike Moses suggested that salaries be raised for math teachers, science teachers, and special education teachers, because of severe shortages in those subjects. "Our members are totally opposed to it," said Annette Cootes of the Texas State Teachers

Association. "We need to pay everyone a decent wage before we start looking at differential pay."[116]

 • In Maryland's Baltimore County, a plan to pay $3,500 bonuses for
one hundred teachers to work in poor schools was opposed by the local
union with a particularly intriguing argument: it released the results of a
survey it had commissioned showing that the teachers themselves were
opposed to the idea.

The Baltimore County union claimed that the vast majority of the
seven hundred teachers who responded to the survey said the money
"wouldn't make a difference in their decisions about where to teach and
suggested that it go instead toward lowering class sizes and providing more
books and supplies in low-performing schools." The teachers consistently
said that money was far less important to them than factors such as class
size, strong discipline policies, adequate supplies, and supportive school
administrators.[117]

This, of course, raises the question: so why does the Teacher Trust keep
demanding higher wages and benefits?

Union officials argue that they must take these stances in order to
ensure that each member receives equal treatment—to the greater benefit
of all. Unfortunately, this argument is undermined by the fact that some
union members are treated more equally than others. It depends on how
important they are to the union power structure. New teachers give up a
great deal, usually to the benefit of veteran teachers.

 • In Boston, over four hundred first-year teachers had their positions
offered to veteran teachers—even veterans who were pushed out of
another school for poor performance. In one instance, the principal needs
the approval of 60 percent of the faculty to even post a job opening.[118]

 • In Los Angeles, teachers with seniority who want a new assignment
can simply bump a junior colleague. One new teacher had been moved
around so much that the *Los Angeles Times* described her as having been
"bounced from grade to grade like a penny on a kettle drum."[119]

Losing an assignment because of union demands may be hard for a new
teacher to take. But it could be worse. A new teacher can lose her job.

 • In Cedar Rapids, Iowa, in 1998, an arbitrator ruled in favor of the
union in a contract dispute, ordering the school district to raise pay and
benefits by 4.19 percent. In order to abide by the decision, the district was
forced to lay off eleven teachers.

"I trust the teachers association will assist in the process of staff reductions by explaining to teachers and parents why they were willing to sacrifice teacher positions for higher salaries," said associate superintendent Greg Reed bitterly.[120]

"The teacher reductions that have been made are not significant," responded Cedar Rapids Education Association director Kathleen Beck. "No one will lose their job permanently."

- In Sonoma Valley, California, in 2000, seventy employees were laid off to satisfy the union's demand for a 7 percent salary increase.[121]

Thus collective bargaining does not contribute to the efficient operation of the government school system. And it doesn't even satisfy the narrow interests of teachers as a group. So what is it for?

Well, it only takes a cursory examination of a contract to see its primary purpose: to benefit the Teacher Trust itself.

Virtually every collective bargaining agreement with a government school has what are called "union security" provisions. These are privileges and perquisites that the union has extorted for itself directly, as an institution.

These provisions can be detailed, numerous, and elaborate. Here are just a few of the twenty or so provisions in the collective bargaining agreement between the San Francisco Unified School District and the United Educators of San Francisco, a dual affiliate of both the NEA and the AFT.

(They make your eyes glaze over. Imagine being a school principal or an administrator confronted with them!)

- *"The Union shall be guaranteed the right to speak on off agenda items at all meetings of the Board of Education if it (the Union) so desires."* This is a right the public does not have.

- *"Neither the District nor the Union shall discriminate* [based on] *membership or participation in the activities of a recognized teacher organization."* This tacitly suggests that both the union and the district *can* discriminate if the teacher organization is not "recognized." Such a provision makes it difficult, if not impossible, for competing teacher groups to be organized.

- "The District agrees that the Union shall have the exclusive right to payroll deduction of dues. A computer printout list and data disk showing the teacher's name and the amount of dues deduction shall be sent to the Union." Since the union enjoys this right exclusively, it also serves the purpose of shutting out competing organizations.

- "Names, addresses, and telephone numbers of all bargaining unit members shall be provided to the Union on or about October 15 of each school year." This provision saves the union the administrative expenses of maintaining up-to-date membership lists.

- "Representatives designated by the Union shall be included on any Superintendent-created task force, committee, or group, that deals with curriculum, instruction, recruitment of new teachers particularly with respect to shortage areas and affirmative action concerns, school facilities, student discipline, industrial health and safety, or any other matters that may affect members of the bargaining unit." This is the union wrapping itself in the teachers' mantle to achieve its ends. It is perfectly reasonable for teachers to have input into school instruction, curriculum, and policies. It is perfectly unreasonable to insist that these teachers must be "designated by the Union." Such provisions are ostensibly included to prevent administrators from choosing compliant teachers. But in fact they simply ensure that the teacher representatives will be compliant to the union's wishes instead.

- "Six (6) Union member teachers shall be granted leaves of absence to conduct Union business. Up to two (2) additional Union teachers shall be granted leaves subject to the District's securing qualified and competent replacements." Generally, the union reimburses the district for the salaries and benefits of teachers released to perform union duties. But union officials are awarded salary increases and ben-

efits for increased "teaching experience," although they
may be spending 100 percent of their time at union
headquarters. Thus a union president who is elected to
serve full-time at the ten-year point may return to the
classroom two years later at twelve-year pay and benefits—at the expense of the school board—even if she
never set foot in a classroom during those two years.

"Thus far, the leading writers of the current school reform movement
have shirked from a critical examination of teacher unions and collective
bargaining," wrote Todd A. DeMitchell and Richard Fossey in their book
The Limits of Law-Based School Reform. "With very few exceptions, one will
search in vain in the school reform literature for even the appearance of the
word *union.*"[122]

School reformers may have shirked examining the Teacher Trust. But
the Teacher Trust has not shirked examining them. For every new reform
proposal, the Teacher Trust is the crocodile lurking beneath the surface.

The teacher unions examine all proposed reforms through the lens of
collective bargaining. The questions they ask are: Will it help or hinder bargaining? Will it (as the California Teachers Association put it in the strategy
document quoted above) "increase the Association's role in educational
decision-making?" Will it enhance the union's standing—either financially
or in the public's eye?

Since most education reformers do not develop ideas with the glory of
the union in mind, it is inevitable that most reforms fail to garner union
approval.

Of course, the Teacher Trust is worried. It does know the public is clam-
oring for reform. So it preemptively generates its own reform proposals.

You can always identify a teacher unions proposal for education reform
by three characteristics:

1. an appealing, commonsense, public-relations-friendly
   concept

2. its enormous tangible benefits to the union

3. its marginal and ephemeral benefits to students, parents, and
   the public

Take class-size reduction. The teacher unions have been promoting class-size reduction for decades. The NEA calls for a maximum of fifteen students per classroom—for regular education.

And, unquestionably, reducing class size has a visceral appeal to parents. They reason that if their child is in a class half its current size, he will get twice as much attention from the teacher.

Class sizes are already a matter for negotiation in collective bargaining agreements. NEA affiliates in particular have lobbied incessantly for statewide class-size reduction. The California Teachers Association has had the most notable success in this regard, winning a statewide 20:1 student/teacher ratio in kindergarten through the third grade in 1996. As we have seen, the measurable effects of class-size reduction on student achievement are arguable, at best. But one thing is not arguable: Class-size reduction is one of the most expensive education reforms possible.

And the rewards to the teacher union stack one on top of the other.

When you reduce class sizes, the first thing you need is: more teachers! And in collective bargaining states with agency-fee provisions, most of these new teachers will either become union members or pay fees to the union. In the first two years of class-size reduction, the California Teachers Association added some 37,000 new members, an amazing 12 percent increase. Each of those new members pays about $420 annually to CTA, another $123 to NEA, and a variable amount to his or her local union.

The second thing you find, particularly with a statewide reduction: an instant teacher shortage. Until the supply catches up with the demand, this creates an upward push on teachers' wages. And, as we have shown above, the government school education "market" policed by the Teacher Trust rarely allows beginners' wages to rise without a corresponding increase in veteran wages. Rising teacher salaries lead to increases in the salaries of administrators, support personnel, and other workers in the system, so that the financial pecking order is maintained.

The third thing you need: room. Soon after class-size reduction became law in California, CTA led the fight for a $9 billion school construction bond initiative. It supported a ballot initiative that lowered the threshold for the passage of school bonds. This money went to the construction and renovation of school buildings. It liberated previously budgeted maintenance funds for other purposes—such as, for example, teacher salaries and benefits—to be negotiated into the collective bargaining agreement.

The fourth thing you find: teacher quality deteriorates. Because the need for new teachers is so great, it's likely that hiring requirements will be waived and school districts will hire many candidates who would have been considered unsuitable previously. When the public complains about these low-quality teachers, the union responds quickly with the commonsense answer: You get what you pay for. It's easier to persuade the public that poor teachers are due to poor wages than it is to persuade them that poor teachers are due to class-size reduction. So school boards, parents, and tax-payers are maneuvered into raising teacher salaries.

But we're not finished yet with the benefits (to the union) of class-size reduction. The fifth thing you find as a result of class-size reduction: because so many employees are being added at the bottom of the pay scale, the average teacher salary tends to be reduced, or at least increase more slowly, compared to previous years. The union promptly steps in with calls for higher teacher salaries to "catch up," or to "match the cost of living" or to "reach the national average."

And the class-size cornucopia (for the union) continues. Class-size reduction opens up desirable teaching slots in wealthy schools in suburban districts. Veteran teachers can now transfer from inner-city districts and leave the new teachers with the worst assignments. Furthermore, teachers in reduced classes have reduced workloads. Teachers in upper grades, who remain in larger classes, complain about the inequity of having the same preparation time for many more students. The union can often bargain for additional aides or assistance for these teachers. Furthermore, because class-size reduction increases demand for teachers, it can prompt experienced private school teachers to take government school jobs, besides drying up the pool of candidates to replace them. Private schools then are forced to lower their standards or increase salaries—and fees. So lowering class size makes private schools a less attractive option, particularly to poor parents, who even under the most ambitious voucher programs are still required to contribute to their child's education.

The teacher unions can also fold the rewards of this class-size "reform" into another "reform" it very much likes to negotiate into contracts—"professional development." With so many inexperienced teachers, the union will step in and offer to provide them with professional training courses. Not only does this place the union in a positive public light, but college credit is often offered for these courses. And accumulating these credits moves teachers up the salary scale.

The professional training may involve classroom management skills or something else of direct use in the classroom. Or it may include training of dubious value to the schools—and of high value to the union.

The University of Alaska at Anchorage offered a Continuing Professional Development graduate credit to teachers who attended NEA-Alaska's fall conference in 1999. What "professional development" training did the teachers receive? Well, they chose from six "training strands":

> Communicating the Association's Message
> Creating Safer Schools in Alaska
> Basic Rights
> Recruit-Retain-Reclaim
> Basic Bargaining Law and Skills
> New Education Initiatives.[123]

But even reforms that originate outside the Teacher Trust can be captured and co-opted. A classic example is Outcome-Based Education (OBE). Paradoxically, this educational doctrine seems to have begun as a Reagan administration attempt to enforce educational standards. But within ten years, it had been turned inside out, downgrading content in favor of nebulous "outcomes," like "thinking skills," "group learning," and associated educrat gobbledegook. Other "outcomes," such as becoming "concerned stewards of the global environment" and "demonstrating respect for the dignity, worth, contributions, and equal rights of each person," were clearly not educational at all, but in the contemporary American context, nakedly political. Conservative and religious parents suspected that their values were under attack. They were probably right.

OBE got the NEA's tenacious support, with opponents accused of belonging to the dreaded "Religious Right." The head of the Pennsylvania Educational Association calls them "voucher vultures . . . for whom OBE stands for Opportunity to Bash Education." One reason for the union's vehemence: the NEA's genuine emotional commitment to the elitist, progressive, social-engineering ideology that pervades America's government-cartelized educational establishment. But another reason was certainly that OBE was labor intensive and yet usually untestable. In fact, in fully implemented OBE schemes, grades and credits could be abolished. This would reduce those embarrassing questions at the bargaining table about teacher performance.

Nevertheless, OBE was also costly to the NEA. Through the 1990s, no other subject provoked so many, often highly articulate, letters from distressed parents to journalists who might possibly be interested in education reform.

I'll discuss the fate of two other reform ideas, vouchers and charter schools, in Chapters 7 and 8.

A frank statement of the NEA's determination to capture educational reform for the collective bargaining process appeared in *Negotiating Change: Education Reform and Collective Bargaining,* a book produced by its Research Division in 1992, when charter schools and vouchers were still just a cloud of chalk dust no bigger than a child's hand:

> Most reform initiatives of the past several years have begun outside the collective bargaining process and are unregulated by collective bargaining agreements. If this trend continues, it could mean that *collective bargaining will have only a tenuous and possibly conflictual relationship* to some of the most dynamic and potentially important aspects of public education. The alternative to this scenario is *to use the collective bargaining process creatively to shape the changes* that are now occurring. [Emphases added][124]

This is the NEA's biggest fear: teachers and school managements will find constructive ways to interact outside of collective bargaining. The NEA manual continued:

> It seems very clear that if school boards and administrations are successful both in creating participative organizational cultures and generating new opportunities for education employees to contribute to education outside of the collective bargaining process and without the support of the local association, over time collective bargaining will become marginalized.[125]

Well—would that be such a bad thing? In states without collective bargaining laws, teachers still teach, NEA still has affiliates, and somehow life goes on.

Tennessee is a state where collective bargaining is allowed, but not required. In a study produced for the Tennessee School Boards Association, Dr. George Nerren concluded:

> For 15 years, collective bargaining has contributed to the erosion of public support and confidence in the schools. Additionally, it has resulted in the deterioration of relationships between teachers, administrators and board members, not to mention the costs in both time and energy for both sides. Certainly it has generated "hard feelings" through its adversarial approach. Rather than resolving conflicts and solving problems it has actually generated conflicts and caused problems. Most regrettably, collective bargaining has forced boards and teachers to focus on bargaining for teachers rather than learning for students.[126]

6

The Inmates Take Over the Asylum

Reform cannot occur in an environment that is indifferent or hostile to it.[127]

—Hayes Mizell, director of the Edna McConnell
Clark Foundation's Program for Student Achievement

It helps to have friends at City Hall—and in state and federal legislatures.

In 1999, Missouri state representative Steve McLuckie (D–Kansas City) carried a bill to establish collective—monopoly—bargaining for teachers in the state. It was ultimately defeated after vocal opposition from the Missouri State Teachers Association, the professional group that broke with the NEA over unionization and the imposition of "unified dues," and to which most Missouri teachers belong.

When not at his job in the statehouse, McLuckie was—drumroll!—*head organizer for the Missouri NEA!*

State and federal politicians are increasingly getting involved in America's government school system. And the Teacher Trust is increasingly getting involved with them. There will be more McLuckies.

But the bulk of the spending and control is still at the local level. Conservatives like this, but it has its own problems. Local politicians, district bureaucrats, and site-level administrators can be just as self-serving and shortsighted as any member of Congress. Even conscientious people can still be manipulated, and talented people can be co-opted. At the local level, those who have the most knowledge and the best organization are the ones who call the tune. All too often, this means the local teacher union.

Local school boards were established to see that curricular, administrative, and fiscal activities are conducted by officials who are elected by—and therefore accountable to—the community. But what if these officials owe their election to special interest groups, particularly groups with a stake in the status quo? Turnout and interest in school board elections are notoriously low. Victories are often decided by a handful of votes. Even a relatively small amount of money can be critical in school board elections. And the Teacher Trust is not shy about tossing money at candidates.

The direct benefits to the union are obvious. Union-friendly school board trustees promulgate union-friendly policies. The trustees hire the superintendent, hire the district negotiator, establish budget priorities, vote on the collective bargaining agreement. A few thousand dollars to ensure allies on the school board is money well spent.

While other school board candidates must raise campaign money on their own, union-endorsed candidates usually receive contributions not only from the local union, but "passed through" money from the union's state affiliate. For example, in 1996, the California Teachers Association funneled at least $235,000 through its local affiliates into school board election campaigns throughout the state. That total does not include contributions to local party committees, local get-out-the-vote efforts, or joint PACs.

A "teacher-endorsed," a.k.a. union-endorsed, candidate has a step up on the competition—particularly if the local union decides to add volunteers and in-kind services to the campaign. In-kind contributions don't have to be reported. Example: Deborah Hawley, campaign consultant for a narrowly defeated pro-school-choice candidate in a recent Wisconsin state school superintendent race (Wisconsin elections are particularly fraught because of Milwaukee's long-running voucher experiment) said her office received reports that the state NEA affiliate ordered teachers to write anti-choice postcards to a minimum number of acquaintances—and to bring the postcards into union headquarters, so that their compliance could be checked. The NEA affiliate denied it . . . of course.

Moreover, election law allows the union to spend without limit to "communicate" with its members, who are quite numerous and influential enough to make the difference in close elections. The union doesn't need to muster these supporters by appealing to their civic duty. It appeals to their pocketbooks.

Thus in Los Angeles in 1997, when the United Teachers Los Angeles sought a salary increase, union officials had no hesitation in spelling out to their members that working for school board candidates would help them get it. "In order for you and I to secure such an increase, we must not only pass Proposition BB [a local bond initiative], but elect Valerie Fields and Julie Korenstein to the LAUSD School Board," wrote UTLA president Day Higuchi in a March 7, 1997, letter to union activists. "Both candidates are committed to a significant salary increase, and, along with David Tokofsky, will provide the 2nd and 3rd votes needed to achieve our goal."

In San Antonio, Texas, in 1998, the San Antonio Federation of Teachers worked hard to win a 4–3 majority on the school board. Soon after, the board approved a 10 percent across-the-board pay raise for all employees and bought out the contract of superintendent Diane Lam, a union opponent. The union got what it wanted. The district got a $16.3 million deficit.[128]

Union participation in school board campaigns is enormous—and often more than even teachers realize. In Milwaukee in 1999, the Milwaukee Teachers Education Association endorsed five candidates for seats on the nine-member school board, intending to create an anti-voucher minority in the city with America's only court-tested school choice program. After a bitter campaign, all five union-backed candidates lost.

It wasn't until months later that the public learned the extent of union participation. The MTEA was fined $5,000 for failing to report nearly $105,000 in expenses related to the campaign.

"I just hope their members find out how much money was really spent on radio, television, lawn signs, mailings, polls, and attorneys' fees, as well as this $5,000 fine, all of which makes the MTEA look incompetent and dishonest," said citywide board member John Gardner, who was the union's primary target for defeat.[129]

The MTEA's activities on behalf of its chosen candidates were legal (as long as they were reported publicly, which they apparently were not). But sometimes unions and their allies engage in patently illegal and/or unethical activities to elect candidates or to get their political way.

The most common of these: using school facilities and supplies for political purposes, such as copying campaign flyers and sending them home with the children. This happened quite often in the 1993 California voucher campaign, and more recently in both California and Virginia.[130]

"Attention students, it's now eight-thirty!" said a student's voice over the loudspeaker at Rio Grande High School in Albuquerque, New Mexico, one morning. Hundreds of students walked out of class to protest low teacher pay. Teachers at the school had previously held informational pickets at the school, and students said some teachers had been discussing the pay dispute in class. The students carried picket signs that had apparently been made using school materials in the school's media center. This was bad enough, but a group of about two hundred students broke off from the main group and began to riot downtown, smashing windows, vandalizing property, and throwing rocks. Some were arrested.

After an investigation, four teachers were suspended and three others received letters of reprimand for their part in the walkout.[131]

Even union allies sometimes flinch. The Mexican-American Political Association accused California teacher Linda Lopez of using learning and physically disabled students, during class, to stuff campaign flyers for the election of county superintendent Herb Fischer and mailing them to homes of members of the San Bernardino County Teachers Association, which supported Fischer.[132]

In Colorado, normally supportive parents chastised the Jefferson County teacher union for telling members to use the emergency phone numbers collected from students to contact parents and lobby them in support of a school tax increase.[133]

The union is able to extend control over the district's budget because of its commitment to learn absolutely everything there is to know about school finance.

Thus the Illinois Education Association offers its local activists a "Financial Analysis Tools for Local Association Leaders" program. It includes a seven-module training packet entitled "Understanding Your District's Finances" and an Internet-based spreadsheet called the Online Financial Analysis System "designed to compare data from your district's most recent Annual Financial Report and Budget. By entering data from these two documents, OFAS tracks shifting district priorities by pinpointing changes in current category allocation and spending patterns." And there's the "District Financial Profile," a twenty-page financial and statistical report that "examines your district's budgeting and spending history over a five-year period. It also compares your district's financial profile with a comparison group of school districts that you designate."

The Teacher Trust's expertise and dedication to a thorough study of school financing are matched only by its mastery of public relations. Unions usually like to keep contract negotiations and other disputes with the district under wraps. But when these problems make it into the press, the unions are much better at getting their message across.

And school districts are very unlikely to spend $30,000 on a two-week advertising blitz at contract time. But that's just what the Boston Teachers Union did in August 2000.[134]

One look at the agendas of union conferences shows how well prepared for battle union activists are. The 2000 Alabama Education Association Leadership Conference included workshops for local presidents "to lead the local association into a new level of activism in the areas of local school board policy, salary schedules, budgets and critical issues." Other seminars taught local union officials how to deal with media coverage, how to make the local a political force, and how to "put together a winning grievance."

The California Teachers Association Summer Institute held workshops on school finance, communications, site-based decision-making, school board elections, campaign techniques, countering threats to public education, managing a field operation, and winning at the polls and the bargaining table.

The National Staff Organization, which is the union of NEA employees, holds an annual Winter Advocacy Retreat, more commonly known as the WAR College. Sessions for 1999 include Advanced Bargaining, Bargaining Insurance Benefits, Bargaining Research, Defined Benefit Retirement Plans, Defined Contribution Retirement Plans, Employee Rights, Interest-Based Bargaining, Introduction to Bargaining, Introduction to Grievance Processing, Introduction to the National Labor Relations Act, Issue Organizing, Mediation of Grievances, Pension Plan Q & A, Preparation for Arbitration, Salary Schedules, Understanding Just Cause, Due Process, and Progressive Discipline.

There may be one, perhaps two, employees in a school district with this much information at hand. But certainly your average school board member has nothing to compare, either in training or data.

Confirming Leo Troy's insight in *The New Unionism in the New Society* that the primary weapon of public sector unions is political, not economic, power, it turns out that most of the NEA's current UniServ directors were trained in the style of the labor organizer Saul Alinsky. A 1982 NEA handbook, "Alinsky for Teacher Organizers," specifically advised union leaders to *"organize the community to put pressure on the superintendent or the school board to get things done for education."* The union negotiator, the handbook said, *"must not resolve issues even though he might be able to."* Teacher Trust members must believe that whatever they receive from the district—however happily the district turns it over—the union has won for them. And they must be persuaded that it was won after a hard-fought battle with implacable enemies.

"Alinsky's strategic and tactical essence is built around conflict," the handbook explains. *"Distance helps to polarize the issue—to make it an us-them affair."*

But in fact the Teacher Trust's task is much easier than the NEA handbook wanted it to appear. Contrary to public perception, school boards, local unions, and administrators are not in constant conflict at all. Instead, they form an "Unholy Alliance," as Gregory Moo, a former teacher, high school principal, and educational administrator, aptly put it in his book *Power Grab*—focused on joint self-aggrandizement.

Explains Dr. Moo:

If you do not cause me too much trouble, say members of the Unholy Alliance to one another, I will not cause you too much trouble, and public education in our community will run smoothly (if fraudulently). . . . The system operates, in large measure, for the benefit of the three major players; and it gives NEA the leverage it enjoys in school district after school district across the states. These out-of-view agreements create the Unholy Alliance, and they allow NEA bosses the power to exact their booty from school districts at the expense of students, teachers, taxpayers, and the democratic process.[135]

Many school boards openly acknowledge their dependence on the unions to lobby for increased budgets. In Clifton, New Jersey, the Clifton Education Association worked with the board on a get-out-the-vote effort to pass an $82.6 million budget in a fiscally conservative area that had rejected nine of the last twelve budgets.[136] In Montebello, California, in 1996, the Montebello Unified School District passed a "Resolution of Appreciation" thanking the California Teachers Association for its efforts to ensure more state money for the district.

In Michigan in 2000, during a campaign for statewide vouchers, the Warren Consolidated school board passed a resolution to "refrain from entering into contracts with any company whose representatives contribute money to the pro-voucher initiative." State officials and the district's own lawyers warned the board that the policy was illegal. In the end, the board backed down.[137]

Sometimes the Unholy Alliance has a very personal dimension. During difficult contract negotiations in Niles, Michigan, the superintendent learned that at least seven phone calls had been made from the high school to the local union office. Confronted with the news, the high school principal, who was on the district's contract negotiating team, resigned unexpectedly to take a new position . . . as a labor negotiator for the Michigan Education Association.

The high school principal/MEA negotiator told the superintendent that the calls were about his new job. Nevertheless, contract negotiations, which had been at a stalemate, were suddenly settled, to the advantage of the district.

Sometimes it's difficult for the Teacher Trust to find political candidates who are sufficiently beholden to its wishes. In those cases, it will if necessary field candidates from its own ranks. NEA and AFT members are prominent in many state legislatures, state policymaking positions, and local school boards.

In Redlands, California, former California Teachers Association vice president Ron McPeck won a seat on the Redlands school board with union help.[138] In Wisconsin, former Madison Teachers Inc. president Bill Keys won election to the school board with the support of MTI, and former Milwaukee school board president Joseph Fisher held elected office in the Milwaukee Teachers Education Association.[139] In Maryland, former

Maryland State Teachers Association counsel Walter S. Levin was appointed to the state school board while Governor Parris Glendening hired former MSTA president Karl Pence as an adviser. In Washington State, superintendent of public instruction Terry Bergeson used to be the president of the Washington Education Association.

Once friendly candidates are elected, the Teacher Trust goes to great lengths to keep them friendly. One union organizer in Missouri described how his local union managed to put six endorsed candidates on the school board:

> The success is due to a long-term strategy of involvement with the school board, not only during elections, but throughout the year. The [union] president and vice president have monthly dinner meetings with the board president and vice president. The UniServ director has frequent meetings with board members. . . . The relationship with the board is a part of the long-term strategy of community organizing. *It has enabled the Association to be a primary player in all aspects of the education system—from instruction and curriculum issues to direct participation in the decision to hire a new superintendent and* [assistant] *superintendent.* [Emphasis added]

The result: a Potemkin village—a cardboard cutout of a government school system in which committed adults devoted unceasing efforts to the education of children. The reality is quite different—and filters down to the classroom.

A California teacher, Diann Myer, summarized the situation poignantly in a letter she published in *U.S. News & World Report:*

> Rigorous, academically oriented teachers who want to maintain high standards in the classroom are thwarted at every turn: by administrators who want happy parents, parents who want happy children, students who want happy lives, and even other teachers who want happy, tension-free classrooms. Teachers are judged by how comfortable their students feel, not by the competence they require of their students by demanding hard work and maximum effort.[140]

Even state governors find themselves kowtowing to union officials when it comes to setting the state education budget. Here is California

Teachers Association president Wayne Johnson, in his own words, describing how $1.84 billion was added to the 2000 state budget—just as the union was about to submit signatures for a school spending initiative and hold a rally on the state capitol steps:

> While you were on your way to Sacramento, I was driving there the evening of May 7, and the governor and I talked three times on my cell phone. The first call was just general conversation. The second call, he had an offer of $1.2 billion above the Prop 98 limit, but we would have to rethink our initiative and call off the rally. I told him we could not do that. On the third call, he upped the ante to $1.5 billion if we would again rethink our initiative and convert the rally into an anti-voucher event. Again I told him that we couldn't do that. . . . [Governor Davis's chief of staff] Lynn Schenk called that evening and asked us to delay submission for 24 hours, and then she asked us: What did we want?[141]

In Hawaii in 1997, during statewide teacher contract negotiations, Governor Ben Cayetano and his budget director invited officials of the Hawaii State Teachers Association to review the state's financial books behind closed doors. Governor Cayetano was trying to convince HSTA that the state was offering all the money it could for teacher salaries. While allowing union officials to rummage through the public wallet for loose change, Governor Cayetano barred reporters from the event.[142]

But how can it be that year after year of increased spending never seems to fix the endemic problems—the schools with broken windows, leaky roofs, inoperable toilets, and obsolete textbooks that are just as much a mainstay of local TV news (and teacher union campaign ads) as they ever were?

The experiences of several states points to the reason: the Teacher Trust wants, not just money, but money spent in certain ways. And textbooks are not a priority.

Minnesota's state legislature increased basic school funding by 4.7 percent in the 1999–2000 school year, and another 3.2 percent for the 2000–2001 school year. Nevertheless, more than one-third of 274 districts reported making budget cuts.

"Right now, it's perplexing to have the legislative auditor say there is no financial crisis, then give the districts more than they've gotten before, then find out they are making cuts and having to lay off teachers," said state education commissioner Christine Jax. "I guess I don't understand how we can put more and more in each year, and it never seems to be enough."[143]

Governor Jesse Ventura was reportedly very unhappy with the continued money problems. But veteran state legislators knew what was wrong.

"He has found out that when you put money on the education formula, salary settlements are higher than that number, no matter what the number is," said Senator Larry Pogemiller, Democrat from Minneapolis and chair of the state senate K–12 Education Committee.

"The pattern repeats itself with uncanny predictability. We give x, the school district negotiates x plus one," added Senator Tom Neuville, a Republican from Northfield.[144]

The St. Charles School District in Minnesota raised the manipulation of the budget to a fine art. A system was instituted by which any year-end operating balance in excess of $600,000 could be used for staff bonuses. Amazingly, the district managed to generate surpluses in excess of $600,000 every year! Annual bonuses over an eight-year period ranged from an average of $900 per employee to $3,200 per employee. Auditors were unable to determine if other district spending was limited in order to keep money in the bonus pool.[145]

Similarly, the Oklahoma legislature generated $177 million in new money for public education in 2000. But $157 million was earmarked for $3,000-across-the-board teacher salary hikes, $10 million for flexible benefits for support employees, and $23 million for a state-mandated 1 percent increase in district contributions to the teacher retirement fund. That left districts $13 million short right off the bat—and no money was left for expected enrollment growth.

"Right now, it looks like every school district will have to cut their budgets 2 to 3 percent," said Keith Ballard, executive director of the Oklahoma State School Boards Association.[146]

In Washington State, the legislature appropriated money for beginning teachers in order to address the oft-quoted problem of "attracting the best and brightest to the profession." Lawmakers soon discovered that many districts were diverting money to veteran teachers. "When you get into the issue of where you're tinkering in the salary schedule, that gets terribly divisive. You're sending the signal that some people are more valuable than other people," said Paul Pritchard, president of the Everett Education Association.[147]

Through politics, the Teacher Trust is in effect capturing America's government school system, beginning with its pervasive presence at the local level. It has reached the point where union officials appear genuinely surprised if they are not allowed to take over management functions.

In Plainview, New York, the local union offered to take over the job of contacting substitute teachers when they are needed. Union president Morty Rosenfeld claimed his organization would be able to do it more efficiently and in a way that would get the district the best-suited person available on any given day. "It is hard to understand why the district appears unwilling to accept our offer," he wrote. "There would be no increase in cost to them and the service would be better." Rosenfeld seemed to see no conflict in having a union choose who works and who doesn't.

In Cincinnati, Ohio, Cincinnati Federation of Teachers president Tom Mooney wanted the union to take on the job of recruiting new teacher candidates for the school district, for the sum of around $100,000. Mooney seemed to see no conflict in paying a union to recruit teachers when its normal business is recruiting members.[148]

In Clark County, Nevada, Clark County Classroom Teachers Association executive director Stephen Conter proposed having the district issue each teacher a $2,750 voucher each year. The teacher could use $500 of the voucher for supplies, and the rest for training. Who would be able to cash in these vouchers? Why, the union of course, through its newly established "academy of teacher training."

The *Las Vegas Review Journal* blasted the scheme because state education funding "would be laundered through the Clark County School District only to flow, in the end, directly to the union offices of the Clark County Classroom Teachers Association."[149]

But perhaps the boldest plot was a 1995 plan by the California Teachers Association to place a one-cent sales tax hike on the state ballot. Seventy percent of the money raised was to go directly to the school site. It would be spent by ten-member "school site councils" consisting of the school principal, three parents selected by the school governing board, and "six teachers selected by the exclusive bargaining representative"—a.k.a. the local union.

The plan was ultimately dropped when the CTA polling showed lack of public support for a tax increase.[150] But they'll be back.

America's government school system is a political bureaucracy. This makes the co-option and/or capture of local school boards by the Teacher Trust just a matter of time. The union is the $1.25 billion gorilla. The school boards are in its cage.

But the inmates are taking over the asylum not only at the school board level, but also in state and federal elections. The NEA's political machine is legendary, and enormous amounts of money keep it well lubricated.

It starts with the union's Political Action Committee (PAC), recently renamed the NEA Fund for Children and Public Education. (Yes, it's pretty saccharine—but the NEA is getting worried about its image.) This is its war chest for hard-money contributions to candidates. For the 1999–2000 election cycle, the NEA's PAC reported that it raised a total of $5,962,464—and spent $6,108,973, drawing down its cash reserves to a mere $354,876.[151]

(It was a tough year. The NEA really, *really* wanted to elect Al Gore and a Democratic Congress.)

But, because of the NEA's hydra-headed nature, the national organization's PAC is only part of its hard-money political spending story. State affiliates and even some NEA locals have PACs too. The NEA has claimed that it does not know how much they spend altogether. Extrapolating from four representative states, however, Leslie Spencer and I estimated in *Forbes* that total state and local spending amounted to a remarkable $16 million in 1992—when it was about seven times what the NEA's PAC spent. If that relationship holds true, PAC spending by NEA state and local affiliates in the 1999–2000 cycle would have been an additional, even more remarkable, $42.5 million. So, the NEA overall may have given roughly $50 million to candidates. By comparison, the Federal Election Commission reports that the total of *all* PAC contributions to *all* federal candidates in the 1999–2000 cycle was a mere $579.4 million.[152] In other words, the Teacher Trust (including the AFT) provided one out of every ten dollars spent in elections.

Historically, as much as 98 percent of NEA PAC money has gone to Democrats. But—unlikely as it may seem—even this is an understatement of the union's partisan slant. Contributions to GOP candidates are invariably made during the primaries, in order to support NEA-friendly Republicans over other Republicans. The NEA will seldom support a Republican in the general election, rarely if the seat is contested, and never if it stands to be a close race.

Interestingly, the NEA raises about $1 million annually for its PAC from the delegates to its Representative Assembly, complete with peer pressure tactics to get 100 percent participation and even a car offered as a prize. (Individual incentives are apparently acceptable in this context.) This raises an interesting logical question: Since money is fungible, some of the stipend that delegates are given by their state and local affiliates to attend the RA might well end up as a PAC contribution.

In fact, the line between dues money and political contributions is hard to draw. Even more important than the Teacher Trust's hard-money contributions is soft money: indirect or disguised contributions. Federal law prohibits the mixing of union dues and political contributions to candidates. But the unions have found numerous ingenious methods to spend money on political activities that do not involve giving cash to candidates. Some of them are actually legal, for example, the union can spend on get-out-the-vote drives as long as it does not restrict its efforts to one party's candidates . . . explicitly. Others of its methods are more dubious.

Each year, the NEA is required to inform agency fee–payers of the amount they spend on activities that are unrelated to collective bargaining. The NEA, with every reason in the world to claim this figure is as low as possible, still admits that non–collective bargaining spending is between 33 and 40 percent of its annual budget (which was $225 million in 1999–2000). Thus, at a minimum, the NEA has $75 million annually for other activities. These could include outreach, advocacy . . . or even education. But most of it is spent on politics.

The NEA's strategic plan and budget in 2000 spelled out its activities:

- *$9.6 million for screening candidates, campaign training and member mobilization . . .*

- *$872,000 to develop coordinated state-specific campaigns . . .*

- *$540,000 to develop strategies for congressional redistricting, candidate recruitment and voter registration . . .*

● *$386,000 to form "organizational partnerships" with political*
parties, campaign committees, and political organizations . . .

The list goes on and on.

As formidable as this may seem, it does not include the resources and manpower devoted to politics by the NEA hydra's other heads—its affiliates in every state and its thousands of local affiliates. Look at it this way: revenues of the whole NEA hydra amounts to some $1.25 billion. Arguably all of what the NEA does is political. But just take the 33 percent that the NEA at the national level admits it doesn't spend on collective bargaining. Applied across the whole hydra, that suggests that the NEA's total spending on politics is over $400 million a year.

But action and reaction are equal and opposite—or at least opposite. For several years, the Herndon, Virginia–based Landmark Legal Foundation has been filing complaints with federal oversight bodies to force the NEA to comply with the clumsy but mandatory filing requirements imposed on labor unions. In its complaints to the Internal Revenue Service and the Department of Labor, Landmark has pointed out that, although the Federal Election Commission found that the NEA had participated in a "National Coordinated Campaign Committee" with other labor unions and Democratic Party officials, aimed at electing Democrats in the 1996 election, the NEA's filings claimed its non-PAC spending on politics amounted to: $0. Nor does the NEA report any of the $70 million or so expended annually on the UniServ directors as political, although the union's own internal documents say that the UniServ director's responsibilities include flagrantly political activities such as raising PAC money and "developing the capacity of state and local affiliates to elect pro-education candidates." Also, Landmark wanted to know, why was no political spending reported to reflect the $400,000 transferred to the Washington Education Association in 1996, responding to the WEA's explicit request for help in "candidate campaigns?"[153]

In the summer of 2002, Mark R. Levin, Landmark's president, seemed quietly optimistic about the course of these complaints. But things do not seem to be moving quite as fast as when the Heritage Foundation and other conservative groups were audited by the IRS during the Clinton administration.

Mark Tapscott, director of the Center for Media and Public Policy at the Heritage Foundation, is even more cheerful. In 2001, he says, we sent letters requesting copies of their most recent 990 filings [expenditure report required by IRS] to the teacher unions representing teachers in the hundred largest public school districts and the state organizations for each state. We received responses from 38 of the 100 and 25 of the 50. This despite the IRS rule that requires copies to be made available upon request to all requesters, with only reasonable copying charges allowed.

The documents Tapscott did get were not very forthcoming about political spending, of course. But they did contain gems like the fact that an average of $200,000 was spent annually on travel—a lot of subway tokens for big city unions, which are supposed to be focused on bargaining with local school boards.

"We will be sending the same requests this year," says Tapscott happily. "I plan to make this an annual project for the Media Center."[154] He knows that if he's feeling really mischievous, he could force the unions to produce the documents by appealing to the IRS.

All of which may seem technical.

But remember, it was income tax violations that finally ended the career of Al Capone.

7

The Workers' Paradise

WEA employees currently have excellent salary, benefit and employment protection in their contract which if widely known by the membership would cause significant unrest within the Association.[155]

—Memo from the Washington Education Association
bargaining team to the WEA Board of Directors

The NEA will take in $130 from each full-time member in 2002–2003. The dues levels for its state affiliates vary widely, but $300 per member is a good estimate, if a bit on the conservative side. Local dues vary even more widely, but $70 per member would be a good conservative estimate. That totals $500 per member for all levels of the union. This means NEA is an industry with, at the very least, a $1.25 billion annual income.

We know where the money comes from. It's extracted from the paychecks of teachers and other education employees. It's collected by each school district and forwarded to the local union, which keeps its share and forwards the rest to the state union, which keeps its share and forwards the rest to the NEA in Washington, D.C. Then the unions spend it. On what?

According to the NEA's strategic plan and budget, in 2001–2002 the union will spend $3.49 of every member's dues "advocating factors that are critical to improving students' readiness, motivation to learn and achievement."

How nice! Almost it's the sort of thing you might expect a professional "educational association" to do.

At all levels, the union's description of its program spending contains language like this, which is designed to persuade teacher members who bother to look at such things that the money is being spent wisely and for their benefit. That may be arguable. ("Advocating" sounds suspicious; maybe it means electing more Democrats?) But what isn't arguable is that large amounts of that money go directly to the union executives and staff. Working for the union is not just a living—it's a good living.

My interest about union compensation is not mere curiosity. (I am curious, of course.) The plain fact is that much of what the union bargains for, lobbies for, and advocates can only be understood if examined through the lens of staff compensation. There are clauses in teacher contracts, bills that work their way through state legislatures and Congress, and campaigns to influence public opinion that have far more to do with the operations and overhead of the Teacher Trust than with teachers or education in general.

Union officers' secrecy about their compensation has always been formidable. Abuses by private sector unions led to public disclosure laws such as the Labor Management Reporting and Disclosure Act (LMRDA) of 1959. But the law's language reflects the concerns of that time. In 1959, public sector unions were either weak or nonexistent. In the forty-four years since that time, growth in public sector union membership, particularly teacher unions, has exploded. The unions' political influence and public policy input have increased substantially as well.

The LMRDA applies only to private sector unions and those public sector unions that have some members in the private sector—just a few of the NEA's state affiliates. Congress has failed to enact federal legislation governing public sector unions. State legislatures are either unwilling or unable to address the issue. These failures make it very difficult for teachers, or taxpayers, to get at the truth about union activities, expenditures, or compensation.

Internal union disclosures run the gamut from A to about D or E— from making information available only to elected state union representatives to complete nondisclosure. An accurate picture can be constructed only by piecing together information from a variety of sources. Furthermore, teachers seem to fear reprisals if they request salary information. For these reasons and more, the task of gathering, analyzing, and disseminating union financial information has often fallen upon education researchers. The ironic result: union members regularly seeking information about union operations from researchers like Educational Intelligence Agency's Mike Antonucci who are entirely outside the union.

In 2002, NEA headquarters planned to send $82.3 million of its dues income (about 35 percent of the total) directly back to its state affiliates to help fund the UniServ program. That money must be spent exclusively to pay UniServ directors. Without this subsidy, state affiliates would have to dramatically raise dues, cut staff, or cut salaries. The NEA will spend another $73 million on the salaries and fringe benefits of its own 560-member staff.[156] Simple arithmetic tells us that comes to $130,357.14 per full-time employee. Not bad, even if a portion of that money goes to people who no longer work for the union, like retirees.

And the NEA compensation is even more impressive when you consider that many officers of local affiliates receive only the smallest of stipends from their parent organizations, and often get along with little or no staff.

The Mountain Valley Education Association in Washington State is a typical local NEA affiliate. It has 313 members and charges $180 in annual dues. Its total income in 1999–2000 was only $56,375.

Even a large local affiliate, like the United Educators of San Francisco, gets by on a $1.2 million budget. More than half of that is dedicated to the salaries and benefits of local-hire staff. The state and national organizations are the cash cows of NEA, often subsidizing local affiliates in various ways to keep them afloat.

The salaries of local union officials are generally governed by the teacher salary schedule of the district they represent. They are considered to be on a leave of absence from the teaching job that they were hired to perform.

Most elected union officials—such as local presidents, members of the board of directors, representatives to state councils or assemblies, and others—are and remain teachers and education support personnel. They conduct classes, grade papers, and meet with parents. They are, however, granted release time for union business. The number of days allowed for release time varies widely. In California, local presidents are usually released half-time, or about ninety school days per year. California members of the NEA Board of Directors get up to seventy-two days of release time. Representatives to the State Council get up to thirty-six days. Presidents of very large local affiliates—such as United Teachers Los Angeles—are released full-time from teaching but are still considered employees of their districts. Locals may also grant other union officers release time.

The government school district continues to pay the teacher as if he or she were present in the classroom full-time. Arrangements vary, but the union usually picks up the cost of the substitute. Of course, even though these release-time officials may make no appearances in the classroom for an entire year (or many years), they continue to move up the district pay scale. The district also continues to pay full-time benefits (including retirement) for a half-time-or-less employee.

Both NEA and its state affiliates have grant programs to help fund routine release time for local presidents. State unions also make special grants to locals for special hiring. In 1996, the California Teachers Association set aside $100,000 to "provide contract-for-service staffing and release time for local activists in order to develop and implement strategic action plans in the arena of school restructuring and improvement."

Teacher union employees come in three categories: executives, professional staff, and support staff. The remuneration of executives (e.g., president, vice president, department heads) is set by the elected board of directors. The remuneration of professional staffers (e.g., mid-level managers, associates) and also support staffers (e.g., secretaries, research assistants) is bargained between NEA's top officials and the staff unions to which their employees belong.

Salaries for employees of Teacher Trust state affiliates naturally vary according to their state's cost of living, size of affiliate, collective bargaining laws, and national union priorities. But in all cases, salaries exceed average state incomes, professional staff salaries exceed average teacher incomes, and in some cases, the salaries of union secretaries and assistants exceed state teachers' pay as well.

In California, the salary of the state union president is pegged to three times the average teacher salary for the previous year. If state teacher salaries increase $500, the union president gets a $1,500 raise the next year. The pay of the union's vice president and secretary-treasurer are pegged to 90 percent that of the president. Many state union executives have six-figure salaries. Several NEA state affiliates have professional staffs whose *average* salaries exceed $90,000 annually.

Press coverage of Teacher Trust staff salaries is minimal—as usual. In 1994, a New Jersey newspaper, *The Trentonian,* published a story on the salaries of employees of the New Jersey Education Association. The story claimed "more than 40 of them are paid at least $100,000 a year."

When asked to verify those totals, NJEA spokesman Ed Gallagher replied, "We don't publish that information at all."

In 1997, *The Detroit News* published a front-page story with the strikingly similar headline "Teachers Union Pays Execs $100,000." The paper described how seventy-five Michigan Education Association employees received over $100,000 in salary and expenses in 1996. The story also noted that three MEA executives earned more than Michigan governor John Engler and ten earned more than United Auto Workers president Stephen Yokich.

Asked to verify those totals, MEA spokeswomen Dawn Cooper replied, "I don't know where they got their figures." She claimed the story was "fraught with errors" even though the figures came from the union's own U.S. Department of Labor report.

The Detroit News story also demonstrated that teachers and union activists are largely unaware of what they are paying union staff—and don't like it when they do find out.

"It's a waste of dues money," said Don Bundy, a former member of the MEA's board of directors. "A lot of members don't think they're worth that much." Tom Lukshaitis, president of the Sandusky Education Association, an MEA affiliate, wrote a Letter to the Editor that contained the classic comment:

> I can honestly say the only time I'm aware of what the brass in our organization gets in salary is when it is reported in the newspapers. . . . The decision as to what each of our executives make is not made by or reported to the general membership.

Also in 1997, a similar front-page story in the *Pittsburgh Tribune-Review,* based on Labor Department figures, prompted the Pennsylvania State Education Association to call the salary figures "so overexaggerated they don't even deserve a response."[157] Since the PSEA certified the numbers when they were reported to the Labor Department, you have to wonder if union officials themselves know what their top staffers make.

Teachers' shock and horror at their union staffers' salaries was also very clear in December 1993, when economist William Styring published a special report in the *Indiana Policy Review* entitled "Inside the ISTA Payroll: Forty bigwigs make over $100,000." Styring analyzed the contract between the Indiana State Teachers Association and its staff union, which had been leaked to him by a disgruntled employee. Forget about the "bigwigs"—the lowliest ISTA clerk received a total compensation package worth more than $36,000, about $4,000 higher than the total compensation of a typical beginning Indiana teacher at the time. Styring did not link specific union officials with salaries. But he later reported that the story had generated hundreds of telephone calls and letters—many of them from teachers who requested permission to spread the story to others.

But paychecks are only part of the Teacher Trust compensation package. There are also benefits. In about a dozen cases, contracts between state unions and their staffs have been uncovered. They are very detailed—as you might expect in a contract between union management and union staff—and reveal that benefits are notably generous, ranging in value up to 40 percent of salary. (Benefits for U.S. workers are typically about half that.)

This was what provided the *Indiana Policy Review* with its eye-catching headline. Only 9 of the Indiana affiliate's 119 employees had been reported in official filings to earn salaries above $70,000. But Styring was able to show that, in 40 cases, total compensation packages that exceeded $100,000, including benefits such as very generous vacations (almost twelve weeks for sixteen-year veterans), cars and credit cards (available to nearly half ISTA's staff), and even allowances for something called "companion travel."

According to the leaked contract, ISTA contributed 22 percent of annual compensation in 1996 to the professional staff's pension plan. Employees contributed nothing. Nineteen of these employees were also ex-teachers and enrolled in the state Teacher Retirement Fund, financed by the taxpayers of Indiana. Thus some Indiana State Teachers Association veterans,

Styring calculated, could retire on more than 100 percent of their final salary, courtesy of Indiana taxpayers—who were in the remarkable position of having to pay the union that organizes against them. In the private sector, such employer-union subventions are illegal.

(And now in Indiana too, as a result of Styring's exposé and Leslie Spencer and my publicizing it in *Forbes*. Let the sun shine in!)

In addition, ISTA staff was covered by a $500,000 litigation policy, $150,000 group term life insurance policy, and up to $150,000 accidental death and dismemberment policy.

The health plan had coverage as follows:

- Basic plus supplemental unlimited major medical coverage

- Long-term disability—two-thirds of salary for five years, 90 percent thereafter.

- 100 percent prescription drug coverage

- 100 percent semiprivate rate for hospital room and board

- 100 percent hospital ancillary charges

- 100 percent extended care facility charges

- 100 percent outpatient surgery charges

- 100 percent voluntary second-surgical opinion

- Up to $200 for a routine physical, up to $50 for spouse and each dependent child

- Usual and customary rates for surgeon, in-hospital medical, diagnostic X-ray lab, emergency accident, nervous and mental, pap smear, mammogram, child immunizations, transfer and ambulance, and home health care hospice

- Maximum out-of-pocket co-payment $500 per individual per year

The vision plan offered usual and customary rates for eye examinations, frames, and lenses. There were no deductibles and the staff was covered for up to $200 for "not medically necessary" contact lenses. The dental plan offered unlimited maximum benefits. Death benefits included: all accrued salary; eighteen months' medical, dental, and vision coverage for dependents; payment for accumulated and unused vacation and personal business leave days; and the right to purchase the decedent's company (union!) automobile.

Not surprisingly, ISTA's turnover was infinitesimal. Thus over a third of its staff had been there sixteen years or more—which qualified them for nearly twelve weeks of vacation. These lucky veterans included a goon briefly jailed after attempting to vandalize a school board member's car during a 1985 teachers strike.

A 1995 contract between the California Teachers Association and its staff has similar benefits. The California staffers and their eligible dependents receive fully paid medical and dental benefits. The employee receives a free annual physical examination, fully paid disability insurance, and fully paid life insurance to provide three times the employee's salary. Retirement benefits are vested after five years and include full retirement available at age fifty-five. The CTA paid a maximum of 21.5 percent of taxable wages into the fund, and retirement payments were based on the highest single year of service. The California staff received another consideration—the CTA paid the employee's share of Social Security.

Based on information from Indiana, plus California and New Jersey, we can get a fairly good picture of what union staff perks are like. Vacation ranges from 22 to 30 working days a year, along with 15 to 20 holidays. Staffers also receive 12 to 15 sick days per year, and additional paid religious leave, personal leave, bereavement leave, birth or adoption leave, and family illness leave. Staffers receive full salary while serving on jury duty. They may take up to 75 days unpaid political leave "to serve in any elected part-time state political position."

In Indiana, anyone required to drive more than eight thousand miles on business receives a company (sorry, union) automobile. The employee selects from among new Chevrolet, Oldsmobile, Buick, or Pontiac models and receives a new auto after three years or forty-eight thousand miles, whichever comes first. The California Teachers Association will reimburse staffers for rental and parking charges for private aircraft used on union business, and for *monthly membership in a flying club*—if it saves the union money (!).

We could go on and on for pages about credit cards, telephone cards, moving expenses, interest-free car loans and . . . incarceration pay! If jailed as a result of conducting union-related business, the employee receives normal benefits and double normal salary during incarceration. . . .

Why can't the state unions get a handle on this extravagant staff compensation, given their budget problems?

An activist who has asked to remain anonymous explained one reason to Educational Intelligence Agency's Mike Antonucci: "The main reason that staff perks are not widely known is that *board members get the same perks.* If the membership knew, they would be furious. So we have a situation where the board negotiates contracts with staff and the board (which is supposed to be representing the teachers) also gets the same benefits that staff gets. This is a pretty good incentive for the board to give staff pretty much anything they want since they will get it, too."

But it's when you reach the top of the heap, at NEA headquarters, that the real money comes rolling in. Union members dole out $2.2 million annually for the care and feeding of the nine-member Executive Committee, six of whom receive only an annual stipend from the union. In 2002, NEA's president, vice president, and secretary-treasurer will earn a combined $616,000 in salary and $544,000 in cash allowances and travel.

Members of the NEA Board of Directors can receive reimbursement for luggage and dependent care. Executive officers receive paid "companion travel" to the union's annual convention plus one international event each year. Members of the Executive Committee receive a free annual physical, "companion travel," and (no doubt very necessary) free assistance with income tax preparation.

Perks received by elected union officers are similar to those afforded the staff, plus a few additional ones, such as:

- First-class airfare if an out-of-state trip exceeds four hours

- Laundry/dry cleaning, exercise facilities, and similar items "comparable to what would normally be available and utilized if not traveling from their home residence" if a trip is three days or more

- With executive-officer approval, chartered short-run air travel due to "constraints of timeliness"

- Reimbursement for one set of luggage and one briefcase for each full term of office

- Reimbursement for travel for one "companion" (i.e., "domestic partner," family member, or similar companion) to three events per year

- One phone line and phone for Association business in director's home

- One phone line and one fax machine for Association business in home

- Reimbursement for office supplies used in home

- Costs of printing, supplies, and postage

- Computer and printer

- Reimbursement for absences from outside paid employment other than teaching

- Up to $300 per month for child or home care

But there's a second reason Teacher Trust staffers succeed in extracting these extravagant packages from Teacher Trust management. The staffs have their own, very demanding, unions. The National Education Association Staff Organization (NEASO) is the largest of these, with approximately 4,000 members working in Washington, D.C., and in each state affiliate. NEASO itself takes in nearly $200,000 a year in dues. It has a single full-time employee who earns $43,163 (not including benefits) to keep track of the staff union's business.

Since the entire membership of these staff unions is largely made up of contract negotiators, they are very good at what they negotiate for themselves. They also are exquisitely aware of the public-relations cost to the Teacher Trust when its own staff have poor working conditions or go out on strike. The staff unions take a hard-line stance when contracts are up. But so, surprisingly often, does Teacher Trust management. What ensues is often bitter and acrimonious . . . and wildly entertaining for union observers.

In the last five years, at least a dozen NEA state affiliates have had their staffs go out on strike or have faced some other work actions. The alleged reasons for the labor unrest are quite eye-opening, especially in light of some demands that teacher unions make of school boards.

In 1998, the Montana Education Association management demanded increased workload from its staffers, a three-year freeze on salaries, and rollbacks in benefits. The MEA Staff Organization held informational pickets outside the teacher union convention in April 1998, drawing press coverage.

"We would prefer that the public not notice it," said MEA president Eric Feaver.[158]

One of the long-standing complaints of the Wisconsin Education Association Council is that state law limits annual increases in teacher compensation to 3.8 percent. But in 1998, when the union staff contract came up, the WEAC offered less than 3.8 percent to its own employees. The staff union set up informational pickets outside the schools where members of the WEAC bargaining team were employed.[159]

Even more ironic was the 1999 strike against the Vermont NEA after the staff union claimed VNEA president Angelo Dorta proposed an alternative pay schedule that in part called for—wait for it—merit pay!

Similarly, in 1997, the Louisiana Association of Educators wanted to tie its staff salary increases to good evaluations and membership increases. The staff went on strike instead.

When union staff go on strike, elected Teacher Trust officials are usually happy to cross those picket lines in order to keep union offices open. This is a little hard to square with NEA Resolution F-7, which begins:

> The National Education Association denounces the practice of keeping schools open during a strike. The Association believes that when a picket line is established by the authorizing bargaining

unit, crossing it, whether physically or electronically, is strike-breaking and jeopardizes the welfare of education employees and the educational process.

Thus, in 1997, Iona Holloway, a member of the NEA Executive Committee, crossed the Louisiana staff union's picket line to help answer phones at union headquarters.

Nor does Teacher Trust management muscle-flexing end at crossing picket lines. There have been several instances of Teacher Trust management filing restraining orders against picketing staffers. In 1997, the Ohio Education Association did this during its staff strike in Columbus.

For their part, the staff unions seem to relish filing unfair labor practice complaints against their NEA employers. In 1996, the Michigan Education Association staff union filed no less than nine charges against MEA during its lengthy strike. These included claims that MEA had: engaged in regressive bargaining (bargaining in which the employer's offer is steadily reduced); engaged in "surface" bargaining (bargaining with no intent to reach an agreement); not provided necessary and relevant information; reduced supplemental benefits; refused to negotiate over workloads; failed to give its representatives the authority to bargain, and bargained directly with workers.[160]

All of these charges will be familiar to school boards and their negotiators. They hear the same complaints from the Teacher Trust at contract time.

"It's a sad day when a union acts like the management it opposes. I just hope they learn that being union is not situational," said MEA staff union president Tom Greene. "You can't be union in public and management behind closed doors."

In 1999, the Pennsylvania State Education Association bypassed the staff union and offered a $1,000 signing bonus directly to its staffers if they would accept PSEA's "final best offer." Despite rejection of this offer by staff union negotiators, the staff accepted it and stayed on the job. The PSEA Staff Organization filed an unfair labor practice charge. In a letter to local activists, the staff union claimed the PSEA had "taken positions at the bargaining table that run contrary to its own bargaining principles and goals. It has employed bargaining tactics identical to those employed by school districts every day."[161]

But for sheer irony, hypocrisy, and lunacy, nothing can match the January 2000 strike against the Kentucky Education Association (KEA) by the Kentucky Education Association Staff Organization (KEASO).

The NEA's Kentucky affiliate has had severe financial, membership, and public relations problems for the last six years. The previous staff contract was settled only after acrimonious negotiations. When the KEA offered the staff a salary proposal that was conditional upon maintaining 28,500 members, the staff union authorized a strike.

A week before the strike deadline, KEA executive director Charlie Vice sent a remarkable memo to the union's staff. In it, Vice claimed that several staffers had approached him with questions about what a strike would mean.

"First, we want you to know that we recognize your legal right to choose to strike or not to strike," Vice wrote. But in a question-and-answer format, Vice went on to provide astonishing advice, considering his position as a union chief of staff.

- [Can staffers decline to strike?] *Answer: Yes. That's up to you. You have a legal right to work and you are welcome.*

- [Can the staff union fine me for showing up at work?] *Only KEASO members can be fined and penalized. If you resign from KEASO, you would not be a member, and would no longer be subject to fines and penalties.*

- [Can KEA replace strikers?] *Answer: Yes, KEA has the legal right to hire what are called "permanent replacements."*

- [Will my job remain open if I strike?] *At the end of the strike, striking employees have the right to return to their former position if it is open or vacant. If not, they would not return until an opening or vacancy in their former position arises.*

Imagine the teacher-union reaction if a superintendent were to send such a memo to teachers contemplating a strike. And the staff union was duly apoplectic. In a letter to the staff, KEASO president Ellen Young called KEA's tactics "reprehensible" and chided the organization for abandoning union principles: "We are embarrassed for members of KEA that this so-called teacher union has become Kentucky's foremost union-buster."

Conveniently for KEASO—and unfortunately for KEA—the NEA was holding a large regional conference in the Hyatt Regency Louisville. Hundreds of union officials and staffers from several Middle Atlantic states were planning to attend. KEASO announced its plans to picket the event. The word got around to the staff unions in other states, who encouraged their bosses to stay home. Most NEA staff did not attend, and estimates of elected union officials who stayed away ranged from dozens to several hundred. Kentucky lieutenant governor Steve Henry was scheduled to address the conference but canceled. KEASO claimed to have twenty-two picketers in front of the Hyatt, including the president of KEA's largest local affiliate, as conference attendees arrived the morning of January 29.

But while many union officials and members refused to cross the picket line, NEA president Bob Chase and vice president Reg Weaver managed to enter the hotel and addressed the hundreds of activists who showed up. When the Educational Intelligence Agency's Mike Antonucci asked why the leaders of America's largest union were appearing at a conference being picketed by striking union workers, the NEA responded that its *employees* may refuse to cross picket lines but "we do not have a policy in regard to governance [officials]."

The contradiction did not go unnoticed by staff unions across the country. "It has always been a puzzlement that unions can and do all too often treat their own employees in a manner that would have them mustering all the power at their command to overcome and defeat if it was happening to their own members," wrote California associate staff president Maureen Keating, in a January 30 letter of support to KEASO.

On the other hand, the *Wall Street Journal* Editorial Page actually had praise for NEA officials, an unusual and no doubt irritating occurrence:

> What's of note is that whenever union management for the teachers does encounter what they consider excessive demands, they don't roll over. They bargain hard and are often willing to take a strike rather than automatically raise dues on all members to pay for more salary and benefits. Would that school boards and the mediators they often employ showed such backbone. Maybe then genuine public school reform would advance in visible stages rather than the grudging lip service the same union leaders give it now.[162]

Still, the Teacher Trust does seem to end up giving the staff unions most of what they want. This leads to many NEA state affiliates having financial difficulties even while they're pulling in huge piles of money from teachers and other education employees. (Hmmm . . . sound familiar?)

In the mid-1990s, the California Teachers Association had a severe budget crisis, leading to demands from some quarters for the union to cut costs.

"I am extremely uncomfortable with the fact that we pay CTA staff salaries and benefits that the fine teachers of this state can never hope to attain. We need to draw the line somewhere," said one local activist at a 1993 CTA Budget Committee hearing. "Members are expressing discontent with CTA's insensitivity to their financial situation. It is time for CTA, for once, to do what its members have to do, live within its current budget," said another.

But the Teacher Trust, and its staffers, don't want to know. In a speech to the CTA State Council in June 1994, president Del Weber nevertheless argued for a dues increase—in the midst of a deep recession in the state.

"The $6 dues [increase] is a bare minimum to maintain our program and represent our members," said Weber. "It would be very easy, with a weaker CTA, for external groups such as the Religious Right to take over the public [government] school system."

Keep the bogeyman from the door! Give generously!

Similarly, the Pennsylvania State Education Association froze hiring in 1999 to deal with a $2.3 million deficit.

And Ohio Education Association president Michael Billrakis and executive director Robert Barkley Jr. sent this memo to local affiliate leaders in April 2000 to inform them about the union's projected $6.3 million deficit:

> Specifically, and regrettably, we can no longer afford to sustain the current number of OEA employees at their current level of compensation and benefits and continue to provide the expected level of services and programs without significantly raising OEA dues for you and every other member. Going backwards is something we all rail against in bargaining. We do not expect OEA's position to be seen as contrary to that philosophy because the OEA can, and will remain an employer that provides high quality benefits and exceptionally competitive levels of compensation.

The final word on union compensation: the amusing saga of the *Board Management Procedures Handbook,* which governs the expenses of elected

officers of the California Teachers Association. The handbook instructs officers nervously:

> Regardless of authorization, expenses should nonetheless be
> incurred *without ostentatious display* on the part of any individual
> which could in any way *damage the image of the Association*. [Empha-
> sis added]

Subsequently, the CTA apparently decided that *any* disclosure of the
privileges awarded to the board of directors and executive officers would
"damage the image of the Association." In July 1997, it restricted access to
the handbook. Previously, it was made available to "any person having a
reasonable interest in it." The language was changed to read "any person
having a demonstrable need to review it."

Well, I think that not just government school teachers but the entire
American public, above all the taxpayers, have a "demonstrable need" to
know what the Teacher Trust is paying itself. Certainly union members
cannot hold union officials and staff financially accountable if they have no
idea where the money goes. The situation is even more invidious for the
non-union teachers who are compelled by many state laws to contribute to
the union treasury.

Teachers are consumers of union services. They will choose the best
value virtually every time. In Georgia, the Professional Association of
Georgia Educators (PAGE), an independent teacher association, has a
smaller staff but more members than the NEA-affiliated Georgia Association of Educators (GAE). Yet PAGE charges about one-third in dues what
GAE charges. Clearly, teachers will decline to subsidize excessive union
management and staff compensation—if they are given full information
and a reasonable alternative.

Disclosure of union operations and finances to the public and its
membership could be instituted by legislation. But internal union reform
is also necessary. The government cannot, and should not, dictate to unions
how they may generate revenues—provided the unions abide by existing
statues against fraud, embezzlement, extortion, etc. But simply the fact that
unions tie their income to increases in teacher salaries—funds extracted
from the taxpayer—necessitates greater public scrutiny. Union staff compensation is a critical component in the problem of the government
school system.

Garages must tell customers how their automobile repair bill was computed. Attorneys must account for time spent on a client's case. Salaries of government school superintendents and other officials are matters of public record.

The NEA and AFT are in the business of providing a service to those who pay dues. They are not charities. Members should be granted the opportunity to judge truthfully whether they are getting their money's worth. So should the public.

8

Kryptonite

Choice is good.[163]

—New Orleans Public Schools chief executive officer Al Davis,
after placing his daughter in a private school.

The Teacher Trust, like Superman, is faster than a speeding bullet, more powerful than a locomotive, and able to leap tall buildings in a single bound. But, also like Superman, it is vulnerable to one thing. In the case of Superman, it's kryptonite; for the Teacher Trust, it's school choice—the creation of a free market in education, rather than the current socialist government school system.

Theoretically, an education market could be stimulated by making school fees tax-deductible—so that parents could write off school costs against income, like interest on their house mortgage—or by giving a tax credit to match school fees, so that parents are compensated for the full value of their spending on their child's education. In effect, the parents would be directing the government's education spending. But another controversial proposal has dominated debate in recent years: school vouchers.

School vouchers were the brainchild of Nobel Prize–winning econo-mist Milton Friedman in a famous essay published in 1955.[164] The idea, simply put, is that, if there is going to be a government subsidy to K–12 students, it would be more efficient to give some or all of it directly to the student and his family in the form of a voucher to be spent in the school of their choice—public, private, or religious. After all, the government fights hunger by distributing food stamps, not by owning supermarkets.

With the freedom to choose the best educational value, parents as consumers will be able force the suppliers of education to improve their services or go out of business. And, unlike tax deductions and tax credits, this means all parents—not just those whose income is high enough to pay tax. Good schools will flourish. Bad schools will decline. Just like supermarkets.

The NEA opposes all aspects of what it calls the "extremist agenda" (see Chapter 9). But it appears ready to do literally anything to stop school vouchers. If vouchers are enacted—as they have been in Milwaukee, Cleve-land, and Florida—the unions will challenge them in court, tie them up with regulations, and delegitimize them in the eyes of the public. Or more.

Reasonable people can disagree about the actual results of a large-scale voucher program. But the Teacher Trust has gone well beyond the point of reasonable disagreement. To union officials, the fight against vouchers is a Holy Crusade. They are quite adamant in their claim that the introduction of vouchers would be directly responsible for the destruction of public education. Indeed, the unions don't stop there. They fervently predict seri-ous consequences to democracy and American society should a voucher program see the light of day.

Teacher Trust rhetoric reflects the fear that it genuinely feels—but for reasons that have nothing to do with education. The public, however, doesn't have the same fear. So the NEA and AFT have to use all sorts of analogies, metaphors, and word pictures to elicit the emotional response they want. They exploit fear of villains from history and politics—left, right, and center:

- "It used to be Marxists who advocated revolution and the withering away of the state. Today, this is the rebel yell of many people who bizarrely call themselves 'con-servative.' "[165]

● "Who supports vouchers? How about the former military dictator of Chile, alleged torturer Augusto Pinochet?"[166]

● "Reminiscent of the Vietnam era, when we heard military leaders justifying the destruction of villages in order to save them, you will hear proponents of vouchers tell you that in order to save public education, we must destroy it first."[167]

They exploit fear of religious cults:

● "The simple fact is, if David Koresh had been in California and the [voucher] initiative had been in effect, the Branch Davidian leader would have been eligible for more than $100,000 in school vouchers this year."[168]

They exploit fear of disease and illness:

● "[Vouchers are] like applying leeches and bleeding a patient to death."[169]

● "[Vouchers for urban schools] are not the cure, but would be one more cancer."[170]

Should all these methods fail, the Teacher Trust will go even further:

● "Vouchers are about fear of life. Vouchers are a diversion. They are a desperate effort of some of our fellow citizens to hold back the profound and scary changes which the 21st century has waiting for us. The private schools which vouchers seek to fund are really a kind of nuclear fall-out shelter and just about as functional."[171]

But only once have we heard a union official even hint at the truth in the midst of hyperbole. In October 1994, while addressing the union's State Council, California Teachers Association president Del Weber said:

Less than a year ago, we trashed Proposition 174, which was designed to eliminate public schools from California and replace them with private schools of a substandard nature. If it had passed, both *our professional and personal lives as teachers would have been shattered,* and the kids we now serve would have been left with virtually nothing. [Emphasis added]

What the unions fear from vouchers is not the effect on education, and certainly not the effect on students. They fear the effect on collective bargaining, on union membership and wages. And they're right. A large-scale voucher system probably would reduce collective bargaining, reduce union membership, and reduce teacher salaries in many cases.

(Teacher salaries might not fall as is usually assumed, at least in the long run. Although many teachers unquestioningly believe that without the union they would be ground into penury, the consensus among labor economists is that in the private sector unions only can raise salaries 10–15 percent—and at the cost of reducing employment in that industry. Teaching is actually a valuable skill. Private tutors in the New York City area can charge as much as $175 or more an hour, which for a forty-hour week could presumably mean a gross of $350,000 a year—albeit with only a two-week vacation! And what if the tutor could handle two or more children? Andrew J. Coulson in his book *Market Education: The Unknown History* reports that top instructors in Japan's *jukus,* the private, for-profit "after-school schools" widely used to supplement government middle and high schools, earn as much as Japanese professional baseball players.[172] In the end, a free-market education system might well use a wider range of teachers, including more part-timers and some superstars. In the short run, of course, the change could be jarring.)

The Teacher Trust's problem: the public will not go to the barricades with it to protect collective bargaining and other union privileges. So it must raise the specter of Armageddon to motivate opposition.

It's a standard political tactic. As described by one political observer, it goes like this: "Stake out the most outrageous position you can and force your opponents to respond; the more they do so, the less outrageous your position will seem, until it appears almost plausible, and then, owing to constant repetition, inevitable."[173]

The NEA offers up numerous arguments against vouchers. Some are specious; others can be overcome through properly crafted legislation or initiatives. None of them really matter—they're not the primary reason the teacher union opposes a voucher system.

The first argument: separation of church and state. Judicial decisions based on the constitutionality of vouchers have gone both ways in lower courts, and the U.S. Supreme Court.*

Yet it is difficult to see how providing grants to parents to spend at a school—any school, no matter its denomination—can violate the Establishment Clause. The unions' public relations arguments, as opposed to their legal arguments, are very interesting on this score. "[Americans] should not be forced to pay taxes for schools which teach religious views they disagree with," declared Florida Education Association executive director John Ryor.[174] But teacher unions make the exact opposite argument when teachers are forced to pay dues to a union whose political views they disagree with. This, too, is a First Amendment issue, though the Florida union's Ryor would probably fail to acknowledge it.

The alleged reason for the unions' opposition is the indirect passing of public funds to private schools. This, union officials say, cannot be tolerated. But public funds are being passed to private schools at this very moment, and have been for many years—with the full knowledge, and even the support, of these same teacher unions.

Hard to believe? Here is a lengthy quote from NEA president Keith Geiger extolling the virtues of America's largest "voucher" program—the G.I. Bill:

> While the war still raged, President Roosevelt, with a nudge from his wife Eleanor, pushed through the Congress the Servicemen's Readjustment Act, which we all know today as the G.I. Bill. This bold measure really launched the postwar education boom. Under the G.I. Bill, the federal government, yes, the federal government paid for the education of returning veterans. Specifically, the government paid their tuition and provided them with a weekly living allowance. For many veterans, the G.I. Bill meant something they had never dared dream of—it meant going to college. And they went in droves. American colleges and universities would never again be the same. To accommodate the bright-eyed veterans, they had to grow faster than ivy. What's more the G.I. Bill changed, fundamentally and forever, how Americans think about a

---

*In June 2002, the U.S. Supreme Court ruled in *Zelman vs. Simmons-Harris* that vouchers could be used in religious schools if parents had options.

college education. Before the war, college had been considered an elite pastime, like belonging to a country club. But by the early 1950s, one in four young Americans was attending college— almost double the prewar rate. It must also be noted that for the sixty percent of the veterans who had not completed high school, the G.I. Bill paid for remedial, vocational, and technical education. In all, eight million of twelve million veterans took advantage of the G.I. Bill. The program ended up costing, in today's dollars, one hundred and nineteen billion dollars. Now that's what I call a national commitment to education! The G.I. Bill turned out to be one of the wisest investments the United States has ever made. It provided the brainpower for America's incredible economic surge that began after the war and carried on right through the 1950s, the '60s, and the early '70s.[175]

This is a remarkable speech to be coming from the leader of an organization unalterably opposed to school vouchers. In 1955, when Milton Friedman first introduced the voucher program in his famous essay, *he used the G.I. Bill as an example of what he meant.*

Antivoucher forces counter that the G.I. Bill is for adults who, they claim, are less vulnerable to religious indoctrination than are elementary school students. (Of course, that is why vouchers would go to adults—the parents of K–12 students). But Geiger's speech undermined even that paltry point. If a G.I. Bill grant could be given to high school dropout veterans for remedial education, why can't school vouchers at least go to civilian high school dropouts today?

Geiger's speech also undercut yet another claim by his own union: that there aren't enough private schools to take in a huge influx of voucher students from public schools. When journalist Matthew Miller attempted to float a voucher plan past AFT president Sandra Feldman in 1999, she repeatedly asked him: "Where are these schools going to come from?"[176] But, as Geiger explained in his speech, in order to accommodate veterans with G.I. Bill money, colleges and universities grew *"faster than ivy."* Why wouldn't the same thing happen today—especially in a technologically advanced society?

Geiger credited the G.I. Bill with creating a national economic surge and calls it "one of the wisest investments the United States ever made." Yet the G.I. Bill was just a voucher allowing people to attend the school of their choice, without regard to income or religion.

Nor is the G.I. Bill the only program that provides public money to attend private schools. There are federal Pell grants, and countless state and local tuition assistance programs. An example of the latter: the District of Columbia Tuition Assistance Program, which provides grants of $2,500 a year for D.C. students attending private schools in the metropolitan area. Over twenty-four hundred students signed up for them.

"But if choice is good at the college level, is it not also beneficial for K–12 students?" asks Matthew Berry of the Institute for Justice, a legal foundation that defends voucher programs in court. "Why do [voucher opponents] support a program that allows students to use federal government grants to attend D.C.'s Catholic University?"[177]

The dirty little secret of the "no public funding for private schools" argument is that the unions oppose the use of *private* money for private schools as well. The NEA will rarely pass up an opportunity to take a swipe at Children First America or the Children's Scholarship Fund, two programs that provide privately funded vouchers to students to attend private elementary schools.

Thus, when such vouchers were offered to the parents of every student in the Edgewood School District in Texas, six hundred signed on. The NEA's reaction was swift and sudden. The union sent operatives from its Washington, D.C., headquarters to organize the community against the program, without visible success. The NEA's Special Committee on Privatization came to this conclusion: "The Committee believes that privately-funded private school voucher programs are undesirable, and that NEA and its affiliates should attempt to educate the public about the pitfalls of such programs."

Since most government school funding is based on a formula related to enrollment or average daily attendance, more students means more money. Therefore any program that might prompt parents to send their children to a private school, or home school, no matter if it is funded privately or publicly, means less *total* money in the government school till. But the effect of voucher programs on *per-pupil spending* is unknown. It depends on what type of school each student was attending prior to accepting a voucher.

This fact has been buried by the rhetoric of the Teacher Trust. It makes mutually exclusive arguments on this issue, either one of which might have validity, but taken together cancel each other out.

Thus the NEA often argues that most parents who take advantage of vouchers already have children in private schools. The government education budget will thus deliver funds to educate students who were not previously in the system.

If a state or municipality failed to provide additional funds to finance these private school students, that could indeed mean reduced funding for all public school students. But what if these private school parents suddenly decided to send their children to government schools after all? The government school system would be required by law to fund their education. Which could also put pressure on its budget.

And what if government school students accepted vouchers in large numbers and attended private schools? It would inevitably mean net savings—because private schools would be educating children for about half the amount the public schools charge. This savings could be applied to per-pupil spending so that those students who remain in public schools would see more funding for textbooks, supplies . . . and, of course, teacher salaries.

The NEA repeatedly disregards this scenario. NEA president Bob Chase responded to a pro-voucher article by Gary Rosen in *Commentary* this way:

> Milwaukee, which now spends nearly $40 million on 8,000 voucher students, avoided deep cuts in its public school budget only by raising property taxes as an offset. In addition, when voucher students leave a classroom, taking their per-pupil state aid with them, the school's fixed costs remain the same; the teacher and the electricity bill still must be paid.

By dealing in total numbers and removing the context, Chase sought to avoid the exact reply he got from Rosen, which was:

> In the case of Milwaukee, this amounts to $5,000 per voucher student, far less than the approximately $9,000 that the public schools would otherwise spend. To my mind, that is a pretty good deal: better schooling for less money.[178]

Contrary to Chase's claims, during the ten years of the voucher program, inflation-adjusted spending by the Milwaukee Public Schools grew more than three times faster than enrollment.

In fact, the NEA seems to feel that the public schools are entitled to specific amounts of spending irrespective of enrollment. In Edgewood, an NEA representative claimed that the private scholarship program "is threatening to gut the services received by children in the public schools. Given the district's heavy reliance on state funding, the loss of 515 students—and more than $3 million of state aid—could stymie ongoing reform efforts."[179]

This is rhetorical sleight-of-hand. The Edgewood district lost 4 percent of its total enrollment to private schools, but it only lost 3.5 percent of its state aid. Additionally, public school funding is budgeted on a district's enrollment for the previous year. So, for a full year, Edgewood received funding for students who weren't there anymore. By any measure, the district had more money for each pupil who stayed behind.

The unions employ the funding issue because their polling says pocketbook issues resonate longer with voters than the church-state, segregation, or any other arguments made against vouchers.

"Experience has shown us repeatedly that, in a contest for the hearts and minds of California voters, victory usually goes to the side that most effectively raises the hobgoblin of higher taxes," said California Teachers Association president Del Weber to his union's State Council before launching its anti-voucher campaign in 1993. And in the years following, that emphasis hasn't changed. Unions in Michigan and California defeated voucher initiatives in 2000 by highlighting the tax issue early and often.

Money aside, the unions claim that any "choice" going on is done by the private schools, not the parents. They claim that, with limited space, private schools will refuse to admit students with low academic achievement, discipline problems, or disabilities—a practice known as "cherry-picking."

"We face a tough, historic choice," said NEA vice president Reg Weaver, addressing the NAACP convention. "Will we go down the path of vouchers, *siphoning the best students and the most motivated parents away from inner-city public school systems?*" (emphasis added).[180]

How about that. All the rallies and legal battles by voucher supporters couldn't mean more than a supporter of the system, Reg Weaver, admitting that, given a chance, the "best students and the most motivated parents" would leave their public schools for a private alternative.

Even so, Weaver is wrong. Students who accepted vouchers in Edgewood were slightly below average academically.

And even if private schools did "cherry-pick," so what? They wouldn't be unique. Government school districts in effect cherry-pick on a regular basis through the use of residency requirements. "Admission to the government school comes only with the price of the house," wrote voucher advocate John E. Coons in 1992. "If the school is in Beverly Hills or Scarsdale, the poor need not apply."[181] (Except where school districts are unified, as in Miami or Hawaii, most American parents already have this—expensive and inefficient—species of choice. Ask any real estate agent. The parents just have to buy a house in the right school district. Real estate prices are their "private school tuition." Economists call this Tiebout choice, after the economist Charles Tiebout, who first drew attention to its significance.)

Reporter Joseph Berger of the *New York Times* found that some states allow parents to buy their way into affluent, suburban public schools. Another sixteen states require districts to accept out-of-town students free of charge if there is space. "Generally, tuition-paying students are admitted only in classes where there are vacancies," Berger wrote. "Most districts screen out students with academic or behavioral problems."[182]

The discrimination is even starker when it comes to special education students. Howard L. Fuller, a voucher supporter who is the former superintendent of schools in Milwaukee, noted that public high schools often have selective admissions requirements, as do gifted and talented elementary (GATE) schools. But his recitation of selectivity in the Milwaukee public schools with regard to special education students was particularly striking. Of the 117 public schools in the Milwaukee system, only 8 accept students with visual impairment, 9 accept those with autism, 13 accept those with hearing impairment, 22 accept those with orthopedic impairment, 60 accept those with emotional disability, 61 accept those with cognitive disability, and 105 accept those with learning disabilities. The only disability that guarantees you a seat in any Milwaukee public school is a speech/language disability.[183]

Ironically, it is not unusual for public schools to unilaterally transfer problem students or students with disabilities to alternative schools. Some of these are private schools—again undermining the "no public money for private schools" argument. A voucher for these students could clearly save taxpayer money. An audit of the District of Columbia special education program found that twenty-two D.C. special education students each had a separate bus transport them to classes at private schools outside the city, at an estimated cost of more than \$2 million, or the price of four hundred vouchers in Milwaukee.[184]

In making their case against vouchers, the Teacher Trust again betrays its very real bias against markets. "Competition—winners and losers—is okay for breakfast cereals, but disastrous for schools" is a typical comment.[185]

This position reflects deep-seated union philosophy. Both NEA and AFT used it in their attempts to push a merger upon reluctant affiliates. It was sold as a way to end "wasteful competition" between the two unions.

But the Teacher Trust's denunciations of "competition" need not be taken seriously. Remember, these are the same people who devote millions of dollars and countless man-hours to winning the ultimate competition: political elections. When its interests are at stake, the NEA and AFT are the most competitive organizations in America. Their efforts not to lose their "market share" of members, of influence, or of income, have made them the force they are today.

Equally spurious are the unions' claims that vouchers will foster segregation because white parents will remove their children from public schools and enroll them in private schools. In taking this stance, the unions are barring the barn doors after the horse has bolted. "Our schools today are more segregated than ever," admits NEA executive director Don Cameron.[186] The enrollment in most inner-city school districts is upwards of 85 percent ethnic and racial minority. Some districts are in the 95–96 percent minority range. It's virtually impossible for these districts to become more segregated. Besides, in Edgewood, as in voucher programs elsewhere, the ethnic mix of those who accepted vouchers was similar to that of the district's enrollment as a whole.

But the worst argument against school choice is that students and parents are "abandoning" public schools by accepting a voucher. When asked why vouchers are bad, Carole Shields of People for the American Way replied: "Fairness. You can't just pluck some kids out of a school and give them more hope and more opportunity and leave the rest behind."[187] This means she thinks parents have some sort of obligation to inflict a miserable education on their children. It's a species of moral blackmail.

And it's particularly heinous because unions don't hold their own teachers to the same obligation.

Teachers abandon lousy schools by the busload every year, and the unions don't denounce them. In fact, unions go out of their way to ease the transfer. Attempts to keep good teachers working in inner-city schools through the use of salary differentials often meet with union opposition.

Schools, districts, and teacher unions go on forever. But individual parents can't wait for the public education system to get its act together. Even three years of awful education is enough to ruin any student's prospects for the future. Parents have an obligation to their children, not to a government bureaucracy.

Close observers of the Teacher Trust are convinced there isn't enough money in the world to buy off union opposition to vouchers. When Matthew Miller of the *Atlantic Monthly* went to NEA president Bob Chase with a proposal that would combine vouchers for inner-city parents with substantially increased funding for the public schools in those districts, the conversation went like this:

> Miller: Is there any circumstance under which that would be something that . . .
> Chase: No.
> Miller: . . . you guys could live with? Why?
> Chase: No.
> Miller: Double school spending . . .
> Chase: No.
> Miller: . . . in inner cities?
> Chase: No.
> Miller: Triple it . . .
> Chase: No.[188]

There is only one thing that would persuade the Teacher Trust to turn down triple funding: survival. Between them, the National Education Association and the American Federation of Teachers have organized about 85 percent of the nation's public school teachers. They aren't worried about students and parents abandoning government schools for private schools; they're worried about *teachers* abandoning government schools for private schools. Private schools are rarely unionized. The NEA and AFT would either lose members, or be compelled to spend large sums of money to hold on to the numbers they already have.

A study by the Mackinac Center for Public Policy illustrated the situation clearly for Michigan. All 583 Michigan public school districts have unionized teachers. Only 5 of 139 state charter schools have unionized teachers. And only 2 of more than 1,000 Michigan private schools have unionized teachers. That's very scary arithmetic if you're a union executive.[189]

Besides simple survival, the Teacher Trust's opposition to vouchers, and to all schemes to marketize education, serves a larger organizational purpose. Unions cannot exist without solidarity. What holds the line together is the same thing that rallies the troops: the idea that you are defending something important and good, that the bad guys want to destroy it, that there's no retreat from this position, and that you are all in it together. What keeps soldiers in the trenches is usually not raw courage, but the fear of letting down their fellow soldiers. It's difficult enough to hold the line together to stop a G.I. Bill for Kids. It is a lot easier, however, to stand solidly against Pinochet, Koresh, witches, and the "cancer" of vouchers.

Nevertheless, with all the resources of the Teacher Trust committed to holding the line against vouchers, there have been some desertions, and they are growing in frequency. They have gotten so large that it would be correct to say that there is a substantial "voucher left" in America today. African American leaders like former New York congressman Floyd Flake and Baltimore mayor Kurt Schmoke support vouchers. They are very pointed in their criticism of unions and other voucher opponents. "Still others will wave their worn-out ideologies to defend a system of educational apartheid while demonizing anyone who promotes a parent's right to choose," wrote former U.S. ambassador to the United Nations Andrew Young.[190]

Liberal journals and columnists have joined the voucher parade. They, too, have been critical of the NEA and AFT. In 2000, the editors of the *New Republic* wrote impatiently:

> The response of the teacher unions to vouchers is to defend endlessly the principle of public education—when, by their implacable opposition to virtually every effort to hold the public schools accountable, they themselves ensure that many of those schools make a mockery of the ideals upon which they were founded.[191]

In 1999, the NEA singled out *Nashville Tennessean* columnist Tim Chavez as a "hero" for his support of public schools and his firsthand analysis of them. But less than a year later, Chavez was a full-fledged voucher supporter. "Bring on vouchers and other competition," he wrote. "The future of the impoverished child must be rescued from the public schools' status quo."[192]

Even industrial unions have fallen into step on vouchers. In 1999, local affiliates of the International Union of Operating Engineers joined the Pennsylvania Conference of Teamsters in endorsing a school choice plan introduced by Pennsylvania governor Tom Ridge.

And even prominent Democratic politicians have climbed aboard. When one of these politicians was asked how to deal with teacher union opposition on the issue, he replied, "We just all have to get together and charge the wall."

The politician's name? Senator Joe Lieberman (D–Connecticut).[193] (Even though he's no relation to the Educational Policy Institute's Mike Lieberman!)

Of course, Lieberman had to do some fancy footwork when he was chosen to be Al Gore's vice presidential running mate in the 2000 election. But the Teacher Trust knows that he's quite capable of softshoeing back.

On the other hand, the voucher movement has problems too. It has lost every single head-to-head electoral confrontation with the Teacher Trust, sometimes overwhelmingly. The battle is always costly for the Teacher Trust, both financially and in public relations terms. But it does win.

Voucher proposals often lack public support for several reasons. Most people don't have children in public schools. They are notoriously querulous about anything that might increase their taxes.

Some principled conservatives and libertarians, articulately represented by the Auburn, Alabama-based Von Mises Institute under its president Llewellyn H. Rockwell, argue that private schools accepting vouchers will be captured by federal regulations. (They also object, not always as loudly, to any government subsidy of K-12 education at all). Paradoxically, many parents with children already in private schools obviously agree, although the NEA insists they will be the main beneficiaries of vouchers.

The voucher movement's fundamental and unspoken problem, however, is race. Government schools in wealthy suburbs are already de facto private schools—and they are de facto segregated, by class if not completely by race. Families who cannot afford to live in these neighborhoods cannot send their children to those government schools. To many suburbanites in these areas, vouchers just look like a new word for busing.

Voucher advocates, naively attempting to show they are nice liberals, often exacerbate these secret suburban fears with publicity material featuring happy inner-city children (coming soon to *your* government school!). Conversely, the Teacher Trust, for all its much-vaunted progressivism, seems to have no ethical scruples against benefiting from these fears.

Diversity is not strength, at least in this instance. It may well be that a perfectly rational way of delivering government services is permanently crippled in America because of the country's profound demographic division.

Ironically, two limited government school voucher programs have been operating quietly in the United States since just after the Civil War: the "town tuitioning" programs in Vermont and Maine. Parents living in rural districts that do not operate schools can send their children to public or nonsectarian schools, even outside of the state, at the home district's expense. A study by Christopher Hammond for the Milton & Rose D. Friedman Foundation does seem to show that schools most affected by town tuitioning deliver better results cheaper. But, of course, Vermont and Maine are both 95 percent white.[194]

While the Teacher Trust has its fears of vouchers bringing death, destruction, and famine, voucher supporters have corresponding fantasies of classical scholarship and dedicated students. Probably neither is likely. From an economic standpoint, particularly when vouchers are minimal and when they are limited to government schools, they represent a form of *perestroika*—market socialism—an attempt to introduce some features of competition into a command economy, which cannot resolve its problems and may prove merely transitional (if we're lucky).

Moreover, as we will see with charter schools in Chapter 11 the Teacher Trust is adaptable, if it has to be. It will adapt to a voucher-expanded private school sector. It is already adapting to the great change that has come over Roman Catholic schools.

Fifty years ago, religious schools were 90 percent staffed with nuns, priests, and other clerics. Today more than 80 percent of Catholic school teachers are laypeople. Many of them are not Catholic. They have families, children, bills. They demand more from their employers.

In some places, these demands will come coupled with union representation. The Teacher Trust, and allied government agencies, are altering their policies toward religious schools. Where once they took a hands-off approach, they are now setting rules and plans for dealing with them. Ten to 15 percent of teachers in religiously affiliated schools are already organized. In Canada, Catholic-school teacher unions are common. They engage in work stoppages, strikes, and other job actions.

Recently, in New York, the federal court of appeals ruled unanimously that the state Employment Relations Board had the power to require Christ the King Regional High School in New York City to "bargain in good faith" with a union representing the school's teachers.[195] The Association of Catholic Elementary Educators promptly bargained a three-year contract with a 22 percent raise and increased benefits. The union is now seeking greater influence in the archdiocese of St. Louis. In northern New Jersey, more than 230 teachers in the Lay Faculty Association protested against the archdiocese. "The church has done more for social issues than anyone," said demonstrator Pat Moran, a religion teacher at Paramus Catholic High School. "The pope preaches it all the time. He supported the union in Poland. He's a union man."[196]

Until now, virtually all union activity in private schools has been independent, or affiliated with the industrial unions, such as the Laborers International Union of North America (LIUNA). But if vouchers boost private schools, both NEA and AFT will begin to move in.

"If they want private schools, we'll just have to organize the private school teachers," said Louisiana Federation of Teachers president Fred Skelton.[197]

Vouchers are the Kryptonite of the Teacher Trust. But should they become inevitable, the Teacher Trust will simply fall back on its traditional rule: If you can't beat 'em, make 'em join.

9

Going to Extremes

Our Association—at the national, state, and local levels—is the only organization standing in the way of the Radical Right taking control of public education.

—NEA president Keith Geiger, speaking to the union's board of directors in December 1994

Considering the Teacher Trust's wide-ranging power and influence, you might expect them to have an equally wide range of opponents and enemies. But a thorough study of union documents and rhetoric leads to the conclusion that it has only one enemy: extremists.

Who are these extremists and where can they be found? Before you go off searching in underground bunkers or compounds in the deep woods, check the mirror. YOU could be an extremist—and not even know it.

In 1997, the Upstate New York Coalition for Democracy—a liberal umbrella group headquartered in the home offices of the New York State United Teachers and composed of twenty-one local labor, civil rights, and other public interest organizations including NEA New York—wanted to know whether there was any "extremist activity" in the Albany-Schenectady area. So it sent a seven-page survey to "organizational leadership" and "key membership." The survey listed, by name, about two dozen extremist groups

and asked which ones were a problem in the respondents' jurisdictions. The
list included the Aryan Nation, Ku Klux Klan, neo-Nazis, and militia
groups. But the survey contained no questions about swastikas, cross burn-
ings, racial incidents, hate crimes, or weapons stashes. Instead, the questions
were about school board meetings, censorship of library books, and school
psychological testing.

Were neo-Nazis storming school board meetings in Albany? Well, no,
actually. But some of the other groups on the coalition's list of "extremists"
might have been causing problems: the Christian Coalition, Citizens for
Excellence in Education, Focus on the Family, Concerned Women for
America, the National Association of Christian Educators, and other mainstream conservative, religious, and family advocacy organizations.

The coalition's survey even named the most dreaded "extremist" group
of all: "Taxpayers' Association: (list specific name)."[198]

Belonging to such a group is enough to label you an "extremist." But
you can be a freelance "extremist" too. Have you ever wanted to reduce or
curtail public funding of the arts? You're an "extremist." Have you voted to
defeat proposed school budgets? You're an "extremist." Do you have problems with the way sex education is taught in your local public school?
You're an "extremist."

It suddenly becomes clear why the Coalition for Democracy limited
the survey to leaders and key members. Too many members of its own
rank-and-file might have had to rat themselves out.

When Christian groups heard about the survey, they—quite naturally—were incensed at being lumped together with racists and violent
fanatics. But coalition leaders were unapologetic. "We label them all as radical right," said co-chairwoman Blue Carreker. "We're saying their goals, as
they outline them, we consider to be radical."[199]

The coalition's definition was also in keeping with Teacher Trust tradition. The NEA Human and Civil Rights Division once warned the union's
board of directors of a very specific "regional extremist activity": a radical
group was setting up "training camps" in four separate areas of Massachusetts. Militia teams set to blow up a government building? No—the Christian Coalition was teaching people "how to run for office and influence
public policy."

The fiends!

According to the NEA, the "Radical Right" includes "free-market conservatives, antigovernment and anti-union ideologues, and religious fundamentalists with a political agenda."[200] But that's hardly a comprehensive list. For example, if white parents want the famous lesbian-nontraditional-family apologia *Heather Has Two Mommies* removed from the elementary school library, they are extremists. However, if African American parents want *Huckleberry Finn* removed from the elementary school reading list for offensive language, they are *not* extremists. But if those African American parents hold a rally in support of school choice—well then, they are extremists after all!

Thomas Toch, author of *In the Name of Excellence: The Struggle to Reform the Nation's Schools, Why It's Failing, and What Should Be Done,* probably didn't know he was an "extremist" in 1996 when he wrote a *U.S. News & World Report* cover story critical of the NEA.[201] But he found out. He was inundated with angry letters from union officials. The NEA Human and Civil Rights Division reported the letter-writing campaign to the board of directors under the heading "Strategic Association Responses to Extremism."

Tennessee state legislators probably didn't know they were "extremists" in 1996 when they introduced a bill to add two additional seats for parents on the state textbook commission. The Tennessee Education Association was instrumental in getting the bill killed. The bill was reported to the NEA board as one of that year's "Attacks on Public Education by Region."

Parents are one of two groups most likely to be "extremists." School board candidates are the other. One NEA document warns local union activists:

> The formation of "concerned parents" groups, and the attendance
> of leaders of such a group at board meetings, for example, usually
> signal a possible censorship attempt.[202]

At one union workshop on the Radical Right, an Ohio Education Association official described the "warning signs" exhibited by one school board member that indicated "extremism." "He had a low profile in the community, refused to undergo the union's candidate screenings, and educated his children at home," the official said.[203]

What can possibly be motivating so many mild-mannered, low-profile citizens to take up "extremism"? In the NEA's mind, there are three factors:

money; racism; religious intolerance. Indeed, according to the NEA's Human and Civil Rights Division, the problems in public schools have been created out of whole cloth by "extremists" in order to generate funds for their crusade against public education. As the division reported to the NEA board of directors in May 1996,

> In the current reality of public education– and NEA–bashing, a manufactured crisis occurs at the same time that extremists mobilize followers, collect money, and divert the public's attention from the real issues in education. In the current reality, those who manufacture and profit from the crisis are one and the same; the money of the duped public is what goes down the hole.

Once the "extremists" have siphoned off the public's cash for a phony campaign, they then *refuse to part with any of it in taxes* to keep the schools running.

"The people who argue that 'money makes no difference' are—it's just this simple—'greed kings and queens,' " wrote Lois Tinson, then-president of the California Teachers Association in 1996. "They resent having to repay American society for the blessings it has given them. They resent paying for the education of children who are not their own. Those nay-sayers are willing to see America suffocate and decline—to see our nation's future and our children's futures atrophy—just to save themselves a few bucks on their annual tax bills."[204]

But these extremist greed kings and queens aren't even satisfied with their ill-gotten gains and their tax dodges. They also want that cold cash that flows through the public school system. "Their major motive is money. They want a big chunk of the $600 billion spent on public education each year," wrote Tinson's successor as CTA president, Wayne Johnson. "They are creating the myth of public school failure for their own greedy self-interest."[205]

New Jersey Education Association president Michael Johnson agrees. "The bad press surrounding our schools and the quality of those employed within them is nothing other than a tactic to create an atmosphere conducive to the corporate takeover of public schools and siphoning off the money used to fund them," he said.

The second factor that the NEA thinks motivates anti-education "extremists" is racism. According to the NEA, there is no difference between today's conservatives supporting vouchers and segregationists barring the schoolhouse doors. As a 1996 NEA issue brief put it.

> The ultimate aim of the extreme right is the destruction of public education in America. Their roots go back at least 40 years to the 1954 *Brown v. Board of Education* school desegregation decision. Then right wing segregationists called for tuition tax credits to pay for white student attendance at private segregated academies. Now they promote tuition vouchers to pay for any student to attend a religious or other private school at taxpayer expense.

Understand that the NEA is *not* saying that segregationists and conservatives share similar ideas. The union is saying they are the *same movement.* As the brief continues,

> What differentiates the right wing today from 40 years ago is its size, its organization, and its status. What was then a scattered assortment of religious zealots and blatantly racist hate groups has become a politically adroit, well-organized network of activist organizations, think tanks, and private foundations that operate both nationally and at the grassroots. From the Christian Coalition to Focus on the Family, from the Bradley Foundation to the American Enterprise Institute, today's ultraconservatives have political clout and the ear of top elected officials, policy makers, and the media."[206]

The third factor motivating "extremism," in the NEA's opinion, is religious intolerance. Not only do the "extremists" want their own sectarian views taught in the public schools, but also they actually want to overthrow democracy and establish a theocracy in America, based on biblical law.
The NEA brief tells it like it is:

> These groups tout their Americanism while seeking to impose their narrow religious and political values on the country. Intent on indoctrinating children with their views, they've launched a concerted and broad-based crusade to discredit the National Education Association and dismantle America's system of public schools. They seek to control public education or to replace it with

private and sectarian schools. Radical right extremists are attempting to impose a rigid and narrow curriculum that mirrors their
values, inculcates fundamentalist Christianity, and devalues people
who are poor, people of color, and people who are in any way different from them.[207]

The NEA raises the specter of a New World Order in which Christian
ayatollahs run a rigid, thought-controlled nation. In the words of one NEA
handbook:

> The overriding goal of the radical right is to impose a new politi-
> cal, social, and religious order on the nation. The ideal New Amer-
> ica, for the radical right, would be one in which citizens
> conformed to the right-wing views on everything from foreign
> policy and constitutional interpretations to the selection of text-
> books in our classrooms. Unfortunately for the extremist point of
> view, free public education provides a strong defense against the
> frantic propaganda and name calling that forms the core of right-
> wing assaults on the American consciousness.[208]

With these horrible extremist monsters out there set to steal away your
freedoms, what power can stand in their way? It can only be—hooray!—
the Teacher Trust!

And they are happy to supply whatever funds, resources, and manpower
is necessary to wipe this scourge from the face of the earth.

The NEA's budget contains funds for the union's various strategic activities, one of which is to assist its affiliates in countering attacks on public education. In 1997–1998, the NEA budgeted $422,303 to "monitor and analyze
forces undermining public education (including laws, contracts, and proposals
relating to charter schools, vouchers, corporate takeovers, and subcontract-
ing)"; $456,600 to "maintain a clearinghouse of information on extremist
groups/individuals and organizations working to dismantle public education";
and $783,180 to "develop and provide workshops, training and conferences to
leaders and staff on barriers and threats to public education (i.e., vouchers, sub-
contracting, sexual harassment, gender equity and sexual orientation)."

This funding, supplemented by similar line-items in the budgets of the
union's state and local affiliates, generates a blizzard of studies, handbooks,

flyers, pamphlets, and assorted documents on the threat posed to public education by radical right-wing "extremists." It appears that if a union staffer isn't too busy, he or she is immediately put to work producing an anti-"extremist" handbook.

The Arizona Education Association has published *Primer on the Extremist Attacks on Public Education,* which described the perceived goals of extremist groups, the terms and "buzz words" they use, along with information about their leaders.

The California Teachers Association has published a fifty-page booklet with the same title, which also included sample questions for school board candidates—presumably to reveal the "extremists," the way their lack of a reflection in the mirror will expose a vampire.

The Michigan Education Association published a thirty-four-page booklet, *Michigan—The Far Right's New Frontier.* It described Far Right tactics such as name-calling, scapegoating, exploiting religion and patriotism, preying on minorities, threatening, and—my personal favorite—"*demanding information immediately.*"

And the Florida, Nevada, Texas, and Washington state affiliates of the NEA have also each produced their own extremist handbook.

The state affiliates then pass this agitprop down to the neighborhood level in the form of training and workshops for local presidents and for the rank and file The NEA Governmental Relations unit has produced "A Checklist for Contending with Right-Wing Extremism," designed to keep union minutemen ever vigilant. "Does your local Association newsletter periodically inform members about the radical right, including its strategies and activities affecting public schools?" it asks. "Is there an Association committee or task force that has the responsibility for monitoring far right activities? Does your Association have an action plan for dealing with the radical right?"

All this heated rhetoric has a practical purpose: It energizes the local base to work hard for union initiatives and support union-backed candidates in school board races. At virtually every state-organized union conference there is at least one workshop, session, or seminar dedicated to the extremist threat—especially as it relates to local school elections. In one nine-month period in 1995, the California Teachers Association held six separate workshops with titles such as "Extremist Attacks on Public

Education," "Extremists—School Board Elections," and "The Politics of the Far Right."

In 1995, the CTA also provided a rare look inside its "extremist cadre training" program by publishing an account of a workshop held in Sacramento. Attendees were divided into various teams for a training exercise. Some were assigned the roles of union leaders, others were school board trustees, some really unfortunate ones were the press, and so on. A mock school board meeting was held in which the main item on the agenda was the establishment of a charter school in the district. The union team was given the job of foiling it.

Why? "The idea was to present a dramatized picture of the overall goals and strategies being employed by extremist groups in their effort to use charter schools as a vehicle for taking over the public schools," the union newsletter explained. "Extremist factions see the state's charter schools act as a way to free the schools from all external regulations."

The role-playing was even further over-the-top than the premise. One union trainer was assigned the role of the "Reverend Barry Farright," whose first action was to admonish the school board and the audience for holding a meeting on Sunday morning.[209]

There is a limit to the effectiveness of fear-mongering, however. The Edmonds Education Association in Washington State evaluated its "extremist" training this way: "Unfortunately, not enough teachers recognize the danger the Far Right poses to public education. In addition, teachers have a limited amount of time and lack the interest to expose the threat from the Far Right."[210]

Yep, teaching kids math and history sure eats into the workday.

Much of the NEA's information on "extremists" is gathered through normal research. But it does extend itself to gather information first-hand—both overtly and covertly. NEA staffers are a fixture at school choice conferences and other meetings of the conservative education reform crowd. They don't advertise their presence, but they don't go out of their way to hide it, either. NEA staff and elected officials are also known to frequent large meetings of the Christian Coalition and Concerned Women for America without identifying themselves by affiliation. When union officials can't or won't attend such events, they can still receive a secondhand account from liberal organizations such as People for the American Way, who attend conservative gatherings as a matter of course.

Sometimes even these outings fail to provide enough information, so the unions may resort to more clandestine means of intelligence gathering. At one Ohio workshop, a union official called on attendees to *join* conservative Christian groups for the sole purpose of keeping tabs on their activities. "The thing they fear most is exposure," said Michael Billirakis, the president of the Ohio Education Association. "You are not doing them any individual harm—you are doing what's right."[211]

Poppy DeMarco Dennis, a union activist who won an award from the California Teachers Association for her work fighting "extremist" groups, described the tactics her organization, something called the Community Coalition Network (CCN), used to gather information:

> CCN read news articles; attended Far Right rallies; and obtained materials from "Christian" bookstores, radio stations, and newspapers. CCN found that the Far Right was more open about their agenda when talking to their own people. CCN members traveled with small recorders and taped Far Right representatives in public meetings."[212]

But perhaps these subtle methods are best left to union representatives at the local level, for use in local school board elections and the like. When the NEA tried to use its research on "extremists" in a grand, well-publicized way at the national level, it was ridiculed and humiliated.

The NEA was troubled, as we have seen, by the initial overwhelming support among its own members for Proposition 226, the Paycheck Protection initiative in California. Proposition 226 was ultimately defeated by a seven-point margin in March 1998. But getting to that victory cost the union a lot of money, including that $500,000 spent on the internal campaign to persuade its own members to vote against it.

There was no denying, of course, that the Paycheck Protection initiative was put together and financed by political conservatives. But that wasn't quite enough for the NEA to ensure that future initiatives, above all ones that put the union in a defensive posture and required internal lobbying, would be kept off the ballot. NEA officials had to show that the forces aligned against them were so wealthy and powerful that union members must stand as one to oppose them. So the NEA put together a task force, hired a consultant, and published an investigative report that purported to expose the "conspiracy."

Naturally, the NEA reached its conclusion first, then marshaled the evidence to support it. The groundwork for the report and the reasons behind it were laid even before the election was held. In December 1997, NEA executive director Don Cameron and general counsel Bob Chanin delivered a presentation to the NEA Board of Directors about the union's opponents. They told the directors that a "far-right ultra-conservative wing of the Republican Party as well as a number of extreme right organizations and think tanks" were coordinating the attacks on public education. Cameron said the union would continue to monitor the attacks and act proactively.[213]

NEA's organs alerted local affiliate leaders to the effort. "Stopping these attacks against us won't be easy," wrote *NEA Now!* editor Steve Lemken in January 1998. "Understand, the people and organizations behind these attacks run a very tight, closely coordinated ship. They are smart and keep on task. They can tap into huge warchests to distort our positions and then make us spend our limited resources defending against their distortions."[214]

Soon after the Paycheck Protection initiative was defeated, Bob Chase telegraphed the NEA's intent. "One of the things that is evident from the campaign against Proposition 226 is that there exists a vast and well-funded national network of organizations that are coordinating a campaign to undermine public education and other parts of our social fabric," Chase said. "These groups are intent upon forcing their agenda on the country, and apparently they believe their first step is to eliminate the ability of unions to speak out on behalf of the average American."[215]

All the pieces were now in place for the NEA to unveil its conspiracy theory and lead its members to the obvious righteous response.

Dr. Daniel Pipes, a scholar on the Middle East and an expert on the role conspiracy theories plays in world affairs, describes the process this way:

> The theories usually contain three basic elements—a powerful, evil, and clandestine group that aspires to global hegemony; dupes and agents who extend the group's influence around the world so that it is on the verge of succeeding; and a valiant but embattled group that urgently needs help to stave off catastrophe.[216]

On October 1, 1998, the NEA held a press conference in Washington, D.C., to launch *The Real Story Behind 'Paycheck Protection'—The Hidden Link Between Anti-Worker and Anti-Public Education Initiatives: An Anatomy of the Far Right*. The title was a little clunky. But the report contained all of Dr. Pipes's elements. The powerful, evil, clandestine group was the conservative network. Although the NEA report didn't capitalize the term, it made clear that this was an exclusive and permanent group, and not a series of temporary alliances organized around single issues. The network, the report claimed, was headed by seven wealthy and powerful individuals: John Walton, J. Patrick Rooney, Richard Mellon Scaife, James R. Leininger, Howard Ahmanson Jr., Grover Norquist, and Bob Williams. The dupes and agents who did the network's bidding were the various think tanks affiliated with the State Policy Network, a coalition of conservative state-based policy institutes. And the valiant but embattled group was . . . the NEA.

The report is replete with classic conspiracy imagery. There is the standard "conspiracy flow chart" straight out of John Birch Society literature, revealing the tangled web of interactions among various segments of the conservative network. The NEA compared the network to a single body, assigning different organizations the various body parts. The Council for National Policy was deemed to be the nervous system, the Heritage Foundation was the head, the American Legislative Exchange Council was the skeleton, the Religious Right was the heart, and the State Policy Network was the arms and legs. Then, for some reason, the NEA abandoned its image of the conservative conspiracy as a body. Instead, it dubbed ultraconservative foundations as "the energy" instead of the stomach. For weeks after the report was released, amused conservatives discussed their nominations for the conspiracy's "left buttock."

The NEA study also noted that corporate support for Proposition 226 came from FedEx, Bristol-Myers, GEICO, USAA Insurance—and Outback Steakhouse. Like any good conservative body, the network apparently subsists on red meat.

The report concluded:

> With the funding and influence of the NEA and other progressive groups eliminated or severely curtailed [by Paycheck Protection], leaders of the conservative network would be free to pursue their

agenda. And that agenda is hostile to public education. *If allowed to continue,* this state-by-state assault would severely limit the effectiveness of the NEA and its affiliates in their pro-education efforts throughout the United States. [Emphasis added][217]

Er—what exactly do they mean, "if allowed to continue"?

The members of the conservative network did indeed have something important in common: they were all conservative. Many of them knew each other through conferences, correspondence, and publications exchanges. Some of them even worked together on particular issues. But the idea that they were being coordinated was met with great merriment among liberals and conservatives alike. The Christian Coalition may support vouchers, but it doesn't care about paycheck protection. The report claims that the National Right to Work Legal Defense Foundation "has taken an active role around the country by supplying the legal muscle for 'paycheck protection' drives."[218] But the National Right to Work organization in fact *opposes* Paycheck Protection initiatives because it feels they divert attention from its own issue: compulsory payment of fees to the union by nonmembers.

Messrs. Walton, Rooney, Scaife, Ahmanson, and Leininger are all wealthy conservatives who donate heavily to conservative causes, particularly school vouchers. But the NEA report presented no evidence that these men even knew each other, much less coordinate. Grover Norquist, head of Americans for Tax Reform, is an influential activist, but his organization has a staff of six, and he has no independent wealth. Bob Williams, head of the Evergreen Freedom Foundation (EFF) in Washington State, is most misplaced of all. Williams is a dedicated man, best known for catching the Washington Education Association every couple of years breaking the state's campaign finance reporting laws. He is not, however, one of the seven most powerful men in the conservative universe. The NEA report itself noted that Williams made less than $50,000 from his work at EFF in 1997.

The report was also strangely padded. The section of "selected biographies" includes people who have nothing to do with paycheck protection, vouchers, or even education. Examples: Elaine Donnelly, president of the Center for Military Readiness; John Lenczowski, founder and director of the Institute of World Politics; Jim Martin, president of the Sixty Plus Association; evangelist Austin Miles (who, the report tells us, used to be a circus ringmaster); Stanley Monteith, a retired orthopedic surgeon who publishes a small newsletter entitled *HIV Watch* (the report tells us his wife's name is Barbara); Lynda Scribante, appointee to the President's Commission of Medical and Bio Medical Ethics; concert pianist Balint Vazsonyi.

For good measure, the report threw in bios of Lt. Col. Oliver North and Gen. John K. Singlaub, presumably insinuating that paycheck protection is a well-hidden subplot to the Iran-Contra affair.

But the most bizarre aspect of NEA's conspiracy report was that its primary author, Robert L. "Bobby" Watson, had done something no member of the conservative network had ever done. He had pleaded guilty to—believe or not—conspiracy.

Watson has a long and colorful history in the political world. In 1992, as a top aide to Senator Chuck Robb of Virginia, Watson worked to deflect inquiries into Robb's alleged sexual peccadilloes. Watson and Robb's chief of staff, David McCloud, blamed the rumors on then-Governor Douglas Wilder, Robb's political foe. To prove their theory, Watson and McCloud released a transcript of a conversation taped from Wilder's cellular phone. Of course, recording and/or disseminating other people's phone calls without their permission is illegal. Watson pleaded guilty to conspiracy and was fined the maximum $10,000.

"In a sane world, McCloud and Watson would have been forced to slink out of town and get real jobs following their disgrace in the Robb scandal. Instead, it seemed to mark a stepping-stone in their careers," wrote John Stauber and Sheldon Rampton for the newsletter *PR Watch*.[219]

But later that year, Watson was hired by the NEA as a "senior political strategist." He became a member of the union's Clinton-Gore "rapid response" team during the 1992 campaign. In January 1994, Watson took leave from the NEA and was hired as deputy executive director of the Democratic National Committee. That spring, Watson was assigned the job of linking the taxpayer-funded White House database with the DNC's donor database.

In November 1994, Watson was named DNC chief of staff. The *New Republic* called Watson's appointment an example of "recycling disgraced hacks who typify insider sleaze."[220] In 1995, he was named DNC executive director and attended one of the celebrated White House "coffees"—

get-togethers meant to connect high-dollar Democratic donors with the President.

In 1996, Watson left the DNC to join the State Affairs Company, a powerful Beltway lobbying group. The company created a political money watchdog group called Contributions Watch. Contributions Watch released a report on the amount of money trial lawyers donate to federal candidates. But the group didn't reveal that Philip Morris Companies—a major backer of tort reform—funded its study. Left-wing reporter Ken Silverstein exposed this and called Watson a "notoriously dirty hitter."

While Watson's background didn't make it into press coverage of the NEA study, reporters were generally dismissive. About the kindest remarks it received were from Associated Press reporter Robert Greene, who concluded: "But if there is evidence, other than by association, that supporters of dues restrictions are motivated by a desire to dismantle public schools, it was not clearly laid out in the NEA's new 144-page booklet."[221]

Members of the conservative network reacted with varying degrees of humor or annoyance. "It's a great address book for funding sources," said Maureen Blum of the Institute of Justice, to which Claremont Institute president Larry Arnn added, "To have the bad opinion of the National Education Association is a badge of honor."[222] The Calvert Institute for Policy Research in Maryland called the report "an exercise riddled with errors and downright idiocy."

Katrina vanden Heuvel of the very liberal *The Nation* magazine has argued that the Left should actually emulate the Right.

"With the different pieces in place (labor commitment, expertise, local coalitions), now is the time to build the progressive equivalent of the Christian Coalition," she wrote, adding that such a group could train people to run for office, introduce ballot initiatives, "and build a network of talk-show guests and pundits with a coordinated message."[223]

Sounds conspiratorial to me.

10

Gaijin

You cannot hope to bribe or twist,
Thank God, the British [read: education] *journalist.*
But, seeing what the man will do
Unbribed, there's no occasion to.

—Humbert Wolfe

The Japanese word *gaijin* literally means "foreigner," but it has a mildly pejorative undertone, somewhat less so than the Mexican term "gringo." Westerners who have lived in Japan, even those who speak the language fluently and have immersed themselves in the country's culture, are very aware that they are always *gaijin*. There are many aspects of Japanese society that Westerners simply don't understand . . . partially because those aspects are designed specifically *not* to be understood by Westerners. So it is with the mainstream press and the Teacher Trust.

On those rare occasions when reporters do cover the teacher unions, they find themselves overwhelmed by the arcane and incomprehensible, much the way a Westerner might feel while watching a kabuki performance. They have little understanding of the interrelationships of the various levels of the unions, little understanding of the interrelationships between union management and staff, and little understanding of the unions' mission. Consequently, reporters' perceptions are often tinted by the ever-helpful union communications people. These are more than happy to explain every little detail to reporters—well, at least the details that portray the unions in a positive light.

A Public Agenda survey for the Education Writers Association found that 81 percent of reporters concur that they are too dependent on school officials for information. When it comes to reporting on the Teacher Trust, that problem is much worse.

Many NEA and AFT affiliates give out awards to newspapers and other media outlets for their coverage of public education. Often these awards are accompanied by banquets and ceremonies. The winners even boast of their accomplishments in their own outlets. But, unsurprisingly, the stories that win awards from the teacher unions are the most uncritical. The *Dallas Morning News,* for example, won three awards from the Texas State Teachers Association, one of which was about a trip by area teachers to the state capital "to lobby for money for teacher raises."[224] It's hard to think of another area where newspapers would brag about awards received from the people they are supposed to be covering.

At other times, the *gaijin* of the press simply get the story wrong. In 1998, coverage of the proposed merger between the NEA and AFT was dreadful. In January 1998, the *New York Times* ran a headline that read, "Two Largest Teachers Unions Announce Preliminary Merger," even though the vote was six months away.[225] No one reported that the merger plan was in trouble as early as April. The Associated Press reported in May that "Teacher Unions Merger Moves Ahead"—on the very day that delegates in the Michigan Education Association, one of the NEA's largest affiliates, were voting to oppose the plan and to spend money to defeat it.

You had to go to the left-wing *Z Magazine* to find any sense of the internal divisions on the merger—which, needing a two-thirds majority, was ultimately defeated when it generated only 42 percent of the vote.

"It's clear that there is a huge gap between the national leaders and the rank and file," Illinois Education Association president Bob Haisman told *Z Magazine* reporter Rich Gibson. "They grossly overestimated their potential votes. They worked this for years, yet had no idea that they would be so completely defeated."[226]

Nothing like this appeared in the mainstream press.

Nor was the merger story unique. In 2000, NEA delegates voted to strengthen their policy against any form of merit pay for teachers. The Associated Press, however, reported:"The nation's largest teacher union took a step closer Wednesday to ending its century-old resistance to paying teachers for performance, instead of just seniority."[227] Newspapers all across the country ran the AP story and then editorialized based on its erroneous conclusions.

Press coverage of the teacher unions also suffers from a unique disadvantage: those assigned to the beat are usually education reporters. They have very little exposure to labor issues. This enables the Teacher Trust to present every issue and controversy as part of its effort to promote quality public education, rather than to extract more from the taxpayer.

The distinction between normal coverage of organized labor and that of the NEA and AFT has become stark if you think about it this way:

Imagine International Brotherhood of Teamsters president Jimmy Hoffa Jr. holding a press conference and announcing a far-reaching plan for reforming the U.S. transportation system.

"Trucks are getting too large for one driver to handle," Hoffa might say. "With the increases in commuter traffic and the higher speeds now allowed in many states, it is simply too dangerous to assume that one person can handle today's big rigs." He might then propose a federal law limiting the size and capacity of trucks, and another requiring that any trucker sent on a trip expected to take more than six hours have a relief driver ride along with him or her, for safety.

Or imagine William Daniels, the president of the Screen Actors Guild, telling reporters that it was unfair for Leonardo DiCaprio to make $20 million for an acting job, particularly since he has much less experience than, say, Martin Landau. And firing bad actors would have to stop. "How can producers or directors judge a performance when they've never acted in their lives?" he might say. "Bad actors merely need added assistance from their peers."

Whatever the merits of Hoffa's and Daniels's plans, we would expect journalists to be skeptical of them, particularly since the solutions seem to serve the union at the expense of the public—perhaps even at the expense of the rank-and-file union member.

Yet when NEA officials propose massive federal subsidies to reduce class size, or increasing teacher salaries to attract "the best and the bright-est," there is very little skepticism because they're, well, teachers. And as such they receive the benefit of the doubt—to an extent that makes indus-trial union officials green with envy.

For twenty-five years the federal government has regarded the NEA as a labor union. The filing requirements placed on the NEA by the Internal Revenue Service and the U.S. Department of Labor are identical to those placed on the Teamsters, the United Auto Workers, or the International Brotherhood of Electrical Workers. But, even internally, the NEA refers to itself as "the Association." And it greatly downplays its union status when dealing with the media.

This spin has been so successful that many NEA members themselves don't realize they belong to a labor union. From November 30 to Decem-ber 2, 1998, the Alabama Education Association polled its members on a large number of questions, including whether they thought NEA was "part of organized labor and the labor movement." Forty-nine percent of those surveyed said yes, but 39 percent said no. When asked what description fit the NEA best, only 5 percent said "a labor union." By far the largest group—48 percent—said "a professional association."

During the 1960s, the NEA had great difficulty competing with the American Federation of Teachers in collective bargaining elections pre-cisely because the NEA was a professional association and not a labor union. It went through a painful transition and much internal upheaval to become a labor union by the mid-1970s. Why wouldn't the NEA trumpet its unionism to the press and the world?

One look at public opinion surveys answers that question. In 1995, the California Teachers Association commissioned a poll and found that 85 percent of the public had a favorable impression of teachers. When asked about teacher unions, the number with a favorable impression dropped to 48 percent.[228]

In a November 1999 Gallup Poll, those surveyed were asked to rate the honesty and ethical standards of people in forty-five professions. Nurses and other medical professionals took the top four slots, but grade and high school teachers came in fifth, with 57 percent of respondents rating them high or very high. Clergy, judges, and police officers all trailed them. By contrast, labor union leaders ranked thirtieth of the forty-five, with only 17 percent rating them high or very high. (Of course, this poll can't be regarded as definitive. Journalists came in nineteenth.)

Given these results, which of the two words in the term "teacher union" would you emphasize?

Since labor unions have such a negative public image, it's important for the NEA to identify itself with other institutions that are more popular. Its solution: emphasize the formula

NEA = teachers = public education = American democracy

Oppose the first item and you oppose them all. Conversely, the NEA, by defending itself, is defending teachers, public education, and American democracy.

The problem, in the NEA's opinion, is that the American people are *just not getting it*. And so, like that algebra teacher you hated so much in high school, the union is going to keep drilling us and drilling us until we get it through our thick heads.

The NEA's self-image and its media strategies for publicizing it are illustrated in the union's 1997 booklet, entitled *Do You See What I'm Saying? Using Message to Reconnect with the Public.*

NEA officials aren't stupid. They do recognize that they and the public are "disconnected." What they're unable to come to grips with is that it has anything to do with NEA policies or operations. They believe they simply have fallen victim to definition by others. They just need a proper public relations campaign to straighten it all out.

Or, as the NEA's booklet explains: "Any American when asked about NEA should be able to readily answer, 'It's that group working to enhance school quality and prepare students for jobs of the future.' "[229]

Oh—*that* group!

The booklet goes on:

Most people are too preoccupied with soccer schedules or the latest scrap with their boss to think too long or hard about the structure of schools, the forces affecting the lives of children, or the relationship of education to the future. We fall so deeply into the trap of wanting to educate people that we've come to believe it's condescending to be simple and direct. It's not. Somebody is going to simplify the issues,

Rush Limbaugh, *Forbes* magazine [say it ain't so!], or the Concerned Women of America. Our critics have a strong motivation to define the issues and us. And most in the media do not think critically about the "analyses" of anti-public education commentators or politicians.[230]

Well, how do these critics win over the public? Easy, the NEA tells us. Because ranting wins out over reasoning.

> Most Association advocates build their arguments around reason. We are used to arguing a case in a hearing, lobbying a state legislator, or making a case before the school board. We can't expect those same arguments to prevail when people aren't engaged. And we can't expect rational arguments to prevail when public school critics appeal to the emotions with concepts like "choice" versus "the failed Soviet-style centralized bureaucracy." [What's emotional about that?] When we try to counter with an explanation of how the public schools aren't a monopoly, that public schools have a wide diversity of choices and options among the 15,000 school districts, etc., we've lost the battle—because we're not talking about our issues, such as public school success, economic opportunity, or local control through elected school boards.[231]

In fact, of course, the NEA is the undisputed heavyweight champion of the emotional appeal. It doesn't even seem to realize that it does it. Thus the booklet goes on:

> We must define ourselves both in terms of what we're for and what the alternatives are by drawing stark contrasts. For example, the Association supports democratic control of public schools, high standards for students, and expanding choices for parents within the public schools. Voucher advocates want to throw education decisions into the marketplace where it's "get it while you can" and "let the buyer beware."[232]

Ah—"stark contrasts." "Get it while you can." Makes all the difference. Typical of centralized organizations, the NEA is reluctant to let its activists ad lib—curiously similar to the Soviet Army's notorious reluctance to give its frontline commanders tactical freedom. The union has perfected the art of "talking points." Long hours are spent ginning up guidelines for any topic that may arise with the press, the public, or the members themselves. The booklet explains:

> With everything in their day, we can't count on reporters giving a lot of thought to our latest opinion. We must talk about a narrowly focused range of topics—children, quality, and the future—to get the kind of repetition necessary to leave the impression we want.[233]

Talking points work on NEA members as well as on the press. In March 1999, the National Right to Work Committee sent e-mails to California teachers pointing out that they did not have to join the union but could stay out and just pay agency fees. (This option is known to labor law cognoscenti as "*Beck* rights," after the Supreme Court decision guaranteeing them in the private sector, parallel to *Abood* in the public sector). Evidently the campaign was effective enough to prompt many teachers to question the CTA about agency fees.

The CTA sprang into action. It produced "Talking Points in Response to the National Right to Work Committee" and distributed them to all its local affiliates.

"Once again, the National Right to Work Committee is soliciting members of the California Teachers Association to drop out of the union or become agency fee payers," the notice began. "This time, their anti-union rhetoric is showing up as unsolicited e-mail. If issues raised in this e-mail come up in your area, consider these responses."

The handout then listed five responses to give to members asking about *Beck* rights. The first response was, guess what: "The National Right to Work Committee is an extremist group that is aligned with other conservative groups in America that have promoted private school tuition vouchers."

Ordinary people manage to deal successfully with all sorts of questions without talking points. But NEA doctrine is that the lack of talking points can lead to blunders.

"Sometimes we can be our own worst enemy," the NEA *Do You See What I'm Saying?* booklet says. "We feel uncomfortable when someone raises an issue to which there is no good argument—or isn't answered directly within the context of our message box. When you have a message and stick to it, you're less likely to say things that can be taken out of context."[234]

The union believes this so fervently that they take it to ridiculous extremes. The Washington Education Association handout entitled "Handling Media and Public Attention" gave this advice to local officials and staff faced with a member accused of sexually abusing a student: "The way we handle things in a crisis determines not only our public image, but can also affect the way future allegations are handled and perceived. It also establishes our ability to positively affect the media in other situations."

The WEA handout suggests that activists

> acknowledge the seriousness of the event and put the association on the "right side" of the issue. If the association and/or the school district has conducted any training or provided any other positive programs aimed at helping education employees and/or students deal with the issue of sexual abuse, emphasize the success of those programs. Sometimes, a negative issue can result in some positive publicity for the good things that are going on related to the issue of abuse.[235]

But you never know. Maybe the NEA is right to stop its operatives shooting from the hip. In September 1999, the Pilchuck UniServ Council, affiliated with the Washington Education Association, published a story in its Board Report, which was posted on the Sultan Education Association's web page, with a rather impolitic headline: "When in Doubt, Shred!"

The item read: "This advice comes from WEA attorney Jerry Painter, as he discussed WEA's Retention/Destruction Policy for anyone who handles WEA documents. Presidents of locals, councils, staff, etc., will all be receiving copies of the new policy regarding how long to retain specific types of documents."

The Evergreen Freedom Foundation, engaged as usual in litigation against WEA, found the story very interesting and disseminated it throughout the state. The union's response was remarkable even by its own standards. The Sultan Education Association simply removed it from its web site, not the Board Report, but just the offending item. Visitors who went to the web page to read the Board Report were treated to a large white space where the shredding story had been.

Since the NEA can be so clumsy in its public relations, how has it managed to shield itself from the type of press scrutiny that dogs unions like the Teamsters and LIUNA?

The answer: sheer decibels. Both teacher unions scream so much when they get bad press that it really does deter the type of investigative reporting that might cause problems.

Every journalist who has written less-than-flattering articles about the Teacher Trust has stories about what happened next. Then-NEA president Keith Geiger wrote an extraordinarily violent response to Thomas Toch's *U.S. News & World Report* NEA cover story that began: "Tabloid-style journalism stooped to a new low . . ." Geiger went on to call Toch's story "the journalistic equivalent of a drive-by shooting: indiscriminate, inaccurate, and destructive."[236]

Geiger also informed the editors of *U.S. News:* "Over the last year, a new wave of scholars and journalists has been reporting not about the 'crisis' in public education, but about the renaissance."

For those of you who missed that particular renaissance, Geiger's letter appeared in March 1996.

The NEA urged its activists to respond not only to the magazine's editors, but also to the *U.S. News* Education Program—a project to sell magazines at a discounted rate to teachers for their use in the classroom. And activists were given an extensive set of—needless to say—talking points to use if parents and taxpayers confronted them with the article's conclusions.

A sample:

- "The *U.S. News* article's authors, as well as many other reporters, ignore or seem to know little about collective bargaining contracts, how school policy is determined, how state laws affect classroom work, and what the NEA is doing in reform."

- "The critics of collective bargaining cannot point to one objective study showing hard evidence of collective bargaining hindering public education or reform."

- "When a fair and equitable way of paying teachers in another fashion is presented, one that shuns patronage and favoritism, local bargaining units give the proposal every consideration."

The NEA also urged: "Identify letter writers who can correct newspaper articles or offer editorial opinions for local op-ed pages. Contact your state affiliate's communications director for training assistance."

In 1994, Arizona State University professor David C. Berliner, recipient of the NEA's Friend of Education award, enthusiastically described to the Representative Assembly this process of generating "spontaneous" (and intimidating) outrage:

> One group of teachers I know created a war room—as the Clinton campaign did—and when a negative story appeared that wasn't true, or needed to be contextualized, they met that evening and were down at the newspaper offices the next morning with a written rebuttal or explanation. The paper printed a few of these. *But more important, it didn't want a meeting with angry teachers every time it printed another school-bashing story, so it stopped printing the silly ones that it had formerly printed with glee.* [Emphasis added][237]

Berliner's remarks received generous applause.

Similarly, in a February 7, 2000, memo to Wisconsin Education Association Council executive director Michael Butera, WEAC communications director Dick VanderWoude wrote:

> We are continuing our work with an external public relations firm developing and encouraging positive letters from the general citizenry to the editors of local daily papers throughout Wisconsin. The project has generated in excess of 100 published letters since the beginning of the school year. Newspaper people advise us that a typical reader of letters to the editor is more likely to be interested in and concerned about public affairs. We estimate that 10,000 individuals will read a typical letter. By these estimates we project that the project has potentially generated a million positive impressions over the last six months. Communications division staff advise the project of current and coming issues and provides issue research.

John Stossel of ABC News was pummeled by the NEA for a report on public and private schools he did for *20/20*. Well, you can see they wouldn't like him reporting this sort of thing:

> At one school, records show a math teacher kept coming in late. One year, he was late or didn't show up at all more than 100 times.

He routinely sent students out to buy him food, and his classroom was so littered with candy wrappers and cigarette butts that the janitors refused to clean the room. When the school tried to fire him, the teacher unions gave him a lawyer, and it took nine hearings, three years and hundreds of thousands of dollars in legal fees before he could finally be let go.[238]

The NEA was particularly incensed by Stossel's description of the public school system as "a government monopoly." The union disseminated to its members a list of companies that sponsored *20/20* on the night Stossel's report aired, presumably so teachers could write and complain. Ironically, the list included the United States Postal Service—a fellow government monopoly.

The major media rarely run reports like these. But the NEA's eyes are everywhere, ready to react to the slightest provocation. *Redbook* and *Good Housekeeping* both published articles about unions protecting bad teachers from dismissal or discipline. The NEA reacted strongly both times, first with letters from NEA president Bob Chase, then calling for letters from activists, followed by talking points for when the public started asking about what they had read in the article.

No publication is too obscure to escape the NEA's wrath. In May 1996, Randy Moore, editor of *The American Biology Teacher,* wrote an editorial critical of teacher unions. He got the same treatment, with the NEA sending an e-mail message to activists directing them to respond with letters.

Don't bother trying to target your criticism very specifically, either. Bruce Murphy of *Milwaukee* magazine tried that in February 1998. Murphy wrote a very critical story about the staff of the Milwaukee Teachers Education Association and its executive director, Sam Carmen. But he treated MTEA president Paulette Copeland sympathetically and quoted her extensively on the obstructionist attitudes of the MTEA permanent staff. Two weeks later, the MTEA newsletter ran a story with the headline, "Unprecedented Personal Attack on MTEA Leaders." The union even insinuated in its newsletter that Murphy's article was some kind of devilish plot.

As the governor is threatening to dissolve MPS [Milwaukee Public Schools] and as difficult contract talks drag on between the school board and the MTEA (as well as all other MPS unions), is this vicious attack on union leaders just a coincidence? Could there be a deliberate attempt to diminish MTEA membership support for its professional staff and elected leaders during these extremely perilous times?[239]

Sometimes union staffers don't even wait for the negative stories to appear before reacting wildly. In September 1997, Trevor Neilson, then the media relations director for the Washington Education Association, warned members in a newsletter article to expect criticism for bad test scores. He wrote:

> The [state test] results are not all together positive and the usual roundup of extremist wackos, voucher-heads and militia members will hee and haw claiming that it is, well, your fault. That's right, you, the educators of Washington. It is also likely that the media will look for someone to blame, and head in your direction.

But the fact is that most American editors, columnists, and reporters lack the proclivity (or the backbone) to provoke the unions. This results in ludicrous puff-pastry journalism.

Here are just a few examples from newspapers and magazines that have taken on the rare duty of profiling teacher union officials.

Imagine Jimmy Hoffa getting press reviews like these!

- "But Chase is gaining momentum, and if he can succeed, prospects for millions of children will be brighter."[240]

- "Chase has taken on some of the toughest issues of any NEA leader in recent history. And he has done it in his characteristic style: by listening to people, reasoning with them, and then pushing on with what he believes is right. . . . His preference for schoolchildren over politics is evident."[241]

- "Yup, Sandy Feldman has dyed her hair blond. Brash, blunt, Brooklyn-Jewish Sandy Feldman, whose saucy voice and straightforward manner—perhaps whose very soul—practically ooze brunette, has gone blond."[242]

- "Her real passion, unmistakable in both her public appearances and on playgrounds, is children. Especially poor children. Although Feldman herself has no children, she seems to consider the 1 million-plus students here her family."[243]

- "In her private life, she [Utah Education Association president Phyllis Sorenson] is a doting grandmother, a master quilter and an antique-shop hound who hunts thrift stores for castoff stuffed animals that can be lovingly refurbished and donated to charity."[244]

- "Colleagues, bosses and friends call [Virginia Education Association president Jean H.] Bankos a natural for the job. They talk about her classroom savvy, dedication to children and teachers, her way of getting people to do things—and her objectivity through years of working for teachers at the local and state level."[245]

Yech!

The Teacher Trust wants the clout of the AFL-CIO, coupled with the public image of the dedicated schoolmarm. And, by and large, it's been getting it. Anyone who questions this fantasy can expect a reaction as subtle as a brick through the window.

A few investigative reporters, with a labor bent and a realization that a brick through the window is a sign you're onto something, would find a treasure trove of stories if they would bypass the unions' "message" and seek out the truth instead.

A good start would be the simple recognition that the Teacher Trust is not just "the teachers" but a special interest group, no different from the NRA, AARP, HMOs, Big Tobacco, or Big Oil.

The teacher unions have as much power over America's economic and cultural future as any group in the country. They deserve at least as much scrutiny from America's journalistic watchdogs.

But don't expect the NEA's Friend of Education award any time soon.

11

The Same Old New Unionism

The campaign should be launched in a speech by President Chase in which he acknowledges the crisis, says some things for their shock value to open up the audience's minds (e.g. there are bad teachers and our job is to make them good or show the way to another career), and then details the Association's substantive programs to improve public schools—those already in existence and those that will be expanded or launched in the months ahead. It should be supplemented by a full-court press blitz, television advertising, and a host of other outreach efforts.

—The Kamber Group, "An Institution at Risk:
An External Communications Review of the National
Education Association," January 14, 1997

The fact is that while the vast majority of teachers are capable and dedicated—professionals who put children's interests first—there are indeed some bad teachers in America's schools. And it is our job to improve those teachers or—hat failing—to get them out of the classroom.

—Bob Chase, "The New Unionism,"
speech to the National Press Club, February 5, 1997

The Teacher Trust's most serious public relations problem is its profound opposition to reform.

We shouldn't be cynical about this (naturally). It isn't that NEA and AFT officials don't care whether a particular reform improves student achievement. They would be as happy as anyone to see test scores rise, curriculum improved, the public satisfied.

But the unions can make the jump from self-interest to high moral principle faster and further than anyone else. They genuinely believe that what's good for the union must be good for teachers, and what's good for teachers must be good for education. And most education reforms are not designed for the unions' benefit. So the unions find themselves saying "no, no, NO!" A lot.

Example: the 1995 position paper on crucial legislative issues put together for a coalition of the California Teachers Association, California School Employees Association, California Federation of Teachers, Service Employees International Union, and the United Teachers Los Angeles. It was marked "Not for General Distribution":

- There should be *no expansion of charter schools* until the legally required evaluation has been completed and has proven the value of the concept. Any future expansion must be contingent upon protection of existing employee rights, including collective bargaining.

- *Oppose* all attempts to limit the collection of dues, agency fees, or political action funds by unions.

- *Oppose* all attempts to weaken or destroy collective bargaining in any manner, including the elimination of PERB (Public Employee Relations Board).

- *Oppose* all attempts to weaken current protections against contracting out and to repeal prevailing wage laws. Non-classroom parent volunteers should not replace current employees, and their use should have the approval of exclusive representatives for the purposes of coordination and quality control.

- *Defeat* any legislation to eliminate existing salary schedule laws and to remove the issue from the scope of collective bargaining.

- *Oppose* all attempts to weaken procedural and substantive due process protections for permanent teachers as
  well as legislation to increase the length of the proba-
  tionary period for teachers without restoration of previous procedural due process rights.

- *Oppose* all attempts at wholesale repeal of the Education Code which would force unions to win back
  existing employee rights.
  [Emphases added]

Opposing every reform idea that comes down the pipeline might be
acceptable if government school systems were exceptionally good. But it is
obviously untenable if they are not. Union officials recognize this. Periodically, they launch campaigns to persuade Americans that they are not the
Abominable Nopersons that the casual observer might conclude.

The latest in the long string of these campaigns is "New Unionism."
Championed by NEA president Bob Chase, New Unionism is purportedly
an effort to deemphasize (his union critics say discard) the old-style industrial union approach in favor of a professional, craft guild approach. That is,
the NEA will spend more time and effort on education quality issues rather
than just salaries, benefits, and working conditions.

Chase officially launched New Unionism in a National Press Club
speech on February 5, 1997.

"Bear in mind," Chase said that day,

> that for nearly three decades now, the National Education Associa-
> tion has been a traditional, somewhat narrowly focused union.
> We have butted heads with management over bread-and-butter
> issues—to win better salaries, benefits, and working conditions for
> school employees. And we have succeeded. Today, however, it is
> clear to me—and to a critical mass of teachers across America—that
> while this narrow, traditional agenda remains important, it is utterly
> inadequate to the needs of the future. It will not serve our mem-
> bers' interest in greater professionalism. It will not serve the public's
> interest in better quality public schools. And it will not serve the
> interests of America's children . . . the children we teach . . . the
> children who motivated us to go into teaching in the first place.

And this latter interest must be decisive. After all, America's public schools do not exist for teachers and other employees. They do not exist to provide us with jobs and salaries.

Chase's remarks received a positive response from the press and the public. They were generally seen as signaling a new direction for the NEA.

Unfortunately, the press and the public lacked the historical background to see that New Unionism was merely the latest "new direction" for the NEA—and for all practical purposes was virtually indistinguishable from the old direction.

Seven months *before* Chase introduced New Unionism to the National Press Club, his predecessor, Keith Geiger, told the NEA Representative Assembly, meeting in Washington, D.C.:

> Let me say this bluntly: We as an Association cannot continue to sidestep accountability for the quality of our members' work. Too often—almost in knee-jerk fashion—we also find ourselves defending failed schools and failed school systems, just because they happen to be public. This is a trap. It is counterproductive.

And five months before Geiger made that speech, he had told attendees of the union's Mid-Atlantic Regional Leadership Conference in Baltimore that the NEA's future "will require a break from the adversarial or subordinate styles that too often dominate relations with school boards and administrators."

But Geiger wasn't launching the new direction that day—February 18, 1996. He was talking about a new direction that had allegedly already occurred. "In the past year," he said, "NEA has stepped forthrightly into the vanguard of the education reform movement in the United States."

And the year before that—in other words, a year before the one when Geiger boasted that the NEA had stepped forthrightly into the vanguard etc., etc.—the minutes of an NEA Board of Directors meeting reported this warning from executive director Don Cameron: "Mr. Cameron said that if NEA continues to do business as usual, the future of public education in America is at stake" (September 23, 1995).

And seven years before *that,* back in November 1988, the NEA's Special Committee on Restructuring Schools issued its final report. The buzzword then was "bilateral decision-making." The report's authors explained:

The authority of the school staff must be expanded to include all decisions related to the teaching-learning process. Specifically, the staff must have the latitude to remove identified barriers to learning imposed by school regulations (e.g., tracking that tunnels students into restrictive learning environments; rigid grade structures; bureaucratic, top-down administration).

The November 1988 report was prompted by an initiative launched by NEA president Mary Hatwood Futrell in March of that year. Futrell's contribution to "New Unionism" was the Learning Laboratory project, described by Futrell in a press conference as an effort to "extend the NEA's leadership in achieving school restructuring."

And two years before *that,* on July 5, 1986, the *Washington Post* published a story under the headline: "NEA Undergoes 'Major Philosophical Shift.' " And a year before *that,* on July 1, 1985, the *Post* published a story under the headline "Futrell Tries to Moderate Union's Stands," stating that "Futrell's efforts at rapprochement yesterday come as she tries to shift her union toward a more moderate stand on issues affecting the profession." That story also noted: "Futrell's efforts at this convention have aimed partly at putting the NEA in the forefront of reform efforts . . ."

Bob Chase himself puts New Unionism even further back in the past. In his 1997 National Press Club speech, Chase said:

> In 1983, after the *Nation at Risk* report came out, NEA president Mary Hatwood Futrell tried to mobilize our union to lead the reform movement in American public education. At the time, as a member of NEA's executive committee, I took a lead role in opposing her. I argued that we should stick to our knitting— stick to bargaining for better pay and working conditions. That, ladies and gentlemen, was the biggest mistake of my career. I was wrong.

It's impossible for "New Unionism" to go back any further than 1983, because the NEA only became a full-fledged union in the mid-1970s. But if the NEA has been, as Chase said in 1997, a "narrowly focused union" for "nearly three decades," then what were all these "major philosophical shifts" since 1983?

Chase seemed to recognize that New Unionism might receive some skeptical reactions. So he told his National Press Club audience, memorably, "to watch what we do, not what we say."

In March 1999, two years after Chase launched his "New Unionism" campaign, NEA released a summary of is impact: "Stepping Forward: How NEA Members Are Revitalizing America's Public Education." For months prior to publication, the NEA had lobbied its locals to contribute examples of "New Unionism" in action.

Some of these alleged Steps Forward failed to qualify as "New Unionism" in any form. The report listed as "New Unionism" more than two dozen examples of its affiliates negotiating bonuses and fee reimbursements for those who achieve national certification. It cited the NEA charter school in Phoenix, even though it failed to open in 1999 (or 2000 or 2001). More than sixty other "reforms" that could be identified by date went back before February 1997—some as far back as 1982.

So if New Unionism isn't new, and it isn't different, what is it—and why did Bob Chase introduce it at the National Press Club in February 1997?

The answers lie in a 1996 decision by the NEA's top officials to hire The Kamber Group, a prestigious Washington, D.C., public relations firm with strong ties to organized labor and the Democratic Party. The Kamber Group was commissioned to study the NEA's "external communications," that is, its public relations as opposed to its relations with its own members. For more than three months the group's researchers interviewed the NEA's elected officials and staff, as well as officials of selected state affiliates. It also reviewed almost three years of news and broadcast media clips, as well as NEA publications and advertising.

On January 14, 1997, The Kamber Group issued its report to the NEA's leaders. Entitled "An Institution at Risk: An External Communications Review of the National Education Association," the report was shared only with the union's 166-member board of directors. Though of course sympathetic to the NEA's mission, the report was devastating. It concluded:

> While the NEA has a surfeit of talented, committed people who work hard to do the right thing, there is an internal political environment which discourages risk-taking. It has a bureaucratic system

of decision-making that involves too many "cooks" and takes too long. To survive, much less to prevail over its critics, the NEA must shift to a crisis mode of operations.[246]

Kamber was very clear as to how this was to be done. So clear, in fact, that Chase put many recommendations into play immediately, even lifting some thoughts out of the report—practically verbatim—to use in his New Unionism speech three weeks later. (See the epigraph at the beginning of this chapter.)

"Stake out a clear risk through a crisis strategy that seeks to win not by silencing the opposition, but by co-opting the other side's turf so the NEA can direct reform discussions rather than having them dictated to it," Kamber advised.[247]

Kamber further explained how this would work:

It will be the means of shifting NEA's approach from that of an industrial union to one that embraces attributes of craft unionism, in which ensuring quality workers is just as important as raising wages and benefits at the bargaining table. It will provide the shock necessary to force everyone from cynical members of the press to the general public to take a second look at the organization.[248]

Finally, the Kamber Report recommended an organizational strategy in which speed and flexibility were emphasized over brute strength.

"In other words," the report explained hopefully, "the NEA spends less time attacking its opponents and more co-opting them—taking some of their positions, molding them to be beneficial to NEA members, and becoming the creator, rather than the receiver, of education reforms."[249]

There was always reason to doubt that the NEA could change its spots (again).

In his speech to the Press Club, Chase admitted that "in some instances, we have used our power to block uncomfortable changes . . . to protect the narrow interest of our members, and not to advance the interests of students and schools."

But after the speech, when a reporter asked Chase how "New Unionism" would deal with clashes between the interests of students and schools and the narrow interests of teachers, Chase replied: "I think I would probably ask the questioner to tell me when they are at odds. Students' learning conditions and teachers' teaching conditions are synonymous. I don't think they're at odds at all. As a matter of fact, I think that exactly the opposite is true."

Chase apparently just couldn't get out of his head that traditional union mantra: What's good for the union must be good for teachers, and what's good for teachers must be good for education.

Even so, Chase's attempt to repair the union's external communications started to jangle its internal communications. Many NEA officials and members suspected Chase was signaling a move away from emphasis on salaries, benefits, and working conditions. They didn't like it one bit. While the press waxed rhapsodic about NEA's new direction, Chase was having to reassure union activists that he wasn't selling out NEA's mission.

In a March 13, 1997, letter to Wisconsin Education Association council president Terry Craney, Chase explained the link between New Unionism and old:

> However, according to polls, critics, friends, the media, as well as our own members, NEA does not possess anything approaching a strong and credible voice in the education reform debate. That reality for NEA is not only alarming, but also dangerous for public education. Without a strong, credible voice in this arena, NEA cannot continue to protect public education; if we cannot protect public education, we cannot protect our members and their jobs.

Chase told Craney:

> NEA is increasingly viewed as an obdurate and powerful protector of the status quo, which translates to the average citizen as the protector of bad public education. Even worse than being seen as irrelevant, we are seen as part of the problem. All the wishing in the world and all the organizational chest pounding we can muster will not change that fact.

But when it came to adding substance to the style of reinventing the NEA, the union fell well short of Chase's rhetoric. At an NEA Board of Directors meeting in May 1997, Chase and the staff gave a three-hour presentation on "New Unionism." One member of the board, reporting to his constituents later, described the meeting this way: "The one universal through all of these presentations was that almost all of us are doing New Unionism things whether we call them by that name or not." The public relations aspects of New Unionism were also described to the board. "It was pointed out that the term 'New Unionism' was used deliberately," reported this director. "Because of this we have received all kinds of positive press on the NEA."

Another member of the board told his constituents that Chase's New Unionism and the report from The Kamber Group were directly linked (a connection Chase has repeatedly denied). "A campaign to implement the [Kamber] report will use the theme New Unionism," the board member wrote, "but state affiliates can use whatever term they wish to reference this new approach."

So if New Unionism doesn't really signal a change in direction for the NEA after all, what are these union programs that Chase and his supporters call New Unionism?

In essence, they are initiatives that directly involve the NEA in the administration of public schools. New Unionism recasts NEA as both labor *and* management.

Once the union has succeeded in making itself the sole voice of teachers, the level of union influence over school policies is directly proportional to the power of the union in that particular district. Significantly, the NEA's favorite examples of New Unionism all turn out to involve districts where the local affiliate is already exceptionally powerful.

Thus the Montgomery County Teachers Association in Maryland negotiated a contract that established more than a dozen task forces composed of administrators and teachers who jointly set school policies in their respective areas. The Glenview Education Association in Illinois negotiated a contract that gives teachers control over a large portion of the district's budget. The Seattle Education Association negotiated a groundbreaking power-sharing agreement with the school district.

But the Montgomery County Teachers Association is the NEA's fourth largest local affiliate and its members are the highest-paid teachers in the state. Teacher pay in Glenview is in the top 25 of Illinois's 900 school districts. And Seattle, NEA's thirteenth largest local, spends more per pupil than any large school district in Washington State.

But the (wormless) apple of Bob Chase's eye was the Columbus Education Association in Ohio. The ninth largest local in the NEA, CEA represents teachers with the third highest starting salary and twelfth largest maximum salary among Ohio's seven hundred school districts.[250] (Columbus is also the home of the celebrated Peer Assistance and Review—PAR—program, which is discussed below.)

But as a model for the collaborative approach of New Unionism, Columbus leaves a lot to be desired. At the very time Chase was championing the Columbus approach, the Columbus Board of Education and the Greater Columbus Area Chamber of Commerce commissioned an "Operations and Efficiency Task Force" to study district operations. After a year of study by eighty researchers, the task force concluded that "the school board's labor agreements with its unions tie managers' hands and hamper efficiency." The task force suggested that teachers had received overly generous pay increases and questioned built-in longevity increases of up to 4 percent annually.[251] It found that Columbus teachers had missed an average of nearly eleven days of work each in the 1996–1997 school year, costing taxpayers more than $5.6 million for substitutes.

What's more, the task force audit revealed that Columbus teachers were spending less than four hours a day actually teaching students.[252] And for all the talk of collaboration with management, Columbus was having great difficulties filling administrator slots.

But "peer review" was the "New Unionism" reform that made Columbus famous. It was endorsed wholeheartedly by Chase, who attempted to make it official NEA policy in 1997.

Peer review was a response to public muttering about teacher tenure—or "due process," as the Teacher Trust prefers to call it. The media is dangerously close to developing a stereotyped story replete with anecdotes about how difficult it is for administrators to fire demonstrably incompetent teachers who have union protection. (Because it *is* hard.) The NEA realizes that these stories resonate strongly and that it cannot simply stand on its utter opposition to tenure reform. So it has acknowledged that there is a legitimate problem and offered its own ready-made solution: "Peer Review and Assistance."

Peer review turns the authority for overseeing teacher performance from school administrators over to the union. The union appoints consulting teachers and the majority of members on a review panel. This has the paradoxical effect of removing the purportedly best teachers from the class-room and putting them to work as consulting teachers—i.e., teaching teachers, not children.

Naturally, there are significant monetary costs associated with peer review. Columbus has twenty-nine full-time mentor teachers who receive a stipend of 20 percent above their regular salary.

Thus peer review disarmed a looming education reform—tenure abolition—that threatened the union. But the NEA nevertheless has developed a list of safeguards that further disarm the reform. NEA Resolution D-11 lists thirteen separate elements that any peer review program should have. These include a mind-boggling proviso allowing "participating teachers the selection and/or approval of their assignment to a consulting teacher."

NEA officials make it clear to their members that the goal of peer review is to retain as many teachers as possible.

"To characterize a peer assistance review program as 'getting rid of bad teachers' is a gross misrepresentation," said Bob Chase. "Quite the opposite is true. Teachers referred to PAR programs are valued colleagues and professionals who deserve the best resources their districts and their local union can provide them."[253]

Indeed, as they approved the peer review resolution, members of the NEA Professional Standards and Practice Committee portrayed "bad teachers" as victims. The committee reported that these teachers "are rarely provided with meaningful and sustained professional support that can help them to again become fully productive members of the school community. More often than not, they are allowed to struggle in an unsupportive atmosphere that offers no constructive approach to the difficulties they are facing."

The difficulties faced by these teachers' students were not addressed.

As it turns out, peer review is *no more efficient* at getting rid of bad teachers than the old-fashioned method. A problem teacher, after dozens of observations and offers of help, can simply refuse to be "counseled out of the profession." Then the procedure for firing him or her is just as demanding, if not more so. In the first eight years of the PAR program, the Columbus school board fired exactly two teachers.

Ivy Featherstone, a longtime Columbus teacher, was placed in the PAR program for incompetence and substandard performance. During the two years he was in the program, Featherstone received seventy-five classroom visits from mentors. He was involved in twenty-nine conferences about his teaching. His case then received sixteen days of hearings before a finding of "gross inefficiency" was rendered. Despite all this, Featherstone was not fired, but merely suspended without pay. He immediately filed a civil rights suit that took another three years before it was finally decided in favor of the district.[254]

In its first eight years, PAR consultants reviewed the performance of only 123 veteran Columbus teachers, or fewer than 16 per year. In a pool of about 4,500 veteran teachers, that comes to about ⅓ of 1 percent annually.

Peer review programs established by the American Federation of Teachers exhibit similar numbers. In Rochester, New York, AFT's peer review program assessed only ½ of 1 percent of veteran teachers. Another AFT program in Toledo, Ohio, assessed only forty one longtime teachers over a twelve-year period—a ³⁄₁₀ of 1 percent. In the nine years the Poway Federation of Teachers has run its program in southern California, a grand total of eight veteran teachers have participated. Six returned to the classroom, one retired and one took disability. Not a single veteran teacher was fired, suspended, or asked to resign.[255]

But peer review is just fine for the Teacher Trust. There are the obvious public relations benefits. The unions frankly admit that peer review "would help reverse the public misperception that the union, and its advocacy of the due process and a fair tenure system, works to protect incompetent teachers."[256] And peer review promotes union membership. As Susan Staub, president of Pennsylvanians for Right to Work Inc., explains: "What better way to whip recalcitrant non-union teachers into joining the union that controlled their review, assistance, and dismissal recommendations?"[257] Finally, and most important, the unions feel "it is far better . . . for teachers to control the induction process and be the gatekeepers to their profession than it is for nonpractitioners to perform this function."[258] Once unions have control over the induction and retention processes, they have control over the labor supply, and thus can inflate wages at will.

But the most outrageous use of peer review by the unions is as a bargaining chip. Though it is completely designed, implemented, and controlled by the union, several NEA affiliates in California treat peer review as a management demand. They refuse to go along unless the district agrees to other union demands, such as agency fees or staff development days.

"It's nice to be in the driver's seat," said one California Teachers Association staffer.[259]

If peer review was the New Unionism reform of 1997, then "pay for performance" was in 1999. The government school system's inability to pay good teachers more than bad ones irks the public probably even more than its inability to get rid of bad teachers. Education reformers are always nagging about the obvious private sector response—"merit pay." So the union has invented the concept of "performance pay."

The difference, which is unclear even to many union members, is that merit pay is awarded based on the subjective recommendation of a school principal or administrator. But performance pay is awarded based on a purportedly objective standard—usually excluding student test scores.

In 1999, the Denver Classroom Teachers Association agreed to a pilot performance pay program. Volunteer teachers were to be evaluated on several different measures. A positive finding after the four-year experiment would result in the abolition of the traditional salary scale in favor of the best performance pay system. Teachers ratified the contract by a large margin. But they weren't very willing to volunteer for the program, and the district had to scramble to meet the minimum number of participants required.

The Denver experiments, coupled with inquiries from several interested state affiliates, persuaded NEA officials to put a committee to work studying performance pay. The idea was to come up with a plan to modify the union's long-standing opposition to merit pay.

Hints of trouble arose almost immediately. California Teachers Association president Wayne Johnson called the Denver plan "sinister." He wrote: "I hope not one teacher or one association in California will even contemplate any merit pay proposal."[260] But after months of research, meetings, and a survey of eight thousand members on performance pay issues, the committee generated a new resolution that would allow the NEA to assist affiliates who wished to negotiate performance pay. However, the resolution had so many ifs, ands, and buts that it was unlikely to lead to any revolutionary change in public school teacher pay scales.

Even so, when the resolution was placed before the delegates of the NEA Representative Assembly in Chicago in July 2000, it was resoundingly defeated. Most of the NEA's largest affiliates—California, New Jersey, Michigan, and Pennsylvania—voted in large numbers against it. In fact, the delegates actually strengthened the union's prohibition against merit pay to include performance pay as well.

Another New Unionism reform: NEA charter schools.

Charter schools were first created in Minnesota in 1991. Laws vary from state to state, but the basic concept is that a group of people open a school and draft a contract, or "charter," that spells out exactly what the school's mission will be, what grades and enrollment it will serve, where it will be located, how it will serve the public interest, etc. Then the charter is presented to the local school board. If approved, it becomes the governing document of that school, which receives public funds. If turned down, its supporters can in most states appeal to a state board. The charter school must abide by its charter, but it is otherwise free from all but the most basic regulation.

Some charter schools achieve outstanding results, others may be indistinguishable from other schools in the district, and a few are dogged by poor administration, mismanagement, or malfeasance. In other words, they are just like every other sector of America.

The difference is that everyone involved in a charter school is a volunteer (except possibly the students, who can be volunteered by their parents). No teacher or administrator can be assigned to a charter school against her will. No parent is forced to accept the school's mission. However, it should be noted that whenever charter schools are closed down or otherwise receive sanctions, legislators—often spurred by the teacher unions—are proving quick to propose reregulation. Watch this space!

The Teacher Trust fought strongly against most charter school laws because the charter usually frees the school from the district's collective bargaining. But it has been losing. Charter schools now exist in virtually every state in the union.

In 1995, the NEA decided to take a big step: it would create its own charter schools. This would serve two purposes. First, the schools would be models for the types of charters NEA could live with. Second, the union could expect positive press coverage—which it got.

The plan was announced with much fanfare. As the NEA's charter initiative put it:

> Freed from the bureaucratic constraints imposed on other public schools, charter schools provide places to develop better ways to improve student learning. If ties to regular schools in the community are strong, charter schools can be an important vehicle to improve educational opportunities for all students.[261]

The NEA needed these charter schools and it wasn't going to let anything stand in its way. It pledged to spend $1.5 million over five years to get them up and running. The original plan was to establish six schools in six states (Arizona, California, Colorado, Georgia, Hawaii, and Wisconsin).

The first to open was in Lanikai, Hawaii. It was a conversion from a "student-centered" school with 360 students, a special state designation that made the transition relatively easy. Lanikai's situation has remained relatively stable, though information on it is hard to come by.

The NEA's other charter schools have not had such smooth sailing. Wisconsin dropped out of the running fairly quickly. But in Colorado Springs, the NEA approved a charter school called the Character, Integrity, Vision, and the Arts (CIVA) school. With 140 students and a staff of 10, the school faced the same difficulties as every other charter school—and, paradoxically enough, the same opponents, the local teacher union.

That's right. While Jan Noble, the president of the Colorado Springs Education Association, was the architect of CIVA, many of her members were adamantly opposed. So opposed, in fact, that they attempted to remove Noble from office. Indeed, Noble's motives for supporting a charter school seemed less than, well, noble. She called the charters a chance "to get the taxpayers on our side."

She feels her efforts were not in vain: "I can't deny that we did this a little because of PR, because now our reputation is one of professionalism."

NEA affiliates have insisted that charters receive the blessing of district teachers before getting approval from the school district or state. Yet when Colorado Springs teachers wanted to vote on CIVA in 1997, Noble wouldn't allow it. She frankly told *Education Week* she was convinced they would have turned it down.

The NEA charters were not faring any better elsewhere. The third charter was supposed to open in East Point, Georgia, where the NEA approved a teacher-led initiative to convert Woodland Middle School to a charter. But after several attempts, the Woodland teachers simply could not generate enough support among their own colleagues for the plan.

This strong opposition from teachers caught the NEA leadership by surprise. But it shouldn't have. It's quite logical. The whole appeal of charter schools is the freedom from rules and regulations. The people who are likely to go through all the trouble to create a charter school don't care where those rules and regulations came from—the state government, the local government, the district, the union, or the labor contract itself. But the charter, the actual agreement, in an NEA charter school contains *all* the rules and regulations that are already in the union contract.

If you're happy with the rules and regulations established by your collective bargaining agreement, why would you want to start a charter school? Why have essentially two concurrent contracts with the school district? A union charter school is perceived by teachers as either unnecessary, or a threat to the status quo. This is what happened in Colorado Springs and East Point. But it was mild compared to what happened next in Connecticut.

When the Georgia plan fell through, the NEA needed a substitute. Union officials found what they thought was an excellent candidate in Norwich, Connecticut. A small group of teachers wanted to create the Integrated Day Charter School for 175 students and a staff of 8.

The officers of the Norwich Teachers League, the local NEA affiliate, opposed the charter school. They held a vote and the charter proposal was defeated. The local school board also rejected the proposal. This was particularly embarrassing, because just as NEA affiliates insist that teachers give their blessing to charters, so also do they generally insist that only local districts—where the local union has most control—have the exclusive authority to grant charters. (Thus the Massachusetts Teachers Association, engaged in its own battle against charter schools, noted in a press release: "We do not believe that districts should be required to host and finance any school that they do not believe is in the best interest of children in their community." Similarly, the Michigan Education Association filed suit against this practice in its state.)

However, contrary to its own lobbying, the NEA used Connecticut's appeals process and got its charter. "Typically, we like to work with the local districts on charter schools," said Teresa Rankin of the NEA. "But it didn't matter in terms of the criteria we had set for endorsing the school. It was just an external event."

Then the NEA constructed the ultimate paradox. The union always insists that charter schools be subject to the existing collective bargaining agreement, and that teachers and staff must remain members of their existing union. Its self-interest in promoting this is obvious: the NEA wants to ensure that charter schools are not used to raid its locals or undermine union solidarity.

But the Norwich Teachers League was an obstacle to the establishment of the NEA's charter school. So the Connecticut Education Association and the NEA allowed the eight Integrated Day teachers to form their own local, and then helped them negotiate a contract with the district. "We felt our responsibility was to continue our commitment to the research effort," said Rankin.

The NEA also let pass other aspects of the Integrated Day plan that it would have opposed in other charter schools. Students and teachers eat lunch together in a makeshift cafeteria. This violates the usual teacher contract provision for a duty-free lunch period. And conditions were unusual—the school is located in the former American Thermos Company factory which was a wreck with broken windows, a partially collapsed roof and piles of trash inside only three months before it opened in the fall of 1997.[262]

The NEA's charter school in Phoenix was slated to open in fall 1999 and would have served two hundred inner-city students in grades seven to nine. Arizona has the least restrictive charter school law in the nation, but the Arizona Education Association was still an odd choice to pursue the project. The AEA's position paper on charter schools had made its reservations clear:

> Through ordaining an array of separate and autonomous special purpose schools within school districts, the charter school movement could have the disastrous effect of fragmenting the shared goals of education communities, lowering educational standards, and exacerbating class, race, and educational stratification in our schools and our society.

Little wonder that Arizona parents, with a variety of choices in charter schools, avoided the union's school en masse. AEA was unable to recruit the

175 students it wanted, even after spending $65,000 on a three-year effort with the cooperation of Arizona State University.

"For ASU and the AEA to venture into those waters and for us not to be able to pull it off the first time is a bit ironic," said ASU associate dean Nicholas Appleton. "Frankly, it turned out to be harder to get established than we thought."[263]

An even stranger place for the NEA to experiment with charter schools was California. The California Teachers Association has fought, and continues to fight, the establishment of charter schools wherever they may appear. Yet the San Diego charter school had the most ambitious schedule of all the NEA charters. It was supposed to open under the name Ixcalli Charter School in fall 1997, or "possibly sooner," explained San Diego Teachers Association executive director Bill Harju. A union design team spent much of 1996 putting together a plan, and even traveled to Celebration, Florida, to study the Walt Disney Company's "school of the future" (more on Celebration shortly).[264]

But the opening of the school was delayed for a year while the team fiddled with the concept. Ixcalli was supposed to start with grades one, two, six, and seven, eventually expanding to become a K–12 school. The school design called for six academic levels to replace grades. Then, for reasons that are not clear, the school failed to open in 1998, the lead administrator was replaced, and, mysteriously, the name of the school was changed to Kwachiiyoa. A new administrator was hired in March 1999, at which time Kwachiiyoa still had no building, no staff, and no students. But it had cash. The California Department of Education gave it a grant of $150,000. The CTA's initial grant was $15,000 and the NEA chipped in an additional $12,000. San Diego State University also contributed $10,000.

Kwachiiyoa finally opened in the fall of 1999. But although scheduled to start with 235 students, it had only 125 and only in grades K–5.

In the fall of 2000, Kwachiiyoa made headlines—but not because of its academic success. *WorldNet Daily's* Julie Foster reported (September 30) that, although taxpayer funded, the school allowed the CTA to hold an anti-voucher rally on campus during school hours and hand out anti-voucher T-shirts to students.

While the CTA was exploiting its own charter school for political purposes, it was also trying to roll back the charter movement. In California, as in most states, charter teachers can remain part of their local union, form their own union, or belong to no union at all. But the CTA-sponsored legislation would have required charter schools to abide by the local government school contract.

"If this passes, we're dead," Yvonne Chan, a charter school principal, said of the CTA bill. "If this passes it will be the districts and the unions that run charter schools."

When *Investor's Business Daily* asked the CTA about charter school teachers who were being treated unfairly, the union couldn't come up with any. "Nothing's come to my attention," said CTA spokesman Mike Myslinski. Do charter school teachers *want* to be represented in collective bargaining, *IBD* asked? "We haven't polled them or anything like that," he said.

In fact, the union knows perfectly well that charter school teachers are generally content. Researcher Julia Koppich performed a survey of charter school teachers for the NEA in 1998. She found that teachers liked working conditions at charter schools—but were losing the sense that their schools are still public schools and had less interest in union membership. "Levels of salaries and benefits are not a big issue," she said. "Even those with lower salaries feel they are compensated for by professional freedom." Teachers felt secure in their jobs even though all they had was a one-year work agreement.

Less interest in union membership? *Satisfaction* with lower wages and benefits?

End of story, so far as the Teacher Trust is concerned.

In fact, the opposition of union activists to charter schools is visceral—and, despite New Unionism, probably insurmountable. This is obvious when they communicate among themselves. A representative of the California Staff Organization, the CTA's staff union, posted this comment for colleagues after attending a charter school conference.

However, it is becoming increasingly evident that the organizers behind charter schools, vouchers and the privatization of public education are cut from the same cloth as those who would outlaw unions, ignore democratic principles and the ills of society. What drives these individuals are profits and an isolationist mental model that emphasizes individual rights while minimizing responsibilities to our communities and society in general. Further, even under the best circumstances, charter schools are often the playground for malcontents, ostracized administrators and ill-advised parents and community members.

Similarly, Idella Harter, president of the Maine Education Association called charters a "counterproductive distraction."[265] Linda Vitiellio, president of the Somerville Teachers Association in Massachusetts, said charter schools "are not just eroding support for public schools, they are destroying them."[266] NEA New York vice president Robin Rapaport called them "clearly a bad idea."[267] And Education Minnesota co-president Sandra Peterson disclosed the union's real preference: "Let's put a cap on creating any more charter schools until we evaluate all the schools we have."[268]

The ultimate New Unionism reform: involving the union in managing the school. When Bob Chase introduced New Unionism in his 1997 National Press Club speech, he happily announced an example—Celebration Teaching Academy in Florida. Chase said:

> And while I'm on the subject of teacher professionalism, I'd like to use this occasion to announce that NEA has entered into a partnership with Stetson University to play a major role in the new Celebration Teaching Academy. This remarkable academy will be part of Walt Disney Company's new town of Celebration, Florida, and it will work hand in hand with the local public school. It will be for educators what a teaching hospital is for doctors. A place where teachers from around the nation can come to sharpen their skills and be exposed to "best practices." NEA professionals on site will help to shape the curriculum and to direct the academy's Master Teacher Institute.

Chase pledged $500,000 in financial and staff support. "As you can imagine," he said, "we are delighted to play a major role in this important project. Indeed, the Celebration Teaching Academy is exactly what the new NEA is all about: a commitment to lifting up teachers as professionals and to revitalizing public education."

Chase was quite right. The experiment in Celebration was exactly what the new NEA is all about.

Celebration opened its school in 1996. "Everyone was starting from scratch," said Don Killoren, the general manager of Celebration in the early years. "Nobody learned from the mistakes of other people. The teaching academy would be a way to bring in people from around the country to preach about the best ideas, teaching methods, and curricula."[269]

But what happened next was entirely predictable. With Disney granting carte blanche, every progressive education fad was instituted in one school: multiple intelligences, cooperative learning, integrated subjects, portfolios instead of tests, self-critique, K–12 in one school, large classrooms with up to one hundred students and four teachers in a room of as much as five thousand square feet. No rows of desks. No fixed time for subjects. No textbooks. Each student was assessed on "social responsibility" and for knowing "the rewards of giving one's energies for a larger good."

Needless to say, the school was an unmitigated disaster. Parents pulled their kids out in droves. "We came here as a family with a dream, and all we received was an educational nightmare," parent Richard Adams wrote to the Disney Company. "My children not only did not progress in this school—they regressed. Not only in their academics but also their discipline." Six of the school's nineteen teachers left after the first year. Indeed, the principal had already notified the superintendent she would not be returning by the time Bob Chase gave his National Press Club speech.

In May 1999, the NEA terminated its relationship with Celebration without fanfare—and certainly without a speech at the National Press Club. It had lost at least $125,000 on the school. Even after that, the NEA continued to tout Celebration on its web page, probably through bureaucratic inertia:

> Ever heard of the Celebration School? It's not a charter school. It's a public school in Orange County. But the Celebration School just happens to be on Walt Disney property. A lot has been invested in the school to make it one of the best in the world. Teachers can go there to take courses. Colleges have student teachers there.

Celebration failed. Will New Unionism follow suit? There is every sign it is about to go the way of new math.

And just as New Math was replaced by *new* New Math, New Unionism has a successor waiting in the wings: "social-justice unionism." Introduced by union activists Bob Peterson and Michael Charney, this new New Unionism expands the role of unionism beyond both teacher working conditions and school management into the realm of liberal social policies.

Leading the Teacher Trust yet further to the political left might seem rather eccentric advice. But Peterson and Charney did (perhaps inadvertently) hit upon a truth that is rarely acknowledged by the union establishment. They pointed out that

> there has been a historic divide between those who commit themselves to union activities and those who commit themselves to improving teaching practices by starting innovative schools, leading district curriculum committees, being active in the community, or participating in state and national professional organizations.[270]

In other words, union activism is fundamentally not about education. The Teacher Trust itself is the problem. Until this fundamental contradiction is resolved, the New Unionism will have about as much significance to improved education as did the New Coke.

12

The NEA Is Worried

The future is here and it does not appear to be union-friendly.[271]

—Kansas NEA UniServ director Steve Lopes

All parents must feel a bittersweet pang on that beautiful fall day when a big yellow school bus comes and takes away their kindergartner for the very first time.

Alexander Brimelow's parents, however, had barely had time to recover from this pang when they received a polite phone call from his young and pretty teacher.

Where, she wanted to know, was Alexander's homework?

Homework? There were several reasons why Alexander's parents had not been delving carefully through his schoolbag—such as the not unreasonable fear that whatever he had put in there might bite. But the most important reason was that, having had little contact with kindergartens in the rather distressing number of decades since they themselves attended, it had simply never occurred to them that five-year-olds got homework.

Five-year-olds can't read, for one thing. If a five-year-old gets homework, that means, in effect, that his parents get it too. And parents and their young children are getting homework, hours of it, often infuriating pedagogically pointless craft projects that involve time-consuming shopping trips, all across the country.

The government school system is eating the American family evening. One survey suggests that elementary school homework nearly doubled from 1981 to 1997; it may be worse at the higher grades.[272] Like the simultaneous epidemic of scheduled soccer, it's something that snuck up on parents unawares. But everybody will admit quickly, when asked, that it wasn't like this in their childhood.

Alexander's young and pretty teacher had not thought up this fiendish scheme to persecute his parents all by herself. Indeed, she probably had nothing to do with it at all. To anyone working as a professional in what might loosely be described as the real world, it is always shocking to find how little discretion government school teachers really have in their classrooms. Detailed lesson plans, homework plans, and much more micromanagement is imposed on them by a hierarchical bureaucracy. Older teachers will tell you they ignore a lot of it—except when administrators are snooping around. Younger teachers don't dare.

The educational value of massive homework is quite questionable. Perhaps surprisingly, U.S. students are already working almost as hard as those legendary Asian children: 24 percent of eighth-graders do more than three hours of homework a night, versus 28 percent in Japan—and only 17 percent in Germany. But international data also shows universally that student achievement hardly improves, and usually deteriorates sharply, once homework passes the point of one or two hours a night.

Signs of a backlash against homework include the San Diego–based Parents for Sane Homework (PUSH—www.sanehomework.com), run by Daria Doering, who describes herself as "an extremely over-extended mother of three" and part-time graduate student.

"It's just one of those educational fashions," she says.[273]

This educational fashion involves, of course, more input. But it's input of an unusual, and extremely cost-inefficient, type: from parents, in kind. It's as if bakers were telling customers that they had to go into the fields and help with the harvest—something which, as a matter of fact, has featured regularly in the history of socialist command economies, like the Soviet Union or Cuba.

One nasty suspicion about why it's happening in the American government school system now: it's another example of the Washington Monument strategy. *The Blob is worried*—all of it, teachers, unions, administrators, even elected school board officials, what Greg Moo calls "The Unholy Alliance." In fact, it's very worried. It knows it's in trouble. And it figures that, by piling on homework, it can make parents afraid to complain, in case it piles on some more.

(Another curious symptom of Blob worry, also requiring more input—and Teacher Trust acquiescence—is the progressive abolition of recess. One recent survey shows that about 40 percent of government schools have cut, or are planning to cut, at least one recess period from the school day. "There's huge pressure these days on superintendents and boards to show that they're serious about achievement," says Paul Houston, executive director of the American Association of School Administrators, "so they do something symbolic—they get rid of recess." This flies in the face of the traditional wisdom, as yet unrefuted by research, which is that children need to break and run around—especially boys. One chilling comment: "Goodbye recess, hello Ritalin."[274])

Within the Blob, the Teacher Trust's worries are particularly acute. The government school system's problems are ultimately its problems. Without its host, the parasite will die. Moreover, the consequence of American teachers' forty-year fling with the industrial labor union model are finally being felt. For a new generation of teachers, the grievances that may once have made unionism attractive are ancient history. (An example: it is impossible for Generation Xers to relate to the fact that women teachers once could not marry—or in some cases even date—without the school board's permission.[275]) But the present and real disadvantages of unionism are all too irritatingly apparent.

This is the sort of symptom that is worrying the Teacher Trust: When ballooning school budgets led to calls for a tax increase in Cincinnati, Ohio, even a retired teacher spoke out against it.

"I highly support public schools; I always have," said Catherine Hill, sixty-four, a retired teacher from Carthage. "But being retired, I can't afford a big tax increase. They have some excellent teachers in the public school system, but if I made $50,000 today, I would get down on my knees and thank almighty God. Teachers deserve a lot, but when they're already making good pay, the schools are crumbling, they cut transportation and they cut librarians, teachers should be willing to take a freeze."[276]

Additionally, the NEA is worried because its attempts to improve its image—most recently through "New Unionism"—keep blowing up in its face.

If the delegates to the NEA Representative Assembly in 2000 had done what the leadership wanted and approved the New Unionism concept of "performance pay," it wouldn't have changed very much. The resolution was already fatally qualified. But their negative vote was a public relations disaster. Even in newspapers normally sympathetic to teacher unions, comment was savage—and worrying:

- "Few professions reward workers merely for showing up. Many public schools do, though."[277]

- "Most parents, in fact, don't quite realize just how much the NEA rank-and-file remain stuck in the mind-set of an industrial union. And for this reason, as go steel and textiles, we suspect, so go the teachers."[278]

- "It was a colossal wasted opportunity."[279]

- "The defeat of the policy change was particularly striking given how conservatively it was worded."[280]

- "The national teacher unions want to be seen as defenders of public education and advocates of reform. But when you move beyond rhetoric, you find them too often simply defending the status quo, even when that status quo means inferior education for too many children."[281]

- "The rejection Wednesday by the nation's largest teacher union, the National Education Association, of even tepid experiments with performance-based pay initiatives shouldn't cause too much worry for those concerned about education reform. Sure, the NEA is again on record as favoring to keep education a profession where educators aren't held accountable or rewarded for the quality of their product; however, in this case their opposition is almost irrelevant."[282]

The unkindest cut of all may have come from the New Dem Daily, online news source of the Democratic Leadership Council. It opined:

> This week the nation's largest teacher union, the National Education Association, rejected a mildly worded resolution endorsing limited experimentation with performance-based teacher pay. The excuses offered for this disappointing action are familiar and largely pointless.[283]

But the shocking and completely unexpected failure of the 1998 RA to approve the NEA leadership's plan to merge with the AFT is the most dramatic evidence to date of why the union is worried.

For months prior to the convention, the NEA's leadership lobbied to get the necessary two-thirds majority. Many state affiliate leaders ardently advocated the merger, warning their wary members of the apocalypse to come should the NEA and AFT fail to merge. In a joint letter to all members of their respective unions, posted on both unions' web sites, Pennsylvania State Education president David J. Gondak and Pennsylvania Federation of Teachers president Albert Fondy wrote:

> We believe that the unification of the NEA and the AFT at the national level and, subsequently, here in Pennsylvania is truly necessary for the survival of public education and of our school employee unions—perhaps even for the survival of the union movement altogether.

But this heavy-handed approach began to produce a backlash. One Missouri NEA member wrote:

> It's scary how this merger seems to be orchestrated. My association was to straw poll its members next week, yet its officers and exec board members voted to endorse at the assembly. This does not seem to be representative governing to me. . . . And is it a generally agreed upon part of the process to keep the membership uninformed during the negotiations?

"This is David versus Goliath," said Buffalo Teachers Federation president Philip Rumore, whose local was opposed to the merger. "The whole leadership of the NEA and their finest PR people are lining up to shove this thing down our throats."[284]

When the 160-member NEA Board of Directors, made up of representatives from every NEA state affiliate, voted to support merger by a 2–1 margin, many delegates were unimpressed. "I believe that very few NEA directors have the guts to vote any way other than what Chase wants," one president of a large NEA local told Educational Intelligence Agency's Mike Antonucci. "They are too political and worry about their own behinds."

At the RA itself, the NEA and its pro-merger allies really turned up the heat. But because the merger required amending the NEA constitution, it was done by secret ballot. And to the shock of almost everyone, the merger gained support of only 42 percent of the delegates. The consensus was that the NEA leadership had pushed too hard.

You don't have to take our word for it. Here are some excerpts from an account by Rich Gibson for *Z Magazine,* the left-wing publication.

First, Gibson quoted Illinois Education Association president Bob Haisman. Haisman was one of the leaders of the opposition to merger. "They gave away our democracy, yet they tried to intimidate people into supporting it," said Haisman. "It half worked. People were intimidated. They had staff all over the country reporting on people. NEA just doesn't do that. So people covered up, then used a secret ballot to vote no."

Gibson then quoted someone he identified only as the head of a large Michigan local. This source explained why the NEA's top officials were so surprised by the defeat of the merger. "It was like Vietnam," he said. "From the top down, and back up again, everybody was lying to everyone else about the body counts. Promotions and jobs were tied to a good count, so the good counts came in. But the people were on the other side, slowly tunneling away."

No one was more surprised than the officials at the AFT. Three weeks later, the delegates to their convention resoundingly approved merger in a symbolic vote.

"The actual voting at the NEA convention reinforced the AFT conviction that no one within the NEA is democratically accountable to anyone else," worried one top NEA official. "That NEA convention delegates could vote overwhelmingly against the merger agreement, after every NEA leadership body had voted at least two-thirds for it, struck AFT delegates as evidence of a fundamental structural disconnect within the NEA."[285]

The NEA-AFT merger did not fail because large numbers of NEA activists had suddenly become convinced that industrial unionism was a bad idea for teachers. (However, the prospect of openly joining the AFL-CIO, like the AFT, was certainly an obstacle in some states.) Still less did the failure of merger mean widespread conversion to the view that the government school system should be privatized. The merger failed because the NEA itself is failing structurally. It has simply become too big and unwieldy to function efficiently.

This does not mean that the NEA should be any the less worried. It was probably structural failure, rather than abstract conviction, that was the key factor in the collapse of the Soviet Union. And the big problem for the Soviet Union turned out to be generational—the zealots of the Revolution, and their Stalin-silenced successors, grew old and were replaced by an age group that had new concerns.

Exactly the same thing is happening to the NEA.

"Teachers find themselves clinging to rules that seem best suited to an assembly line where workers are interchangeable even as they demand to be treated as professionals with specialized skills," wrote *Los Angeles Times* reporter Richard Lee Colvin.[286] With veteran activists retiring and so many new teachers entering the government school system, the NEA's worries can only grow. As has long been obvious in the private sector, Generation X is not union-friendly.

At the AFT/NEA Conference on Teacher Quality in 1998, the AFT publicized a nationwide Peter Hart poll it had commissioned. Teachers had been asked to complete the sentence "The union should concentrate on . . ."

Forty percent said professional issues. Only 24 percent said collective bargaining. Thirty-three percent said both. The last number makes the first all the more remarkable. It means that 40 percent of those surveyed think the union should not concentrate on collective bargaining at all.

The NEA knows that teachers are growing disillusioned with the industrial labor model. But it appears unable to believe it. As a recent NEA manual put it:

> Today the myth that professional relationships are constructive and devoid of rancor while collective bargaining is a largely adversarial process dedicated to the status quo is held not only in the larger society but, more disturbingly, *by many within the NEA family* [Emphasis added][287]

NEA officials have long known about the disconnect between the union's deliberative bodies and the members.

"I think we are naive if we think those elected represent the majority of the membership," wrote one official of the NEA's Delaware affiliate. "My experience is that the average member is less involved and aware of union activities than at any time in the past."

"We figured out a long time ago that our Rep Council isn't necessarily representative of the views in the building," wrote another, from Florida.

"I think there is a real danger that those leaders at the pinnacle of the organizational pyramid—local, state, national—become so certain of the rightness of their cause that they lose sight of the much less 'lofty' feelings of the minions in the trenches who pay the dues (and surprisingly often don't know or care if they belong to the EA or FT)," a staffer from Minnesota told the Educational Intelligence Agency's Mike Antonucci.

The ever-quotable Lois Tinson, when president of the California Teachers Association, wrote this plaintive "get-acquainted" editorial in 1995 in the union newspaper *CTA Action,* shortly after being elected.

> What I've found is that the "typical" member, the "grass-roots member," is not heavily involved in association activity at any level—local, state, or national. Many are —thousands upon thousands are—but most are not. The grass-roots member is likely, as well, to know rather little about CTA policies and programs—or how those policies are set and how those programs are developed and implemented.

Tinson added toward the end of her editorial:

> If you have read this far—and if our recent membership survey is valid—you have read more and further than four out of five CTA members.[288]

If getting members to read union publications is hard, getting them to participate in the union is really tough. The La Porte Education Association in Texas posted this telling message on its web page:

> LPEA is in desperate need of people who are willing to become officers in our local. If we are not able to recruit new officers, our local is in danger of being dissolved and turned over to the state [union].

Sometimes the chasm between members and unions becomes so wide that, in states without monopoly bargaining laws, it can lead to deteriorating membership and (*this is serious!*) reduced revenues. The travails of the Kentucky Education Association are a case in point. In January 1998, an internal report of the KEA concluded:

> The handwriting is on the wall, and we cannot ignore the overwhelming evidence that KEA is at risk [there's that phrase again!] as an organization. Only 27 percent of our members report being "very satisfied" with their membership. The majority is only "somewhat satisfied," indicating a high level of apathy and a low level of commitment. Typical KEA members do not volunteer to assist the Association, nor do they have much contact with it. Only half of all members have had minimal contact with their UniServ office, their local association, or the state association, and a mere third of our members have volunteered to assist their local associations in the last year. Only one in ten has volunteered to help their UniServ office.

The news got worse.

> Feelings that KEA has lost touch with teachers in the trenches and that KEA does not represent their interests anymore permeate the surveys. Factionalism and politics in the leadership ranks were cited as complaints over and over.

The report even dared to suggest a *really* horrible thought:

> The current perception of KEA is that we are an organization far removed from the rank-and-file membership. Some perceive that a few elite, power-hungry leaders and management personnel sit in Frankfort in ivory towers making all the decisions. We are seen as uncaring toward the real problems or real teachers in real classrooms. Leaders and staff alike are seen as self-serving, disrespectful to one another, jealous, and sometimes resentful of one another.

Teacher indifference naturally extends to elections. An election for top union officials in Clark County, Nevada, one of the NEA's largest locals, could garner only 13 percent of eligible voters. "Apathy is running rampant through our ranks," complained one member.[289]

This teacher indifference doesn't necessarily lead to direct consequences for the rank-and-file union member. But it leads to vast and crucial consequences for those who do involve themselves in the union and work to set its policies. The question is a simple one: If the teachers don't seem to care about what the union does, what does the union do?

Or, as one Illinois delegate explained it to the Educational Intelligence Agency's Mike Antonucci: "I really wonder whether even one out of a hundred individual members back home ever whip out the vote tally sheets and say to lounge colleagues, 'Hey, did you see how Sandra voted on paragraph c of by-law D-5?' "

In some cases, indifference begets indifference. In January 1999, the Oakland Unified School District was in an uproar because of the decision by the Oakland Education Association, the local NEA affiliate, to hold a "teach-in" on the death penalty and on the case of convicted Philadelphia cop killer Mumia Abu-Jamal. Some in the community protested this as a waste of instructional time. So the OEA called a meeting of its 250-member representative council to vote on whether to go ahead with the teach-in. For a vote that was sure to be contested, and with national media attention, only 101 council members showed up.

In other cases, indifference begets independence—or the desire for it. Linda Bacon, an influential NEA activist from Pinellas, Florida, wrote of her experience on a New Unionism task force, which consisted of local leaders and staffers from NEA headquarters, on a New Unionism e-mail bulletin board:

> At one point we were asked to respond to a question (and I'm paraphrasing) about what our locals needed from NEA that was really important, that we couldn't do without. One local leader responded by basically saying "absolutely nothing."
>
> He told the group that his members probably wouldn't notice much if his local left NEA tomorrow and that the local would find a way to provide the services that were important to his members. He went on to say that NEA had not been particularly helpful in doing any of the cutting-edge things they were involved in, and often put up roadblocks. He wasn't nasty about it, just very matter of fact.

When he basically blew off the national, the reaction of the staffers in the room was incredible. Faces were stunned, angry, dumbfounded—I thought one woman was ready to do physical violence!

Several people were so upset that I think they stopped listening, as evidenced by their reactions to him in their comments. They failed to hear his message: the members were looking for something different that NEA wasn't giving them.

If that happens in enough locals, NEA will be obsolete.

Staffers aren't too thrilled with the elected leadership either. Elizabeth Arnett, a longtime staffer for the Ohio Education Association, posted her views on an NEA-sponsored listserv:

I have worked here at OEA for 23-plus years. Between 1988 and 1998, this has been a truly dysfunctional system. The cause of dysfunction was not because we were more enlightened and were more conscious. It was because it was oppressive and designed to stifle creative thought, thwart exploration of new ideas, and punish those who thought differently, tried to be creative, or explored new ideas. The oppression was purposeful. The work setting was depressing, both visually and in attitude. There was no plan. Persons in high places used resources for personal gain rather than for the organization. Character and ethics were nonexistent in persons placed in leadership positions. These were the factors that caused low morale.

Are the fat years over for the Teacher Trust?

In the early summer of 2002, Mike Antonucci wrote to readers of his *Educational Intelligence Agency Communiqué*:

It used to be relatively easy for EIA to obtain accurate, up-to-date membership numbers for NEA and its state affiliates, but recently it has become a lot more difficult. Perhaps it is coincidental that the numbers are becoming harder and harder to find just as the news becomes less and less cheerful. The tremors are small: lots of talk about needing inroads with Generation X teachers . . . financial problems here . . . possible layoffs there.

In the past, membership problems were localized in the chronic, hard-to-organize states that had competing organizations. Today, the sounds are more widespread. NEA has grown every year since the mid-1980s, but for the first time the end of the boom may be in sight. The union experienced an increase of some 37,000 members this year—about half of what it achieved in 2000–2001. More alarming if you're an NEA official is the fact that 20 state affiliates had a decrease in membership last year—even as the number of potential members nationwide continues to grow at a fairly steady 2 percent annual clip.

EIA cannot yet identify which state affiliates are growing and which are not, though it seems safe to assume that the large states—California, New Jersey, Michigan, Illinois, et al.—continue to enjoy solid growth, while perennial weak sisters are now having serious problems.[290]

Significantly, all of these states where the NEA is still enjoying strong growth are ones where the union has been granted very favorable legal privileges. Reluctance among Generation X teachers will not, by itself, dismay the Teacher Trust. It will simply fall back on its traditional rule—if you can't beat 'em, make 'em join.

Thus the NEA Board of Directors granted $175,000 to the Mississippi Association of Educators for additional organizing in that right-to-work state. And the North Carolina Association of Educators is preparing a lobbying offensive in support of collective, a.k.a. monopoly, bargaining legislation in one of the last two states where collective bargaining by teachers is still banned by law.

Nevertheless, the ultimate worry for the NEA is that it is inextricably committed to an economic system that cannot work—just like the Communist Party in Leonid Brezhnev's Soviet Union. As the Education Policy Institute's Mike Lieberman put it in his classic *Public Education: An Autopsy:*

> The pro-market forces have one ineradicable advantage in the years ahead. That advantage is the inherent futility of conventional school reform.[291]

13

What Is to Be Done?
A Twenty-four-Point Wish List

*The NEA may be the only thing that stands between
the survival of public education and social chaos.*[292]

—Denise Rockwell Woods, member of the NEA Executive Committee

What Is to Be Done? was the title of V. I. Lenin's famous 1902 pamphlet, which argued that the only way to achieve a revolution in Russia was through a disciplined, elite vanguard—the Bolsheviks, a.k.a. the Communist Party. Amusingly, we can ask the same question, exactly a century later, about America's own homegrown socialist government school system and its disciplined vanguard—the teacher union.

Note that this Wish List, unlike every other education wish list you've ever seen, does not pontificate about teaching techniques. For example, it does not advocate Open Classrooms, closed classrooms, just-ajar classrooms, or *any other type of classroom*. As I have argued, I think these educational issues should be left to the market—i.e., teachers (sellers) and parents (buyers). The problem with the government school system right now is precisely *that there is no market*.

Nor does this Wish List consist of whatever the Education Establishment Blob currently wants to do anyway for other reasons. (Although I'm less sure of this—the Blob, especially its Teacher Trust component, is very tricky. It has survived many reform waves before. In particular, I think it's quite capable of capturing the charter school reform wave—see Chapter 11. However, I do think that all of these Wish List reforms taken together will give the Blob a Bloblem.)

It is also important to note that I am deliberately Listing our Wishes while totally ignoring the secondary question of whether or not they are "politically possible." These Wishes are what Bill Bennett's Department of Education staffers used to call, ruefully, "Full Moon Proposals" (as in throwing your head back and baying at). They assume an ideal world, except possibly for union executives.

I ignore the question of what's politically possible for two reasons.

Firstly, it actually helps to know where the moon is. You can navigate by it. In other words, by looking at the ideal, we throw into sharp relief the deep, systematic problems of the real world and avoid the minutiae that is typical of so much education policy discourse.

Secondly, the plain fact is that *no one really has the faintest idea what is politically possible.* Least of all professional politicians. They appear to have been designed by evolution to snuffle along like blind shrews, following their exquisitely sensitive snouts from one day to the next, reacting savagely if asked about next week—let alone next year—and thus able to perform 180-degree turns without rupturing their consciences.

Or even noticing. On innumerable issues—price and wage controls, welfare policy, the efficacy of military intervention overseas—the American conventional wisdom has changed out of all recognition over relatively short periods of time, without the conventionally wise seeming to feel much need to reproach themselves for being wrong. It can happen in education too.

Or, to put it another way: the Soviet Union—completely unexpectedly—collapsed.

The National Education Association doesn't look any healthier.

Although there is much pious talk about education during federal elections, the government school system still basically remains in the hands of state and local officials. Nevertheless, federal politicians cannot escape our Wish List so easily.

This point was explained to us by Dick Morris, the political consultant associated with President Bill Clinton's famous "triangulation" strategy, whereby Clinton was to win reelection in 1996 by distancing himself from the congressional Democrats and stealing the Republicans' issues. (It worked, of course, but Morris himself had by then been evicted from the White House inner circle after a scandal involving a prostitute that was colorful even by Clinton administration standards.)

In a remarkable passage in his memoir *Behind the Oval Office,* Morris considers the hypothetical question of how he would have gone about winning the 1996 presidential election for the Republicans—which he would have certainly been happy to do, on payment of the appropriate fee. He writes:

> Had I been running Dole's campaign, I would have said, "President Clinton did a fine job of helping to get our economy in order. He did well to set us toward a balanced budget. But now we must turn to the *new* issues we face, the values issues." Then I'd have focused on a host of issues that the president was afraid to touch or that *his interest-group support* wouldn't let him touch— *ending teacher tenure, school choice,* school prayer, an end to school busing, the balanced-budget amendment, a moratorium on immigration, *passage of a federal right-to-work law. . . .* I'd have piled it on. [Emphasis added][293]

Five of Morris's proposals were government school–related; three— with our emphasis added—strike directly at the Teacher Trust (lightly disguised here as a part of President Clinton's "interest-group support").

Morris did not make these proposals because he had spent time in long and careful study of education or the teacher union problem. He just thought they would work with the electorate. This is a measure of the NEA's very real political vulnerability. Someday, Dick Morris (or someone like him) will be advising a national candidate who has the freedom—and the courage—to run on these issues.

But what about the fact that teacher tenure is hardly a federal issue? Isn't it between the teachers and the school boards? Interviewing Morris for *Forbes,* I naively raised this question.

Morris waved it aside airily. "Oh," he said, "you just threaten to withhold federal funds from the states unless they comply. It would be like the 55-miles-per-hour speed limit."

Of course, this is distressing if you worry about the grand old American constitutional principle of federalism—the respect for the autonomy of local communities that has been critical to keeping this continent-sized country together. And it certainly seems to confirm the fears of those grinches who opposed federal funding of education because it would tend to centralize education policy in Washington's paws.

But Morris's proposal does show what could be achieved by enterprising, not to say ruthless, education reformers—both in the White House and in Congress.

The Wishes on my List are in theory the responsibility of different levels of governments: federal, state, local. But in practice, these categories are fluid. So we proffer our Wish List generally, to whoever can figure out a way to implement any part of it.

Our Wish List has two overall themes:

- *Disinfect the apple.* The problem with America's government school system is socialism. The solution is capitalism—the introduction of a free market.

Or, to put it another way, just as economists realized in the nineteenth century that the tariff was the mother of trusts, so in the twenty-first century we must recognize that the government school system is the mother of the Teacher Trust—and American education's chronic qualitative and quantitative failure.

Viewed from this perspective, dealing with the National Education Association is both a means and an end.

As it happens, desocialization is something with which economists have much more experience now than even a few years ago, because of the collapse of the Soviet Union and the liberation of Eastern Europe. One interesting development: quite often privatization actually meant that former Communist apparatchiks seized control of, i.e., stole, government enterprises and assets, emerging as newly fledged capitalists. Whatever the abstract justice of this, the economy benefits—investment allocation decisions are more rational.

Perhaps, after the Revolution, Wayne Johnson will emerge as president, not of the California Teachers Association, but of Combined Teaching Associates, earning much more than his reported $150,000 annual salary (not including benefits).

Hey—whatever it takes.

It's also quite possible that a reduced but galvanized government school system might be right in there, pitching. The reformed economies of Eastern Europe are still pretty well government-dominated by American standards. Or look at a parallel American case: the U.S. Postal Service. As Harvard's Caroline Hoxby says: "Few analysts expected the Postal Service to be able to compete with its new rivals [when competition was allowed in package-delivery], yet several decades later it is a worthy opponent."[294]

(However, it's important to realize that this happened because the Postal Service was confronted with competition from private enterprise from without—not because it was transformed through incremental *perestroika*-style, market-socialist reforms from within. Moral: charter schools may not be enough.)

Our Wish List's second theme:

- *Extracting the worm.* The teacher union is a creature of
  legal privilege. The way to deal with it: *remove its legal
  privileges.*

When it dawned upon Americans, just over a century ago, that the modern corporation was here to stay—news brought to them largely by muckraking journalism, most famously Ida Minerva Tarbell's *McClure's Magazine* articles, published in book form as *The History of Standard Oil*—they passed laws aimed at combatting monopoly, notably the federal Sherman Antitrust Act. And then they insisted that governments enforce those laws. Economists and lawyers argue about whether this was an appropriate response, and how antitrust laws should be interpreted today. But antitrust is undeniably part of the American business landscape.

Which brings us to our first Wish:

[1] BUST THE TEACHER TRUST

Well—why not? Federal antitrust law prohibits any contract, trust, or conspiracy in restraint of trade. The Sherman Act actually says that no person "shall monopolize, or attempt to monopolize, or combine or conspire with any other person or persons, to monopolize" trade or commerce. And the entire purpose of a labor union is exactly to "monopolize the supply of labor"—in order to extract a higher price for it.

Turnabout is emphatically not fair play in labor law. Various hopeful employers did attempt to point out to the courts that, if capital is not supposed to collude, then maybe labor should not collude either. The courts did not want to know. But courts are not oracles. There is nothing sacred about their rulings. Legislators can correct them by statute. (See—I meant it when I said I'm ignoring what's politically possible!)

At the very least, a federal antitrust statute could be aimed at preventing Teacher Trust collusion across state lines. This could end the flow of funds from the locals up to the national level—reestablishing something like the situation that prevailed before the "Michigan Mafia" succeeded in unifying NEA local, state, and national membership dues as part of its unionization drive in 1971—and from the national level to subsidize local action that locals could not afford. It could result in the NEA being broken up into state-only units, rather like antitrust litigation broke up John D. Rockefeller's Standard Oil Trust into Standard Oil of New Jersey—the ancestor of Exxon Corporation—Standard Oil of California ("Socal"), Standard Oil of Ohio ("Sohio"), etc.

A state antitrust statute, attacking any "attempt to monopolize" the supply of teacher labor by the union, could effectively cut the Gordian knot of state collective bargaining statutes, which would otherwise have to be disentangled strand by strand. (See below, Wish II.)

Most industries don't have legislation aimed specifically at them. But it's by no means unprecedented in cases that are considered especially vital to the public interest. For example, railroads are governed by the highly specific Railroad Labor Act of 1926.

So: is K–12 education vital to the public interest—or not?

[II] Reform Public Sector Collective Bargaining Statutes

The modern Teacher Trust is the creature of legal privilege. The basis of its power is the collective bargaining legal regime as it exists in each state.

As we have seen, the most extreme versions of state collective bargaining law allow the union to claim, and compels the school board to accept, the right of monopoly bargaining. After bitter dispute, the courts have established the constitutional principle that Americans cannot be forced to join a union to get or keep a job. But monopoly bargaining means that a union can claim to speak for them, whether they like it or not. And in many states they can be forced to pay fees to it.

Monopoly bargaining also means that the Teacher Trust and the school boards decide public policy in conclave. Not just non-members of the teacher union, but also members of the public, are effectively excluded. However, the U.S. Supreme Court has rejected Edwin Vieira's argument that this is a violation of the equal protection clause of the constitution.

"But Congress could easily reverse that under Section Five of the Fourteenth Amendment, which would apply to the states," says Vieira animatedly. "Congress could say exclusive representation violates equal protection, freedom of assembly, freedom of speech. They could restrict exclusive representation to matters of wages, hours and so on. That could leave a union of truck drivers pretty much the way it was. But it would reduce teacher union power dramatically."

There are state-level solutions to this problem. The simplest, of course, would be for a state whose government school teachers are covered by a collective bargaining law *to just up and repeal it*. Then school boards would no longer be forced to deal with the union just because a majority of teacher voting in a certification election supported it. School boards could still choose to deal with the union—unless the state got really enterprising and prohibited it, as is the case now in North Carolina and Virginia. Life would not come to an end, the union could still organize and lobby, but it would lose its monopoly access.

Of course, most commentators assume that collective bargaining legislation is somehow like a ratchet and can never be reversed. But that's what the British thought about nationalizing industries—until Margaret Thatcher came along.

Or the collective bargaining laws could be picked apart piecemeal. A state could establish the right of teachers to opt out of union contracts and bargain for themselves, as attempted in Michigan in 1993 and in Indiana, more comprehensively, in 1995.

One proposal, advanced in *Education Week* by Henry F. Cotton, a former school administrator, is "Educational Free Agency." He argues that it will establish a link between reward and performance in the teaching profession.

I suggest that the teacher be his or her own salary negotiator and be allowed to accept or reject an offer, as is the case in the sports world. . . . Unions and boards could set minimums and maximums, but every teacher would be able to negotiate within that range. A look at the sports environment shows clearly that when the best have been rewarded better, all the players have ultimately done better. The young talented teacher will be able to be rewarded right away, the best of the experienced will benefit commensurably, and the mediocre will be driven out by the talented who will have incentive to enter the profession.

When such ideas are proposed, the unions always want to know: how will administrators fairly and equitably distribute reward? Cotton has a sensible answer:

The complaints about who will evaluate teachers and how it will be done are begged every time one spends more than a day in a school. Yet students know who the best teachers are. Parents know, too. Even the teachers know who the best teachers are. It's only the teachers' organization that apparently is not privy to this information.[295]

(Professor J. E. Stone of the Education Consumers Clearinghouse argues there is an objective method: "Since 1993, Tennessee has measured teacher performance by looking at how much students gain as opposed to their progress in previous years. It's objective, impartial and works regardless of entering differences among students. Even unions"—he concludes, possibly optimistically—are starting to like it!")[296]

Similarly, school boards could be allowed to opt out of mandated collective bargaining, a less radical approach than outright repeal of the collective bargaining statute.

Individual bargaining may be, at first, too much of a culture shock for teachers. (And for some school boards. Employers get used to living within union rules, like blind pit ponies.) Milton Chappell, a senior staff attorney with the National Right to Work Legal Defense Foundation, has a modest and comforting alternative: adopt what he calls the "Europe Model," under which unions can represent only employees who agree to be represented, and no one union has the exclusive right to represent workers. There could be several different unions competing—and any individual union would be less able impose its ideological agenda.

Some of Chappell's other recommendations for progressively unpicking the collective bargaining knot give an idea of its complexity:

- *Resignation at will*—teachers enrolled in the union should be allowed to leave whenever they want, not just in the summer or—as has been the case in states like Pennsylvania and California—only when each multiyear contract expires.

- *Mandatory recertification elections*—the union's monopoly bargaining privileges should be reviewed by the teachers every three years or so, with provision for competing organizations to be considered.

- *Contract ratification by all bargaining unit members*—that is, including teachers who don't want to join the union but whom the law decrees that the union represents anyway. Excluding them from voting puts them under pressure to join anyway.

- *Reduction of mandatory subjects of bargaining*—to hours, wages, conditions, etc., helping taxpayers and parents resist the union's progressive takeover of the entire education complex.

- *Mandatory discussion with public, independent groups*—basically to prevent the school board from being cowed or co-opted.

Chappell notes that, in some states with extreme prounion legal regimes, teachers who resist being dragooned into the union "are denied both membership on school committees and any voice in the day-to-day workings of their school."[297]*

---

*While this book was in galleys, Myron Lieberman published a Cato Institute pamphlet proposing legislation to promote a market in teacher representation, instancing the United Educators Association in Fort Worth (www.ueatexas.com), a for-profit company representing 11,000 teachers.

[III] PASS STATE AND/OR FEDERAL RIGHT-TO-WORK LAW

Although teachers cannot be forced to join the union, they can be compelled to pay their alleged share of the costs of collective bargaining. This forced tribute could be ended through more state right-to-work laws (there are currently twenty-two) or through laws that specifically target teachers or government employees. (Teachers do not pay agency fees in another eight states—see Appendix A). Alternatively, how about a federal right-to-work law reversing the U.S. Supreme Court's questionable 1977 *Abood* ruling?

The teacher unions would still exist under right-to-work laws. But it might turn out that many teachers don't want to pay $400 to $600 dues a year.

[IV] PASS PAYCHECK PROTECTION

Right-to-work weakens the union by allowing teachers to work without being forced to pay any tribute to the union, thus weakening it financially. And *Abood* did weaken the union in non-right-to-work, agency shop states because non-union teachers are not compelled to pay that portion of their union tribute that goes to political activity. "Paycheck Protection" (they have people sitting around thinking up these terms) would weaken the union even further, by allowing union *members* to opt out of paying the political portion of their dues. This means no teacher anywhere would be forced to finance politics of which they disapprove, which those who belong to the union effectively are doing in many states today.

Paycheck Protection sounds so reasonable to most Americans that the CTA and other unions had to spend $30 million to defeat it, in the shape of California's Proposition 226, in 1998. Paycheck Protection was then pronounced dead, but it promptly rose like a phoenix in other states. In 2001, Paycheck Protection was established by legislation in Utah and by an Executive Order in Colorado.

The enforcement of Paycheck Protection—as with all reforms affecting the tricky Teacher Trust—will have to be watched carefully. In California, for example, the CTA had an ingenious backup plan. The union drew up two budgets. If paycheck protection had passed, all the money that would have gone to the union's PAC was instead to be shunted over to a newly formed "Public Policy Center." Among other things, this Center would have allowed the union "to engage in organizational outreach to other interested groups with common goals and objectives to obtain visibility and coordinated advocacy on educational issues." Obviously, the Public Policy Center, although barred by state law from providing funds to candidates or initiatives, would have simply provided "outreach" money to other organizations. If those organizations deposited that money in their general funds, they would be free to do with it what they wanted thereafter—even form PACs or donate to candidates.

Something like this happened in Washington State, where voters in a 1994 referendum liberated teacher members of the state NEA affiliate, the Washington Education Association, from being forced to contribute to the union's Political Action Committee. It turned out that (surprise!) only 13 percent of them really wanted to do so.

The WEA responded by spending at least $700,000 out of its mandatory general fund to influence the 1996 elections. Amazingly, in 2002, a Washington State Appeals Court judge ruled that this amount was not "meaningful" in relation to the WEA's $20 million annual expenditures. Lynn Harsh, the executive director of the Evergreen Freedom Foundation, noted that this apparently meant that Boeing Aircraft, Washington State's largest employer, could have poured $52 million into an election without reporting it—because that would have been equally "meaningful" in proportion to its annual expenditures.

But courts, as we have pointed out before, can be corrected by legislation.

Paycheck Protection could possibly be imposed federally. Governor George W. Bush actually proposed it while attempting to counter Senator John McCain's advocacy of campaign finance reform during the 2000 Republican presidential primaries.

Nothing much has happened since Bush reached the White House. But you never know.

How many teacher union members really want to go to the trouble of putting up their hands and asking to be allowed out of the political portion of their dues is perhaps questionable. But the idea certainly annoys the Teacher Trust, which is a good thing.

[V] Give Teeth to Anti-Strike Laws

Attempts to prohibit teacher strikes have been so ineffective that, paradoxically, strikes are at least as common in the forty states where they are illegal. But real penalties can be imposed: A Michigan law now docks teacher pay for every day on strike—and in Iowa, not just the public employer but any district resident can sue if unions break no-strike agreements . . . so they don't.

In Middletown, New Jersey, in 2001, teachers refused to return to work during an illegal strike. Judge Clarkson Fisher began giving teachers individual hearings and jailing them in alphabetical order. The Middletown Township Education Association agreed to return to work soon after the Rs had been jailed. By an amazing coincidence, the union president had a last name that began with an S—Diane Swaim.

[VI] Support Independent Teachers Associations and Unions

Conservative and even some liberal pundits have generally gotten the message about the government school monopoly. But, significantly, they are for the most part blissfully unaware of the even more harmful oligopoly of teacher representation held by the NEA and AFT. If these two organizations do succeed in merging, choices for most education employees will sink to one (1).

A monopoly "management"—government—will negotiate with a monopoly labor force—the merged NEA/AFT.

It is not commonly known, however, that there are several independent education associations. In some states, they thrive. In Texas, Missouri, and Georgia, the membership of independent teacher organizations, which are not unions, exceed the membership of both the NEA and AFT affiliates in those states. The Association of Texas Professional Educators has a membership of over one hundred thousand. A national independent group, the Association of American Educators, helps organize education employees who don't have a large independent association in their states.

Further, there are actually local teacher unions that are unaffiliated with any state or national teacher unions. In Ohio, the Akron Education Association represents two thousand members. In Indiana, there are ten districts with independent local unions. In California's Warner Springs, after the decertification of the CTA affiliate, the teachers' contract was negotiated by the fledgling Associated Warner Educators (AWE).

"Pitting attorneys against each other on opposite sides of the table has never been the best approach," says AWE president Doris Burke. "We're all in this together, so we believe it will serve everyone in the district better if we negotiate King Arthur–style around the table. AWE will always strive to put the needs of our students first. If we do that, there will be much less conflict in negotiations."

These local groups still generally oppose vouchers, support class size reduction, etc. Some may have education agendas barely distinguishable from NEA/AFT's. But in each case, the independent organizations are less militant, more professionally oriented, and a lot easier to get along with.

If you add the membership of all the independent professional associations and unions together, it comes to about 300,000—roughly one-tenth of NEA/AFT's membership. Nevertheless, the Teacher Trust is terrified that these organizations are gaining a foothold among government school teachers.

During the 1994 NEA Representative Assembly, Carolyn Hart of the Georgia Association of Educators, the NEA affiliate in that state, called on delegates to destroy the independents.

"Help us to eradicate—no, better yet, help us to stomp them out in nonbargaining states before their poison spreads," she shouted.

Sounds like they're doing something right!

What independent professional associations and local unions need, above all: *a favorable legal environment in their state.*

It is no accident, as Marxist polemicists used to say, that independent professional associations are strongest in Texas, Missouri, and Georgia—all states without compulsory monopoly bargaining or agency fees. Where a state government has already conceded compulsory monopoly bargaining, independents have great difficulty breaking in. Where a state considers introducing such a collective bargaining law, independents face a ruinous winner-take-all battle with the better-funded national unions in order to get control of each local bargaining unit.

That's why the Missouri State Teachers Association spent some $300,000 opposing a proposed collective bargaining law in Missouri—it was a mortal threat. And it's why Missouri state representative Steve

McLuckie (D–Kansas City) proposed it—he was the Missouri NEA affiliate's head organizer.

[VII] APPLY PRIVATE-SECTOR-TYPE RESTRICTIONS
TO UNION ENCROACHMENT ON MANAGEMENT

The National Labor Relations Act, which governs the private sector, specifies "management prerogatives"—such as questions of product quality, marketing, and the like. These prerogatives have been violated in the government school industry—if for no other reason that that teachers, spouses of teachers, and even spouses of union officials often sit on school boards and vote on salary increases. Prohibitions on these obvious conflicts of interest could be extended and enforced in most states.

Another possible solution: forbid teacher unions, and all other groups that stand to benefit directly (textbook publishers?), from contributing to candidates in school board elections.

After all, U.S. corporations are banned from giving money to federal and state legislative candidates.

[VIII] END "UNFUNDED MANDATES"

A common union-backed "school reform" tactic is the "unfunded mandate"—state legislation that end-runs local voters to impose duties and costs on school districts. "Massachusetts' 1993 reform law imposed teacher protections like restrictions on school board authority to hire and fire," grumped Peter Rogers, a disgruntled former chairman of the Nahant, Massachusetts, school board management study committee, in 1995.

[IX] END BARGAINED TAXPAYER SUBSIDIES TO THE TEACHER TRUST

As a rent-seeking parasite, the NEA is quite open-minded about who exactly it parasites upon. Normally, the victim is the government school system. But, quite often, the victim is *you*—the taxpayer—directly. The union bargains its way into your pocket in a number of ingenious ways—resisted feebly, if at all, by your nominal defender, the school board.

As the Education Policy Institute's Mike Lieberman repeatedly says (in effect), it takes one to tell one—only an ex-union operative, like Lieberman, can anticipate all these ingenious scams:

● *Taxpayer funding of retirement benefits for union staff.*
When teachers metastasize into union officials, the
government school system often continues funding
their pensions. Rhode Island general treasurer
Nancy J. Mayer said in 1995 that legislation ending
this practice was saving her state $13 million annu-
ally. The NEA affiliate suit challenging the Rhode
Island law backfired: One local chapter began with-
holding dues to its parent in protest against union
financing of the appeal.

● *Release time with pay for teachers to conduct union business.* Similarly, taxpayers get to pay union activists to
organize against them. Currently bargained into
union contracts far in excess of private-sector
equivalents, this could be restricted by state-level
legislation.

● *Government agencies' collection of PAC contributions.*
Many school districts agree to deduct union PAC
contributions from payrolls. This cuts NEA fund-
raising costs and requires individual teachers to take
positive, sometimes difficult, steps to opt out.

[X] PROVIDE ALTERNATIVE SERVICES, BENEFITS, AND DISCOUNTS TO TEACHERS

"I'm in it mainly for the magazine discounts," a New England teacher once
replied when I asked him about his membership in his state's NEA affiliate.
He seemed sincerely puzzled by the question. For many teachers, the NEA
really is like the American Association of Retired Persons, a sort of cooperative that you join to get good deals on a vast range of purchases. (Rather
unsportingly, the union struck *Forbes* magazine off its discount program
after our first cover story about it.)

Or, in the memorable words of the Michigan Education Association
lobbyist Al Short, quoted in Chapter 4, "You take members that don't
believe in collective bargaining, that don't believe in our political ends, but

you talk to them about MESSA; they'll stand in the middle of a highway to defend it."

Breaking this tie requires school boards and states to interpose themselves between the teachers and the union, brandishing these services. And, of course, they have to figure out what the services are.

[XI] End Teacher Tenure

And what about Morris's proposal to abolish teacher tenure? It strikes me as a fairly marginal reform—the mirror image of merit pay, dangerously close to being a tough-talk version of the panaceas that are epidemic in the government school industry. Not being able to fire bad teachers is, of course, unquestionably a problem for many schools. But abolishing tenure (or awarding merit pay) only alters one part of the complex of incentives and disincentives—rather like Soviet commissars deciding to shoot Russian peasants for drunkenness.

Some teachers might be stimulated, for a while. But the deeply dysfunctional system—particularly the "Unholy Alliance" of unions, administrators, and co-opted school boards—would remain the same.

Thus the state of Oregon actually did eliminate tenure for teachers in 1997, putting them on two-year renewable contracts. When the first two-year period expired, most districts simply rehired everyone. One exception was Portland, the largest school district in the state. Portland fired six teachers and one principal and non-renewed five teachers. (They have one more year to improve). Ten teachers and two administrators resigned. That total is still less than 1 percent of certified employees. Nevertheless, Richard Garrett, president of the Portland teacher union, denounced it as "barbaric."

"We give them a tool to be able to get some of the poor teachers out of the system, and they just don't use it," said Oregon senate majority leader Gene Derfler, author of the tenure elimination law.[298]

Similarly in Georgia, Governor Roy Barnes made tenure elimination a centerpiece of his school reform package. But while Barnes was working his bills through the legislature, Georgia Association of Educators affiliates in Clayton and DeKalb counties were working with their school boards to get tenure protections written into local policy. Of the nine people on the Clayton school board, three were teachers.

"This is an attempt to see if the local boys will allow through the back door what he and the General Assembly have prevented through the front door," said Barnes spokesman Howard Mead.[299]

Abolishing tenure without other counterbalancing reforms might well result in abuse by administrators, which the NEA would certainly use to discredit any non-Blob reforms at all.

Nevertheless—it's better than nothing.

[XII] ALLOW MERIT PAY

See pages 87–89.

[XIII] TWO, THREE, MANY SCHOOL CHOICE INITIATIVES

(For those too old to remember, "Two, three many Vietnams!" was a slogan of the international Left during the Vietnam War.)

In many respects, the NEA resembles nothing so much as Leonid Brezhnev's Soviet Union after the fall of South Vietnam in 1975. It appears everywhere triumphant. Its political organizers, like the Red Army, are unmatched and undefeated. It even has its equivalent of Eurocommunism— the easier sell so ardently desired by many of its apologists in the *gaijin* media—the "New Unionism." And it has its Brezhnev doctrine, the equivalent of the rule propounded by Brezhnev when he ordered an invasion to suppress the reforming government of Czechoslovakia: Socialism, in the form of government monopoly schooling, cannot be rolled back anywhere.

But, like Brezhnev's Soviet Union, the NEA has problems. It has shown it can defeat school choice—at least in the form of vouchers—anywhere. But it can afford to lose nowhere.

"If I was running a school choice referendum," the AFT's Al Shanker told Leslie Spencer and myself in 1993, "it would win."

(He declined to say how. But the Education Policy Institute's Mike Lieberman helpfully suggested one essential: Buy off the incumbent teachers, perhaps with guaranteed benefits, just as British prime minister Margaret Thatcher bought off union member opposition to privatizing nationalized industries with stock options.)

And the danger is growing. There is always the danger that some new, virulent way of marketizing education may be discovered—for example tax deductibility or tax credits—that does not have the convenient but unspoken racial and other negatives that voucher programs seem to have.

The moral of this story: Like Brezhnev's Soviet Union, not even the NEA can fight on all fronts at once. Increasingly, however, it must. Thus the National Taxpayers Union's Jim Davidson has a simple antidote for NEA opposition to his state-by-state antitax insurgencies: "We like to see a school choice initiative started. That distracts them."

It works. In 1990, the Oregon NEA affiliate defeated a state choice initiative. But a property tax-cap initiative passed. In 1993, when the Wisconsin NEA affiliate narrowly defeated Deborah Hawley, the school choice candidate for state school superintendent, after a bitter battle—this was the case in which the union allegedly ordered teachers to write antichoice postcards to acquaintances and to bring the postcards in to union headquarters, so that their compliance could be checked—Republicans took control of the state senate for the first time in two decades.

In 1998, the California Teachers Association's Herculean effort to defeat the paycheck protection initiative left the field open for software millionaire Ron Unz to get Proposition 227 passed. The measure effectively ended bilingual instruction in California. Students who had previously languished for years in bilingual classes were immersed in English for one year, to greatly increased test scores and higher academic achievement.

Every school choice initiative is a financial victory for the forces of government school liberation. The union always has to raise more than opponents, just to defend the status quo. The special levies that are required put pressure on the union and on its grassroots members' loyalty—often already pretty tenuous.

Hit them again!

[XIV] EXPLORE TAX CREDITS, TAX DEDUCTIBILITY OF EDUCATION COSTS

The free-market liberal coalition is split on vouchers. Some normally reliable members fear that any private school that accepted vouchers would rapidly be captured by the Blob, because of the inevitable accompanying regulation. However, it does seem to be generally agreed that making school fees tax-deductible, or even instituting a tax credit for money spent on K–12 education, would not give the government camel quite as much chance to get its snout under the private school tent. Of course, tax deductions and credits would only be helpful to parents who pay taxes, not the poor. But perhaps some sort of aftermarket could be instituted whereby tax credits could be sold to those who could benefit from them. Explore!

[XV] LIBERATE THE GED!

"The big difference between my kids today and kids when we went to school," a high school teacher friend once told me (making a tactful assumption about my age) "is how tired they are in the classroom. They're always falling asleep. It's because they all have evening jobs working in the malls. That's why they can afford these great cars. You can always tell the teachers' cars in the parking lot. Look for the clunkers."

Part-time work is a great American tradition and an example of American society's superior flexibility. It's how generations of American students have put themselves through college. Even today, labor force participation for American men aged sixteen through twenty-four is almost 70 percent, as opposed to just over 30 percent in France, although more Americans will attend college.[300]

But for *high school students*? What we are seeing here is further support for the proposition advanced in Chapter 3: *comprehensive high schools have never worked, and can never work, for everyone.* But in these cases, the teenagers are not on the street corner (or worse). They are not incompetent. They want to work. But school is getting in the way.

Liberating these kids from high school earlier, with a sound basic education, should be a goal of public policy. And, indeed, it is possible for them to leave school and take the General Education Development (GED) certification. The problem, as we have seen, is that the GED is under a cloud. Employers do not regard it as a true equivalent.

The cloud over the GED should be removed. A reformed program certifying genuine basic education should be designed. Then students who want to get out of school and go to work would have a goal to aim for. (Free at last!)

The economy would benefit. What economists call the "opportunity cost" of keeping kids in the junior and high school—the value of the work they would otherwise have done—has been estimated to be possibly as much as $140 billion a year, about 1.4 percent of GDP.[301] And the taxpayer would no longer be paying to keep these kids awake.

Remember, these kids can always top up their education with evening classes later. Part-time adult education is another example of the superior flexibility of American society—and, it should be acknowledged, the American education system.

Plus getting those great cars out of the school parking lot would make teachers feel a whole lot better.

[XVI] HANDS OFF TEACHER TRAINING AND ACCREDITATION!

"The teacher unions exert inordinate control in the certification process," says Professor Michael Podgursky of the University of Missouri. "They have extensive representation in the dominant Education School accrediting organization—NCATE, the National Council for Accreditation of Teacher Education—and also in the national teacher certification organization—NBPTS, the National Board for Professional Teaching Standards. The unions are pushing to shift control of teacher training and licensing from state boards of education, which usually have lay members, to teacher-controlled 'professional boards,' patterned after medicine, dentistry. They've succeeded in about fifteen or sixteen states."

Some of these states are union strongholds—like California and Hawaii. But some are not—Wyoming and Texas do not require collective bargaining or agency fees; North Carolina, of course, prohibits both.

Moral: it's really very tricky, this Teacher Trust. If it can't get in through the door, by getting its rented politicians to vote mandatory monopoly bargaining, it tries to get in through the window, by controlling the teacher certification process.

"Not only is there power to be had but there's money to be made by controlling America's teacher accrediting system," says Sylvia Crutchfield of the Alexandria, Virginia–based Foundation Endowment.[302]

To an economist like Michael Podgursky, controlling the certification process means one thing: in economistspeak, *barriers to entry*. In other words, by reducing the supply of teachers able to enter the business, the union will be able to increase their price (salaries). "Combined with the extensive monopoly power the NEA already has through the collective bargaining process, this would really be an unprecedented concentration of economic power," he says.

The consumers in the K–12 education market (parents, taxpayers) have little choice, Podgursky notes: "Moreover, unlike medicine, they cannot sue for malpractice. So even if you think that these 'professional boards' work well in medicine (and most economists think they don't), it's important to recognize that consumers in these markets still have the protection that comes from markets—choice—and tort law."

(Sue the Teacher Trust for bad education, increasing costs? Now there's a Full Moon proposal!)

Podgursky's recommendations: *Keep the regulatory process in the hands of lay state boards. Don't insist on NCATE accreditation of teacher training programs. Don't subsidize National Board certification of teachers. Don't set up "independent"—hence easily captured—professional boards.*

"Most of all," says Podgursky, "don't buy the idea that only education professionals are competent to make decisions about teacher training and licensing. These are the same professionals who gave us whole language learning!"

As usual, the NEA has contrived to get taxpayers to fund some of its attempts to restrict teacher supply—federal money has gone to the NBPTS. *Eliminate this subsidy.*

Education is an industry, not a religion. Teachers need to be trained, not ordained by some higher power. Training is a production process that could easily be done by private firms—Podgursky suggests the tutoring franchise operation Sylvan Learning Systems Inc. (NASDAQ symbol SLVN)! Neither the government nor the union should be involved in production process decisions—any more than they are in any other industry.

[XVII] INSTITUTE ALTERNATIVE TEACHER CERTIFICATION

Not only should prospective barriers to entry into teaching be stopped—the current barriers should be relaxed. Why should former Vice President Al Gore teach journalism at Columbia University's Graduate School of Journalism, when he can't teach a high school English composition class without a credential and a year of student teaching?

Paradoxically, national politicians expound on the necessity of having "qualified" and "certified" teachers in government schools. Then they send their own children to Washington, D.C., private schools like Saint Alban's or Sidwell Friends. These do indeed have instructional staff with great skills and varied experiences—but they do not require their staff to hold a teaching credential.

More than forty states have alternative teacher certification programs. Though they differ greatly, none of them requires a degree in education from a teacher college. They target mid-career professionals—people with life experiences in business or the military—who receive accelerated training in areas such as classroom management and lesson planning. They perform student teaching and are paired with a mentor while they get their feet wet. These programs also draw a disproportionate number of males and minorities into an overwhelmingly white female teaching force.

"There are a lot of people who would make excellent teachers but are discouraged by the bureaucracy of the certification process," says Arthur Moore, a graduate of the Troops to Teachers program who began teaching fourth grade in Baltimore after twenty-one years in the Army.[303]

These teachers reportedly excel in the classroom. Graduates of the seven-week Massachusetts Institute for New Teachers, designed for mid-career transfers, received higher ratings from their principals than those who became teachers through the traditional route.[304] In New York City, graduates from the alternative program passed a licensure exam at a much higher rate than graduates of the biggest education school in the state.[305]

"The data is unequivocal," say researchers Dr. Vicky Schreiber Dill and Delia Stafford-Johnson. "In 1998–1999, 24,000 new teachers have entered teaching through alternative certification routes: in total, nationwide, since about 1985, about 125,000 individuals have been added alternatively. Unlike graduates of traditional routes, these individuals share characteristics that make them a superior choice to teach all children, especially children at risk."[306]

Final word to Professor Podgursky:

The best way to check the power of the unions and the Ed Schools is—*create competition.* Let school districts make their own choices as to whom to hire. Districts can be held accountable through monitoring—and through parental choice. If Ed schools train nitwits, schools hire them, and unions protect their jobs, then empower parents to avoid them. Ultimately, the best protection from incompetent teachers is—*parental choice.* [Emphases added][307]

[XVIII] LIBERATE CHARTER SCHOOLS

It should be clear that I am generally well disposed toward the charter school movement, as discussed in Chapter 11. But I have more moderate expectations of charter schools than many of their supporters, because I view charter schools as an attempt to import market features into a fundamentally socialist system—a form of American *perestroika*—and therefore inevitably limited, probably transitional.

Charter schools are entering their first period of backlash. They should be defended against it. Of course, charter schools that do not serve students well should be closed. Of course, administrators who misuse funds should be fired and indicted. But we don't close down a whole chain of supermarkets because one grocery manager was stealing lettuce. Generally speaking, whatever success charter schools have is directly related to the amount of freedom they have to pursue their own visions. Their ultimate responsibility is, and should be, to the people who patronize them, not to school boards, teacher unions, or state agencies.

But in the last analysis, the charter school is, to paraphrase the first American to put foot on the moon, a small step toward market education—a giant step for the American government school system.

[XIX] BREAK UP LARGE SCHOOL DISTRICTS

Funny thing: class-size reduction is at the top of the unions' education reform list. Ask a union official whether class size should be reduced (certain answer: YES!). Then ask if school size should be reduced (likely answer: yes.)

Then ask if school district size should be reduced.

(Pause . . .)

Your victim realizes that he has been led into a trap.

The reform wave of the 1960s left the government school system with monstrously large school districts. They are often in poor urban areas, which are home to the worst problems in education. Unions don't control the size of school districts directly, but they do resist efforts to break up large ones. Why?

Because it's a lot easier for union officials to organize, administer, and oversee one local union of eight thousand teachers than to have eighty local unions with one hundred teachers each. Similarly, the Roman emperor Caligula once remarked that he wished the Roman people had only one neck, so he could cut it through.

But Caligula, of course, was mad.

Large districts are nicer for administrators too. The larger the district, the larger the bureaucracy and the higher the career ladder.

The American government school system suffers from *penalties of scale*. Through the principle of bureaucratic bloat know as Parkinson's Law, the larger a school district gets, the more resources tend to get diverted to secondary or even nonessential activities.

The average American public school district has six schools and approximately 3,600 students—for an average school size of 600 students. By contrast, the Los Angeles Unified School District averages 1,039 students per school. In Florida, Dade County averages 1,059, and Broward County averages 1,133.

The differences are even more jarring if you look at individual states. The entire state of North Dakota enrolled about 120,000 students in 1996. If all those students were placed in one district, it would rank only nineteenth in the nation in size. But North Dakota doesn't have one district, it has 236.

The large-district effect is disproportionately hard on minorities. The average American school district has an enrollment of 35.8 percent ethnic and racial minorities. But of the twenty-five largest districts, twenty-two have a higher percentage of minorities. In some districts the ratios are extreme: Houston, 88.9 percent minority; Los Angeles and Dallas, 89 percent; Chicago, 89.5 percent; Detroit, 94.8 percent.

Minority students in these large urban districts bear a double burden. They are stuck in school districts that do not have the tax base of surrounding suburban districts. And the available funding gets diverted to areas unrelated to the district's primary mission—educating students. Suburban schools may spend more per pupil. But how many, like Philadelphia, have two bus attendants, three non-teaching assistants, four noontime aides, and nine custodians for every school?

Breaking up large school districts will increase the relative influence of parents and the community on the district's actions. And in the process, it will lessen the power of the unions in the process.

[XX] PRIVATIZE SCHOOL SERVICES

Teacher unions fight privatization of any school district service in order to maintain solidarity. But when private companies can perform a district function more efficiently and at less cost, the teacher unions are maintaining solidarity at the expense of their own members. Money that is being overspent on support services could be available to help teachers with textbooks, supplies—even salaries.

The Mesa School District in Arizona contracts out its transportation and food services. "We're in the business of education," said Chuck Essigs, Mesa schools assistant superintendent of business services. "Anything we can do to be more efficient in support areas puts more money into the classroom."[308]

The Detroit Public Schools have discovered the same thing. "Our core competence is education," said district chief information officer Thomas Diggs. "It's not food service. It's not transportation. It's not information technology."[309]

Some companies, like Standard and Poor's and SchoolMatch by Public Priority Systems Inc., even evaluate school systems to see if they are spending their money wisely—a commonplace service in the business world, but almost unheard of in public education.

Private enterprise is already heavily involved in the public schools. It provides textbooks, curriculum, and tests. But it is now entering the world of classroom instruction. The OPIS company in New England, an affiliate of the U.K. firm Select Appointments PLC, and Kelly Services Inc. nationwide, now contract with school districts to provide substitute teachers. Kelly says it already has two hundred districts signed up, mostly in the South and Midwest.[310] In Denver, Aspen Learning Systems, a subsidiary of financier Michael Milken's Knowledge Universe company, opened Colorado's first privately run reading center. The company has a nine-week program that emphasizes heavy phonics. In the first quarter of 1999, students gained an average of two years and four months in reading ability.[311]

The federal government provides school districts all across the country with additional funds through the Title I program to help their neediest students. Some districts, like Chicago, used Title I money to hire Success Labs Inc. to help teach kids how to read. The school district in Pasadena, Texas, uses Sylvan, while Los Angeles and New York City use Kaplan Inc. for the same purpose.[312]

Ironically, perhaps the most prominent case of education industry privatization is Bob Chanin. Originally a union employee, he is now a partner in the Washington, D.C., labor law firm Bredhoff and Kaiser, but still NEA general counsel and the union's gray eminence.

[XXI] PROMOTE UNION DEMOCRACY

Or: *Repeal the Iron Law of Oligarchy.* Congress has long been concerned about the capture of labor unions by their permanent officials. In 1959, it passed the Labor-Management Reporting and Disclosure Act (the "Landrum-Griffin Act"), which regulated union affairs and finances, including the requirement of internal free speech and regular secret elections. *Extend Landrum-Griffin-type rights to the Teacher Trust, federally and/or state by state.* (Carefully, because we don't want to infect states with monopoly bargaining.)

For many years, the teacher unions have had a stranglehold on their internal communications. The only place to get news about the union was the union itself. But the Internet has changed all that. It enables previously isolated individuals to communicate with each other. The Internet bypasses union filters, and empowers the vast majority of union members who don't listen to what their union tells them, and who don't believe what they do hear.

Ironically, the Teacher Trust is dropping millions of dollars into cyber-technology, using the Internet to hook up its activists all over the country. But there is reason to think that grassroots union members will no more pay attention to the unions' electronic messages than to the printed messages they already get. And once they get a horizontal flow of information, instead of the current vertical flow, they will find more and more opportunities to cooperate with other dissident teachers on internal union issues.

The Teacher Trust is not monolithic. There are many contrary voices within NEA and AFT. But they are disjointed, unorganized, and easily drowned out by the zealots. If the contrary voices can form a critical mass, they may eventually form opposition factions, with competing interests that run the gamut from A to, oh, say G or H, instead of the current A to B. The unions may develop true democracy.

It would be helpful, of course, to give these contrary voices something to talk about. Legislation can help provide information. *Establish Teachers' Right to Know.* Improve current labor union reporting laws so that members can easily find out union officials' pay and benefits. *Make notification of Beck/Abood Rights mandatory,* so that teachers know they can opt out of paying the political portion of their fees. *Make sure teachers know that they can't be forced to join the union.* The U.S. Supreme Court ruled in *Marquez vs. Screen Actors* that everyone knows employees don't have to join a union, even if the contract says they do. But (not for the first time) maybe the Supreme Court was wrong.

[XXII] Empower Parents Through Choice

Whatever method of school choice is devised, it is essential that parents become the ultimate arbiters of their child's educational future. If government transfer payments are necessary, they must follow the child and its parents should decide where it goes.

Parents need information. The government school system controls the information flow, and it tries to create a rosy impression. Good news is trumpeted, bad news spun, even—perhaps especially—in report cards. Frequently, it is only when students start college that their true level of preparedness becomes apparent. Parents who work at staying informed are corralled, not least through Blob-captured Parent Teacher Associations.[313]

Grassroots consumer organizations are emerging as an alternative channel. For example, the Education Consumers Clearing House, www. education-consumers.com, is a paid subscription service for parents, policymakers, and taxpayers.

[XXIII] Empower Teachers Through True Professionalism, or, Give Teachers a Stake

In poll after poll, teachers say they want to be treated like professionals. Who can blame them? Despite the best efforts of their unions, teachers are not mine workers or ditch diggers.

The aspect of professionalism that has most interested the Teacher Trust is, as we have seen, the ability of some professions to restrict entry into their field. But in the real world, being a professional is high-risk as well as high-reward. Educators who compared their measly salaries with those of computer programmers and web designers in Silicon Valley haven't said much after the high-tech bust, when many of those folks lost their jobs.

By continuing to build castles to protect their members from risks and consequences, teacher unions are also building prisons—confining their members to being little more than hourly wage-earners.

A better model than "professional" might be "entrepreneur." Why can't teachers run their own schools? Why can't they receive stock options instead of just step increases on the salary schedule? Under a completely open system, teachers could be the movers and shakers, at least as much as doctors in hospitals or in private practice. Teachers could seek out—or perhaps even hire—the best support and administrative staff available. Educator/entrepreneurs would not tolerate the mismanagement and bureaucracy if it was their money.

There's a lot of money in the education business. Remember, average per-pupil spending is currently over $7,000 a year. Every extra child that a teacher can take in her class, every extra child that she can help graduate a year early, is $7,000 that could go to her. She needs a system that permits her to claim her reward.

Think about it.

(Actually, I think this "profession" stuff is overblown. Journalism is not a "profession." It's a trade. Anyone can start writing, there is no code of conduct or particularly vital common body of skills that anyone—apart possibly from journalism schools—can see. But generally, reward depends on individual effort, and some individuals do very well, which is stimulating. It's fun. I recommend it.)

[XXIV] Abolish the U.S. Department of Education

The NEA wanted this federal toehold. *Chop it off.*

Epilogue

The (Possible) Shape of Things to Come (Aaargh!)

Oh, call back yesterday! Bid time return! And thou shalt have twelve thousand fighting men.

—The Earl of Salisbury, from *Richard II,* Act III, Scene 2

In January 2001, the U.S. Bureau of Labor Statistics delivered a body blow to the nation's unions when it released its annual report on membership. The survey of the American labor force showed that the percentage of workers belonging to unions had fallen to 13.5 percent, its lowest share since World War II. Not only did the percentage decline, but the absolute number of union members fell by two hundred thousand, even while the economy boomed.

Despite these sobering statistics, the story is not the decline of union membership—a trend that has been steady for almost two generations. The real story is one that deserves a lot of attention, not only from union members and researchers, but from economists, sociologists, and public policy experts. It is the rise of government unionism.

Today, the most unionized sector of the entire U.S. economy (at 43.2 percent) is local government—a category that includes police officers, firefighters, and, of course, government school employees. Though the BLS data did not separate these occupations, a reasonable estimate of the percentage of local public school employees who belong to unions is somewhere in the 70 percent range. Mike Antonucci's research suggests that, after the 1960s–1970s surge, NEA/AFT membership is growing at almost the same rate as the public school employee workforce.

Should present trends continue, we will see in our lifetimes the total number of public sector union members overtake the total number of private sector union members. We may also see a labor force in which public school employees are the *only* growth sector in union membership.

The implications of such a trend are enormous. First, we will have a private sector almost devoid of unions, being regulated by a large plurality of unionized government employees, whose unions' membership growth will be directly tied to the size of government itself. For organized labor, it will mean either dragging the NEA into the AFL-CIO in order to bolster its failing numbers, or it will mean that the education unions will displace the AFL-CIO, effectively putting it out of business and replacing it with a new coalition dominated by the NEA (or, more likely, by a merged NEA/AFT).

The time may come when teacher unions may *be* the organized labor movement. Such a possibility compels us to expend a lot more energy examining what these unions are and where they are going. Will they slowly become extinct, like the dinosaurs, or will they survive and thrive? And if they are dinosaurs, will they continue to trample government education in their search for sustenance before they finally disappear?

Georges Clemenceau, the prime minister of France in World War I, is reported to have said, "War is too important to be left to the generals."

We subscribe to the sentiment more recently expressed by Mark Yudof when he was president of the University of Minnesota:

> If war is too important to be left to the generals, then education is too important to be left only to professional educators.

> Or, above all, to their unions.

APPENDIX A:
THE STATES AT A GLANCE

State	NEA State Affiliate, Membership	Independent Teachers Organization (where available)	Collective Bargaining Laws[1]	Strikes Are Legal[2]	Agency Fee Laws[3]	Comments
Alabama	Alabama Education Association 67,972	Alabama Conference of Educators	No		No	Alabama Education Association executive secretary Paul Hubbert is the most powerful political operator in the state, despite a failed run for governor.
Alaska	NEA Alaska 9,952		Yes	Yes	Yes	Animosities with NEA–Alaska management led to a staff strike in January 2001.
Arizona	Arizona Education Association 28,560	Arizona Professional Educators	No		No	The relative weakness of unions in the state is best illustrated by Arizona being home to the most charter schools in the country and having the least restrictive regulations on them.
Arkansas	Arkansas Education Association 14,195	Arkansas State Teachers Association	No		No	The Arkansas Education Association had a rare case of a union vice president who was defeated in a bid for the presidency.

State	Organization				Comments
California	California Teachers' Association 291,595		Yes	Mandatory	By far the most powerful and most militant NEA affiliate in the nation.
Colorado	Colorado Education Association 32,423		No	No	Colorado has been a battleground state on vouchers, tuition tax credits, and paycheck protection.
Connecticut	Connecticut Education Association 34,318		Yes	Yes	The Connecticut Education Association delivered a body blow to the NEA/AFT merger in 1998, when it voted to oppose merger right after favorite son NEA president Bob Chase gave a speech promoting it.
Delaware	Delaware State Education Association 9,326		Yes	Yes	Opposed to merger, the Delaware State Education Association quietly engineered some of the highest teacher salaries in the country.
Florida	Florida Education Association. Approximately 121,000 members after statewide merger with the Florida AFT affiliate.	Professional Educators Network of Florida	Yes	No	Despite numbers, the Florida Education Association's influence is waning in an increasingly Republican state government.

State	NEA State Affiliate, Membership	Independent Teachers Organization (where available)	Collective Bargaining Laws[1]	Strikes Are Legal[2]	Agency Fee Laws[3]	Comments
Georgia	Georgia Association of Educators 30,198	Professional Association of Georgia Educators	No		No	The Georgia Association of Educators plays second fiddle to the independent teachers organization in the state, the Professional Association of Georgia Educators, which has over 51,000 members.
Hawaii	Hawaii State Teachers Association 12,090		Yes	Yes	Yes	A three-week strike in 2001 highlighted its ongoing feud with Governor Ben Cayetano, a man the Hawaii State Teachers Association endorsed twice, once over the objections of the rank and file.
Idaho	Idaho Education Association 11,172		Yes		No	Sleepy union woke up in 2002, holding a large rally at the state capitol in favor of increased school funding.
Illinois	Illinois Education Association-NEA 106,263		Yes	Yes	Yes	Took the extremely rare step of endorsing the Republican gubernatorial candidate in the general election over the Democrat in a close race. The Republican won.

State	NEA Affiliate	Alternative Organization			Notes
Indiana	Indiana State Teachers Association 46,152	Indiana Professional Educators	Yes	No	Not a very strong union, but strongly opposed to new charter school law.
Iowa	Iowa State Education Association 37,270	Professional Educators of Iowa	Yes	No	Surprised observers by agreeing to a statewide performance-pay plan for teachers, which may soon disappear due to lack of funding.
Kansas	Kansas NEA 25,914	Kansas Association of American Educators	Yes	No	Commissioned poll that found 60 percent of Kansans favored school vouchers; quickly distanced itself.
Kentucky	Kentucky Education Association 32,776	Kentucky Association of Professional Educators	No	No	When the Kentucky Education Association staff went on strike, its executive director threatened to hire "permanent replacements."
Louisiana	Louisiana Association of Educators 17,914	Associated Professional Educators of Louisiana	No	No	The only state other than New York where the AFT state affiliate is larger than the NEA state affiliate.
Maine	Maine Education Association 20,187		Yes	No	Supporters of "old unionism," they were strongly opposed to the merger.

State	NEA State Affiliate, Membership	Independent Teachers Organization (where available)	Collective Bargaining Laws[1]	Strikes Are Legal[2]	Agency Fee Laws[3]	Comments
Maryland	Maryland State Teachers Association 50,029		Yes		Partial	As a parting gift to the Maryland State Teachers Association, outgoing Governor Parris Glendening signed a bill that expanded the scope of collective bargaining in the state.
Massachusetts	Massachusetts Teachers Association 85,597		Yes		Yes	Strongly anti-merger, the Massachusetts Teachers Association supports bilingual education and the antitesting movement.
Michigan	Michigan Education Association 129,316		Yes		Yes	Stung repeatedly by influence of the Mackinac Center for Public Policy, the Michigan Education Association formed its own "independent" think tank.
Minnesota	Education Minnesota 73,818		Yes	Yes	Yes	First NEA state affiliate to merge with that of the AFT, Education Minnesota is looking to oust its nemesis—Governor Jesse Ventura.
Mississippi	Mississippi Association of Educators 6,902	Mississippi Professional Educators	No		No	Very weak union, but home of NEA Executive Committee member Michael Marks, who is future NEA president material.

State	NEA Affiliate	Membership				Notes
Missouri	Missouri-NEA Missouri State Teachers Association	26,756		No	No	The Missouri NEA failed to pass a collective bargaining law due to the opposition of the much larger independent organization, the MSTA.
Montana	Montana Education Association	10,724	Yes	Yes	Yes	Merged with the state AFT affiliate, MEA–MFT is very active in the state AFL–CIO.
Nebraska	Nebraska State Education Association	21,937		Yes	No	The Nebraska State Education Association vaunts its opposition to "contract deviation"—a school district paying teachers more than the contract specifies.
Nevada	Nevada State Education Association	22,836		Yes	No	If the Teamsters succeed in winning over 8,000 school support personnel who currently belong to the Nevada State Education Association, this NEA affiliate may disappear.
New Hampshire	NEA–New Hampshire	12,155		Yes	Yes	NEA–New Hampshire endorsed a Democratic primary challenger to Governor Jeanne Shaheen when she vowed to veto a bill to establish a state income tax.

State	NEA State Affiliate, Membership	Independent Teachers Organization (where available)	Collective Bargaining Laws[1]	Strikes Are Legal[2]	Agency Fee Laws[3]	Comments
New Jersey	New Jersey Education Association 147,290		Yes		Yes	The New Jersey Education Association has the most "wall-to-wall" units in country—that is, it represents all employees in a school district.
New Mexico	NEA-New Mexico 7,188		No		No	NEA New Mexico was severely weakened when the state's collective bargaining law lapsed.
New York	NEA-New York 38,998		Yes		Mandatory	NEA New York is dwarfed by the AFT—fully half of the AFT's teacher membership comes from this one state.
North Carolina	North Carolina Association of Educators 51,117	Professional Educators of North Carolina	Banned by law (3)		No	NEA executive director John Wilson is from North Carolina. The state's ban on teacher collective bargaining influences his strategies on organizing, membership, and lobbying.
North Dakota	North Dakota Education Association 7,335		Yes		No	Two members of the North Dakota Education Association's government relations committee resigned when the NDEA leadership overruled the committee's endorsement of the Democratic gubernatorial candidate. The union was neutral in the race.

State	Affiliate (membership)		Competing Association			Notes
Ohio	Ohio Education Association 114,307	Yes		Yes	Yes	The Ohio Education Association's participation in the lawsuit against the Cleveland voucher program went all the way to the U.S. Supreme Court, where it lost.
Oklahoma	Oklahoma Education Association 25,528	Yes	Association of Professional Oklahoma Educators	Yes	No	Whenever the NEA's liberal political agenda makes headlines, membership in the Oklahoma Education Association suffers markedly.
Oregon	Oregon Education Association 38,507	Yes		Yes	Yes	Like all the Pacific Coast teacher unions, the Oregon Education Association is a prime player in ballot initiative battles.
Pennsylvania	Pennsylvania State Education Association 134,663	Yes	Keystone Teachers Association	Yes	Yes	The Pennsylvania State Education Association is a leader in the effort to unionize charter school employees.
Rhode Island	NEA–Rhode Island 8,905	Yes		Yes	Mandatory	NEA Rhode Island has the unusual distinction of having had a sitting union vice president run and defeat an incumbent president.
South Carolina	South Carolina Education Association 11,156	No	Palmetto State Teachers Association	No	No	Probably the weakest NEA state affiliate.

State	NEA State Affiliate, Membership	Independent Teachers Organization (where available)	Collective Bargaining Laws[1]	Strikes Are Legal[2]	Agency Fee Laws[3]	Comments
South Dakota	South Dakota Education Association 6,706		Yes		No	The South Dakota Education Association is small but active.
Tennessee	Tennessee Education Association 46,996	Professional Educators of Tennessee	Yes		No	Strongly opposed to charter schools, the Tennessee Education Association is best known for its unbridled support for a state income tax.
Texas	Texas State Teachers Association 49,721	Association of Texas Professional Educators; Texas Classroom Teachers Association; United Educators Association	No		No	The Texas State Teachers Association hemorrhaged members and money until forced to lay off staff and shut down offices. Its merger talks with the state AFT affiliate are going nowhere. The 100,000-member Association of Texas Professional Educators is the largest independent teachers organization in the country.

State	Organization					Notes
Utah	Utah Education Association 18,753		No	No	No	In a staunchly Republican state, the Utah Education Association is constantly on the defensive.
Vermont	Vermont-National Education Association 8,892		Yes	Yes	No	Vermont NEA made the news when its union president transferred his son to a private high school.
Virginia	Virginia Education Association 53,265	Virginia Professional Educators	Banned by law[4]	No	No	The Virginia Education Association strongly opposed the NEA/AFT merger.
Washington	Washington Education Association 71,946	Northwest Professional Educators	Yes	Yes	Yes	The Washington Education Association was twice assessed the largest penalties in state history for campaign-finance-reporting violations.
West Virginia	West Virginia Education Association 14,755	West Virginia Professional Educators	No	No	No	Very quietly, West Virginia teachers have, dollar for dollar, the best benefits package for teachers in the country.

State	NEA State Affiliate, Membership	Independent Teachers Organization (where available)	Collective Bargaining Laws[1]	Strikes Are Legal[2]	Agency Fee Laws[3]	Comments
Wisconsin	Wisconsin Education Association Counsel 84,731		Yes	Yes	Yes	The Wisconsin Education Association Council has severe problems with vouchers in Milwaukee, state caps on education spending, and perennial battles with its local affiliate in Madison, but still remains a powerful player in state politics.
Wyoming	Wyoming Education Association 5,856		No		No	The outgoing president of the Wyoming Education Association made news when she warned that Generation Xers had little affinity for unions, seeing them as "being about collective negative action."

[1] States with a collective bargaining law require school boards to negotiate with the union if it can get a majority among the teachers voting in a certification election. In states without a collective bargaining law, school boards are not legally impelled to negotiate with the union, regardless of how many teachers it represents, but may choose to.

[2] Government school strikes are generally illegal.

[3] States with agency fee laws allow the union to negotiate them if it chooses. In California, New York, and Rhode Island, agency fees are mandatory. In states without agency fee laws, they are generally prohibited.

[4] In North Carolina and Virginia, school boards are legally prohibited from negotiating a binding contract with the union. However, the union can lobby, meet with board officials to make its views known, etc.

APPENDIX B:
THE GOOD GUYS (AND SOME OTHERS):
EDUCATIONAL REFORM GROUPS

	Web site	Description
Alabama Policy Institute (Birmingham, Ala.)	www.alabamafamily.org (205) 870-9900	A research and educational institute that promotes free markets and limited constitutional government as envisioned by the Founding Fathers. Educational focus is on preschool and day care.
Allegheny Institute for Public Policy Research (Pittsburgh, Pa.)	www.alleghenyinstitute.org (412) 440-0079	The institute supports competitive market processes in the delivery of government services, and the evaluation of services based on outputs rather than inputs.
Alliance for the Separation of School and State (Clovis, Calif.)	www.sepschool.org (559) 292-1776	Founded in 1994. Supporters believe that politics and education don't mix, and want to liberate K–12 schools from state, local, and federal government control.
American Legislative Exchange Council (Washington, D.C.)	www.alec.org (202) 466-3800	A nonpartisan partnership among state legislators and the private sector to promote principles of free markets and limited government.

Apple Tree Institute for Education Innovation
(Washington, D.C.)

www.appletreeinstitute.org
(202) 488-3990

Strives to increase the number of effective school choices through innovation. Track record includes successful launch and opening of five schools in Boston and Washington, D.C., serving well over 1,000 students.

Arkansas Policy Foundation
(Little Rock, Ark.)

www.reformarkansas.org
(501) 537-0825

Tax policy, education monitoring and reform

Association of American Educators
(Laguna Hills, Calif.)

www.aaeteachers.org
(949) 595-7979

A national, professional alternative to teachers unions, offering many of the same benefits without the politics.

Association of Education Practitioners and Providers
(Watertown, Mich.)

www.aepf.org
(800) 252-3280

AEPP brings together educators who view education as an entrepreneurial venture.

Association of Texas Professional Educators
(Austin, Tex.)

www.atpe.org
(512) 467-0071

The largest independent association for public school educators in the nation, ATPE employs a full-time professional staff and serves as a alternative to NEA membership.

	Web site	Description
Becket Fund for Religious Liberty (Washington, D.C.)	www.becketfund.org (202) 955-0095	A bipartisan and ecumenical public-interest law firm that protects the free expression of religious traditions.
Black Alliance for Educational Options (Washington, D.C.)	www.baeo.org (202) 544-9870	An organization that has members and local chapters nationwide working to increase educational options and to empower families to meet their children's educational needs.
Calvert Institute (Baltimore, Md.)	www.calvertinstitute.org (410) 662-7272	A nonpartisan public policy research organization that serves as a clearinghouse for information on the benefits of a society based on regulated government. K–12 education is one of several policy areas studied.
Capital Research Center (Washington, D.C.)	www.capitalresearch.org (202) 483-6900	A nonprofit education and research group studying critical issues in philanthropy, with special emphasis on nonprofit foundations and advocacy groups, their funding sources and agendas, both hidden and open.

Cato Institute
(Washington, D.C.)

www.cato.org
(202) 842-0200

Public-policy research organization dedicated to limited government, individual liberty, free markets.

Center for Civic Renewal, Inc.
(Sweet Briar, Va.)

www.civic-renewal.org
(804) 381-6480

Founded in 1999, the Center supports Sweet Briar College's efforts to foster civic engagement and participation in the United States.

Center for Education Reform
(Washington, D.C.)

www.edreform.com
(202) 822-9000

An independent nonprofit organization providing support and guidance to individuals working to bring fundamental reform to their schools.

Center for Equal Opportunity
(Sterling, Va.)

www.ceousa.org
(703) 421-5443

Conducts research and education on bilingual education and other issues related to race, ethnicity, and assimilation.

Center for Public Justice
(Annapolis, Md.)

www.cpjustice.org
(410) 571-6300

The center articulates a Christian political philosophy, providing educational resources for leaders, public policy research, and coalition building strategies.

	Web site	Description
Center for School Change (Minneapolis, Minn.)	www.hhh.umn.edu/centers/school-change/ (612) 626-1834	A program of the Humphrey Institute of Public Affairs of the University of Minnesota, the Center works with educators, parents, and businesspeople to increase student achievement, raise graduation rates, and strengthen communities. Daily posting of important school choice news and commentary. The web site provides an invaluable archive of such materials going back to January 1999.
Children First America News Children First CEO America (Bentonville, Ariz.)	www.childrenfirstamerica.org/NEWS/index.html www.childrenfirstamerica.org (501) 273-6957	Promote school choice through private tuition grants and tax-funded options.
Children's Scholarship Fund (New York, N.Y.)	www.scholarshipfund.org (212) 752-8555	Started by Ted Forstmann and John Walton, the Fund offers partial-tuition scholarships enabling low-income families to attend private schools in grades K–8.

Christian Educators Association International
(Pasadena, Calif.)

www.ceai.org
(888) 798-1124

Encourages and equips educators in public and private schools to strive for educational excellence and a focus on the preservation of Judeo–Christian heritage and values.

Citizens for Educational Freedom
(St. Louis, Mo.)

www.educational-freedom.org
(314) 997-6361

Founded in 1959, CFEF promotes parents' right to choose where their public education funds are spent.

Clare Booth Luce Family Institute
(Herndon, Va.)

www.cblpolicyinstitute.org
(703) 318-0730

Takes conservative ideas to young women, mentoring them into effective leaders and parents guiding the education of their children.

Clearinghouse for School Reformers

www.schoolreformers.com/

The organization aims to introduce people to the market-based school reform movement and to enable school reform advocates to become effective activists by giving them opportunities to get involved.

	Web site	**Description**
Common Sense Foundation (Raleigh, N.C.)	www.common-sense.org (919) 821-9270	Founded in 1994, the Foundation acts as a center for the progressive-conservative movement in North Carolina, publishing research and providing advice to activists.
Commonwealth Education Organization (Pittsburgh, P.A.)	www.comedorg.org (412) 967-9691	The Commonwealth Education Organization is a nonprofit, nonpartisan organization, primarily but not exclusively focused on Pennsylvania, that researches and disseminates information on a broad array of school issues to parents, taxpayers, educators, school directors, and public-policy makers. Publishes newsletter.
Commonwealth Foundation (Harrisburg, Pa.)	www.commonwealthfoundation.org (717) 671-1901	A conservative, independent public policy organization committed to goals of economic growth and individual opportunity for Pennsylvanians.

Competitive Enterprise Institute
(Washington, D.C.)

www.cei.org
(202) 331–1010

A promarket public policy group committed to advancing principles of free enterprise and limited government.

Council for Basic Education
(Washington, D.C.)

www.c-b-e.org
(202) 347-4171

Founded in 1956, CBE advises states and local districts on upgrading academic content and performance standards, providing professional development programs for teachers and principals.

Discovery Institute
(Seattle, Wash.)

www.discovery.org
(206) 292-0401

Institute develops visions of the future through books, reports, articles, and public conferences.

Education Consumers Clearinghouse
(Johnson City, Tenn.)

www.education-consumers.com
(423) 282-6832

Online networking and education information for parents, taxpayers, and policymakers.

Education Excellence Coalition
(Seattle, Wash.)

www.wacharterschools.org
(205) 634-0589

Founded in 1994 by dissatisfied public school parents and teachers, the Coalition's mission is to revitalize public education through legislative reforms based on deregulation, competition, and parental choice.

	Web site	Description
Education Intelligence Agency (Elk Grove, Calif.)	www.eiaonline.com (916) 422–4373	Education research, analysis, and investigation from a position skeptical of unions and public schools.
Education Leaders Council (Washington, D.C.)	www.educationleaders.org (202) 261–2600	A network and voice for state and local officials who believe true education reform requires parental choice, school accountability, and empowerment of both parents and teachers.
EducationNews.org (Houston, Tex.)	www.educationnews.org Editor@EducationNews.org	"The World's Leading Source of Education News." Daily updates of education news and commentary from the United States and around the world. Daily, 365 days a year.
Education Next (Cambridge, Mass.)	www.educationnext.org (617) 495–6954	Quarterly publication on school reform.

Education Policy Institute
(Washington, D.C.)

www.educationpolicy.org
(202) 244–7535

A research group striving to promote greater parental choice, a more competitive education industry, an enlarged role for the for-profit sector, and other policies that address the problems of both public and private schools.

Education Week
Education Week's Daily News
(Bethesda, Md.)

www.edweek.org
(301) 280–3100
(800) 346–1834
www.edweek.org/clips

Weekly education research publication. *Education Week's Daily News* contains "The best education articles from newspapers around the country, updated daily by noon Eastern time." Monday through Friday.

Empire Foundation for Policy Research
(Clifton Park, N.Y.)

www.efpr.org
(518) 383–2877

A nonprofit research organization focused on New York State public policy.

Empower America
(Washington, D.C.)

www.empower.org
(202) 452–8200

A political advocacy organization that formulates and promotes progressive-conservative policies based on principles of economic growth and cultural renewal.

	Web site	Description
Evergreen Freedom Foundation (Olympia, Wash.)	www.effwa.org (360) 956-3482	Provides research on education reform and other public policy issues. Its governing principles include responsible self-governance, individual rights, and limited government.
Florida Tax Watch Inc. (Tallahassee, Fla.)	www.floridataxwatch.org (850) 222-5052	Supports research to enhance productivity of government services and to explain the economic benefits of limited government.
Focus on the Family (Colorado Springs, Colo.)	www.family.org (800) 232-6459	Organization devoted to the preservation of the home, the sanctity of human life, and the permanence of marriage and the family.
Foundation Endowment (Alexandria, Va.)	www.fe-ednet.org (703) 683-1077	A nonpartisan, nonprofit public policy research organization with a special focus on educational issues. Sponsors research; exhibits at state and national educational meetings; conducts seminars and conferences.

Frontiers of Freedom Institute
(Fairfax, Va.)

www.ff.org
(703) 246–0110

Founded in 1995 by Senator Malcolm Wallop, FFI promotes freedom from unwarranted government regulation and controls.

Georgia Family Council
(Norcross, Ga.)

www.gafam.org
(770) 242–0001

The organization's mission is to strengthen the family by shaping public policy, informing public opinion, and training leaders to be effective advocates for the family.

Georgia Public Policy Foundation
(Atlanta, Ga.)

www.gppf.org
(404) 256–4050

The foundation acts as a catalyst for policies that promote private enterprise, limited government, and personal choice in Georgia.

Goldwater Institute
(Phoenix, Ariz.)

www.goldwaterinstitute.org
(602) 462–5000

An independent, nonpartisan organization devoted to promoting conservative economic and social policies in Arizona.

Greater Educational Opportunities Foundation
(Indianapolis, Ind.)

www.gecfoundation.org
(317) 283–4711

The foundation's mission is to raise the awareness and understanding of school choice across the country.

	Web site	Description
Harvard—Program on Education Policy and Governance (Cambridge, Mass.)	Executive summaries: www.ksg. harvard.edu/pepg/execsum.htm Research papers: www.ksg.harvard.edu/pepg/papers. htm (617) 495–7976	A joint initiative of the Kennedy School's Taubman Center and Harvard's Center for American Political Studies, PEPG brings together experts on K–12 education with specialists in governance and public management to examine strategies for education reform and to evaluate important education experiments.
Homeschooling Today (Fort Collins, Colo.)	www.homeschooltoday.com (970) 493–2716	
Hoover Institution (Stanford, Conn.)	www-hoover.stanford.edu (650) 723–1754	Education policy for primary and secondary schools.
Hudson Institute (Indianapolis, Ind.)	www.hudson.org (317) 545–1000	Hudson scholars develop concrete solutions to policy issues facing government, business and industry, and the public.

Indiana Family Institute
(Indianapolis, Ind.)

www.hoosierfamily.org
(317) 423-9178

A research organization dedicated to preserving the family and the public square.

Institute for Contemporary Studies
(Oakland, Calif.)

www.icspress.com
(510) 238-5010

Founded in 1974, the Institute promotes self-governing and entrepreneurial ways of life, sponsoring programs and publications on a wide range of issues.

Institute for Justice
(Washington, D.C.)

www.ij.org
(202) 955-1300

A nonprofit, public interest law firm that through strategic litigation, training, communications, and outreach advances school choice and other libertarian causes.

James Madison Institute
(Tallahassee, Fla.)

www.jamesmadison.org
(850) 386-3131

Florida-based organization advances economic freedom. Limited government, federalism, traditional values, and the rule of law.

John Locke Foundation
(Raleigh, N.C.)

www.johnlocke.org
(519) 828-3876

A nonprofit research institute that studies state and local public policy issues from a free-market limited government perspective.

	Web site	Description
Josiah Bartlett Center for Public Policy (Concord, N.H.)	www.jbartlett.org (603) 224-4450	A nonprofit think tank focused on state and local public policy issues in the state of New Hampshire. Education—especially the promotion of charter schools—is a major priority.
King for America (Atlanta, Ga.)	www.kingforamerica.com (404) 756-5675	A faith-based organization whose primary issue is school choice, headed by Dr. A. D. Williams King, brother of Martin Luther King Jr.
Landmark Legal Foundation (Herndon, Va.)	www.landmarklegal.org (703) 689-2373	The organization litigates cases involving school choice, free enterprise, and free speech, while promoting government accountability and exposing official corruption.
Lexington Institute (Arlington, Va.)	www.lexingtoninstitute.org (703) 522-5828	The Institute's goal is to inform and shape the public debate on education reform, focusing on nongovernmental, free-market solutions.

Liberty Fund Inc.
(Indianapolis, Ind.)

www.libertyfund.org
(317) 842-0880

A private foundation devoted to the study of free and independent individuals through conferences and book publishing.

Link Institute
(Libertyville, Ill.)

www.linkinstitute.org
(866) 828-5465

A nonprofit organization committed to promoting and supporting schools with vigorous academic content and virtue-based character education.

Mackinac Center for Public Policy
(Midland, Mich.)

www.mackinac.org
(989) 631-0900

A full-time research staff analyzes state and local government policies in Michigan.

Manhattan Institute (Center for Educational Innovation)
(New York, N.Y.)

www.manhattan-institute.org
(212) 599-7000

A nonpartisan, independent research organization that develops public policies at all levels of government to allow individuals the greatest scope for achieving their potential.

Michigan Family Forum
(Lansing, Mich.)

www.mfforum.com
(517) 374-1171

The organization's research department formulates a legislative agenda and strategy to guide and educate citizens in the state of Michigan.

	Web site	Description
Milton & Rose D. Friedman Foundation (Indianapolis, Ind.)	www.friedmanfoundation.org (317) 681-0745	Promotes K–12 education reform, stressing the role that competition through parental choice can play in achieving that reform.
National Center for Education Information (Washington, D.C.)	www.ncei.com (202) 362-3444	Founded in 1980, NCEI is a nonpartisan research organization specializing in survey research and data analysis. NCEI's primary focus is on teacher preparation and certification.
National Center for Policy Analysis (Dallas, Tex.)	www.ncpa.org (972) 386-6272	NCPA seeks to discover and encourage private alternatives to public policy problems in education and other public policy issues.
National Council on Teacher Quality (Washington, D.C.)	www.nctq.org	This web site, an information clearinghouse on teacher quality issues, should be bookmarked by anyone with an interest in teacher preparation, teacher quality, and alternative teacher certification. It provides up-to-date information on news, research, literature, and policy options, together with many links to other useful web sites.

National Institute for Labor Relations Research
(Springfield, Va.)

www.nilrr.org
(703) 321-9606

A research organization providing analysis needed to expose the inequities of compulsory unionization and how union monopolies harm workers.

National Right-to-Work Committee
(Springfield, Va.)

www.right-to-work.com
(800) 325-7892

Dedicated to providing free legal aid nationwide to thousands of employees whose human and civil rights have been violated by compulsory unionism abuses.

National Taxpayers Union Foundation
(Alexandria, Va.)

www.ntu.org
(703) 683-5700

Founded in 1977, NTU Foundation disseminates information on the effects of spending and tax policies on taxpayers.

Nebraska Center for Policy Research
(Omaha, Nebr.)

Contact:
rthayer@scholars.bellvue.edu
(402) 334-1241

The organization advances the development of charter schools, school vouchers, and other free-market, nongovernmental alternatives to the various economic and social problems Nebraska's neighborhoods and communities face.

	Web site	Description
Oklahoma Family Policy Council (Bethany, Okla.)	www.okfamilypc.org (405) 787-7744	Council's mission is to strengthen families and to educate Oklahomans on public policy as it impacts the family. A public interest, nonprofit legal foundation whose mission is to protect individual and economic freedoms.
Pacific Legal Foundation (Sacramento, Calif.)	www.pacificlegal.org (916) 362-2833	Through its litigation, PLF combats race and gender preferences, quotas, and set-asides in government hiring, education, and contracting.
Pacific Research Institute (Los Angeles, Calif.)	www.pacificresearch.org (415) 989-0833	PRI promotes the principles of individual freedom and personal responsibility in education and other issues, striving to foster a better understanding among leaders in government, the media, and the business community. Peter Brimelow is a senior fellow!
Partnership for Choice in Education (St. Paul, Minn.)	www.pcemn.org (651) 293-9196	A nonprofit organization that provides public information on the benefits of educational choice.

Pioneer Institute for Public Policy Research
(Boston, Mass.)

www.pioneerinstitute.org
(617) 723-2277

A think tank that devotes half of its efforts to the reform of K–12 education, with a focus on competition and the expansion of parental choice.

Professional Association of Georgia Educators
(Atlanta, Ga.)

www.pageinc.org
(770) 216-8555

Founded in 1975 as an alternative for Georgia educators who opposed the forced unionization policy of the NEA.

PTOtoday
(Wrentham, Mass.)

www.ptotoday.com
(800) 644-3561

Reports on individual Parent Teacher Organizations set up in opposition to the PTA.

Reason Public Policy Institute
(Washington, D.C.)

www.rppi.org
(310) 391-2245

National research organization conducts peer-reviewed research in education reform and other public policy issues.

School Reform News
(Chicago, Ill.)

www.heartland.org/education/whatis.htm
(312) 377-4000

A 24-page monthly newspaper reporting on school reform efforts nationwide.

Social Philosophy and Policy Center, Bowling Green State University
(Bowling Green, Ohio)

www.BGSU.edu/offices/sppc
(412) 372-2536

The center examines public policy issues from an ethical perspective, reflecting the belief that policy questions cannot be adequately addressed by empirical investigation alone.

	Web site	Description
South Carolina Policy Council (Columbia, S.C.)	www.scpolicycouncil.com (803) 779-5022	The council promotes state and local public policy based on the traditional South Carolina values of individual liberty and responsibility, free enterprise, and limited government.
Susquehanna Valley Center for Public Policy (Hershey, Pa.)	www.susvalley.bhcom1.com (717) 361-8905	A Pennsylvania-based research organization established to promulgate local government efficiency, accountability, and responsibility.
Tennessee Family Institute (Nashville, Tenn.)	www.tennesseefamily.org (615) 327-3120	A conservative state-based think tank devoted to the ideas of freedom, the free market, private property, educational choice, and strong families.
Texas Public Policy Foundation (San Antonio, Tex.)	www.tppf.org (210) 614-0080	The foundation's mission is to improve government by generating academically sound research and data on education reform and other public policy issues.

The Brookings Institution
(Washington, D.C.)

www.brookings.edu
(202) 797-6000

The Brookings's Brown Center for Education Policy conducts research on American education, with special efforts to improve academic achievement in K–12 schools.

The Family Foundation
(Richmond, Va.)

www.familyfoundation.org
(804) 342-0010

A statewide organization, TFF helps develop economic, education, and social policies that strengthen families and family values.

The Heartland Institute
(Chicago, Ill.)

www.heartland.org
(312) 377-4000

Founded in 1985, Heartland is an independent nonprofit public policy research organization, and an information source for journalists and the nation's 8,000 state and local elected officials.

The Heritage Foundation
(Washington, D.C.)

www.heritage.org
(202) 546-4400

Formulates and promotes conservative public policies based on principles of free enterprise, limited government, and individual freedom.

	Web site	Description
The Lone Star Foundation and Report (Austin, Tex.)	www.lonestarreport.org (888) 472-6051	The foundation seeks to create a community of leaders committed to conservative thinking. Presents original research and analysis to further define the state's policy agenda.
Thomas B. Fordham Foundation (Washington, D.C.)	www.edexcellence.net (202) 223-5452	Supports research, publications, and action projects of national significance in K–12 school reform, as well as educational reform projects in Dayton, Ohio. Affiliated with the Manhattan Institute for Public Policy Research.
Alexis de Tocqueville Institution (Washington, D.C.)	www.adti.net (202) 548-0006	Founded in 1986 to study and promote the principles of classical liberalism.
Traditional Values Coalition (Washington, D.C.)	www.traditionalvalues.org (202) 547-8570	The coalition comprises 43,000 churches of various Christian denominations, serving as a lobbying and education group.

Urban Family Council
(Philadelphia, Pa.)

www.urbanfamily.org
(215) 663-9494

An interracial, urban-based progressive organization dedicated to Philadelphia, its children and its families, and to penetrating public policy with the Judeo-Christian ethic.

U.S. Supreme Court Decisions
(Ithaca, N.Y.)

www.supct.law.cornell.edu/supct/index.tml

The complete text of the U.S. Supreme Court decisions is available from this Cornell Law School web site.

Washington Research Council
(Seattle, Wash.)

www.researchcouncil.org
(206) 467-7088

The council promotes effective public policies and efficient government through independent research on policy questions.

Wisconsin Policy Research Institute
(Thiensville, Wisc.)

www.wpri.org
(262) 241-0514

A nonprofit organization established to study public policy in Wisconsin in order to improve government efficiency and accountability.

Yankee Institute for Public Policy Inc.
(Hartford, Conn.)

www.yankeeinstitute.org
(860) 297-4271

The institute produces white papers, seminars, and media releases on education reform and other public policy issues affecting Connecticut and the nation.

NOTES

1. Jeff Archer, "Academics Square Off over Unions' Role in Reform Efforts," *Education Week,* October 7, 1998.
2. Fred M. Hechinger, "Spending: Attack and Counterattack," *New York Times,* January 6, 1987.
3. See Diane Ravitch, *Left Back: A Century of Failed School Reforms* (New York: Simon & Schuster, 2000); *The Troubled Crusade: American Education 1945–1980* (New York: Basic Books, 1983).
4. See Michael Fumento, *The Fat of the Land: The Obesity Epidemic and How Overweight Americans Can Help Themselves* (New York: Viking, 1993).
5. Christina Hoff Sommers, *The War Against Boys: How Misguided Feminism Is Harming Our Young Men* (New York: Simon & Schuster, 2000).
6. Michael X. Delli Carpini and Scott Keeter, *What Americans Know About Politics and Why It Matters* (New Haven, Conn.: Yale University Press, 1996).
7. Quoted in *The Education Intelligence Agency Communiqué,* July 5, 1999.
8. Andrea Billups, "Washington's History a Mystery to Collegians," *Washington Times,* February 21, 2000.
9. Susan Reimer, "Why Johnny Can't Tell 'Their' from 'There,' " *Baltimore Sun,* February 22, 2000.
10. Quoted in Andrea Peyser, "Poor Excuse for Teachers," *New York Post,* May 16, 1999.
11. U.S. Department of Labor News Release, Table 1, "Employment and Average Annual Pay for 2000 and 1999."
12. Quoted in Debra J. Saunders, "Those Who Can't, Sue," *Weekly Standard,* March 4, 1996.
13. All SAT data from The College Board, "2001 College-Bound Seniors," 2001.
14. All NAEP data in this section from U.S. Department of Education. Office of Educational Research and Improvement, National Center for Educational

Statistics, "NAEP 1999 Trends in Academic Progress: Three Decades of Student Performance," August 2000.

15. Richard J. Herrnstein and Charles Murray, *The Bell Curve: Intelligence and Class Structure in American Life* (New York: The Free Press, 1994), pp. 420–421.

16. Quoted in Peter Brimelow, "Claiming Credit Where No Credit Is Due," *Forbes,* October 20, 1997.

17. Third International Mathematics and Science Study (TIMSS), 1998–1999 (Boston: Boston College Lynch School of Education, 2000), p. 35.

18. Quoted in Diana Jean Schemo, "U.S. Students Prove Middling on a 32-Nation Test," *New York Times,* December 5, 2001.

19. Peter Brimelow, "Disadvantaging the Advantaged," *Forbes,* November 21, 1994.

20. Herrnstein and Murray, *The Bell Curve,* pp. 143–145; Jay P. Green, "GEDs Aren't Worth the Paper They're Printed On," *City Journal,* Winter 2002.

21. Peter Brimelow, "Diploma Missing," *Forbes,* May 28, 2001. Note also that the graduation rate increases a couple of points if measured against the broader eighteen- to twenty-four-year-old cohort—i.e., allowing for late graduations, etc.—but the trend remains the same.

22. Herrnstein and Murray, *The Bell Curve,* pp. 146–147.

23. Peter Brimelow, "Private School Surge," *Forbes,* November 27, 2000; citing *Digest of Education Statistics, 1999.*

24. Estimate by Dr. Brian D. Ray, National Home Education Research Institute; e-mails to author.

25. Thomas Fordham Foundation, "Remediation in Higher Education: A Symposium," 1998.

26. E-mails from Steven Goldberg, March 25 and 27, 2002.

27. American Society for Training and Development, "Sharpening the Leading Edge," 2001; www.astd.org/cms/templates/index.html. Calculated as $1,100 times the 142-million-person labor force.

28. Herrnstein and Murray, *The Bell Curve,* p. 421.

29. OECD, "Education at a Glance 2001," Table B2.1C (data refer to 1998).

30. *Digest of Education Statistics, 2000.*

31. See, for example, Eric Hanushek, "The Evidence on Class Size," in Susan E. Mayer and Paul Peterson, eds., *Earning and Learning: How Schools Matter* (Washington, D.C.: Brookings Institution, 1999), pp. 131–168.

32. Eric Hanushek, e-mail to Peter Brimelow, February 25, 2002.

33. CSR Research Consortium, Summary of Findings; www.classize.org/summary/9901/index.htm.

34. Department of Education, Center for Education Statistics, *Digest of Education Statistics, 2000,* Table 70.

35. Ibid., Table 80.

36. Ibid., Tables 70, 136, 168.

37. Peter Brimelow, "Top-Heavy," *Forbes,* November 2, 1998.

38. Caroline M. Hoxby, "School Choice and School Productivity (Or Could School Choice Be a Tide That Lifts All Boats?)," paper presented to the

National Bureau of Economic Research Conference on the Economics of School Choice, February 23–24, 2001.

39. Productivity numbers from Bureau of Labor Statistics, interview by Edwin S. Rubenstein.

40. Richard K. Vedder and Joshua Hall, "For-Profit Schools Are Making a Comeback," *The Independent Review,* Spring 2002, pp. 753–754. E-mail from Richard Vedder.

41. Richard K. Vedder, *Can Teachers Own Their Own Schools: New Strategies for Educational Excellence* (Oakland, Calif.: Independent Institute, 2000).

42. Caroline M. Hoxby, "Rethinking Public Education: School Choice and the Teachers Unions," speech to Manhattan Institute, New York, March 25, 1997.

43. Caroline M. Hoxby, "How Teacher Unions Affect Education Productivity," *Quarterly Journal of Economics,* August 1996.

44. Terry M. Moe, ed., *A Primer on America's Schools* (Stanford, Calif.: Hoover Institution Press, 2001), pp. 162, 182.

45. Wayne Johnson speech July 24, 2001, cited in Pamela Riley et al., *Contract for Failure: The Impact of Teacher Union Contracts on the Quality of California Schools* (San Francisco: Pacific Research Institute, 2002), p. iii.

46. Linda Charles, Micaelia Randolph Brummett, Heather McDonald, and Joan Westley, *MathLand: Journeys Through Mathematics Guidebook, Grade 6* (Mountain View, Calif.: Creative Publications, 1995), p. 124.

47. Speech to the California Teachers Association State Council, October 19, 1996.

48. Quoted in Gregg Zoroya and Kristen Hartzell, "Teacher Shortage Just Doesn't Add Up," *USA Today,* August 30, 1999.

49. Quoted in *The Education Intelligence Agency Communiqué,* September 27, 1999.

50. Quoted in *The Education Intelligence Agency Communiqué,* August 30, 1999.

51. Quoted in Kenneth J. Cooper, "Best and Brightest Leave Teaching Early, Study Says," *Washington Post,* January 13, 2000.

52. Paul Glastris, "When Teachers Should Be Expelled from Class," *U.S. News & World Report,* June 2, 1997.

53. Faith Johnson, "Records: Teachers Not Fired," *Augusta Chronicle,* February 21, 2000.

54. Anemona Hartocollis, "Speed Is Urged in Disciplining of Teachers," *New York Times,* March 1, 2000.

55. Quoted in Associated Press, "Schools Pay Convicted Thief to Stop Teaching in District," September 18, 1997.

56. Associated Press, "Teacher Resigns After Sex Conviction—and After Collecting Year's Pay While on Suspension," May 28, 1998.

57. Quoted in David Sharp, "Outcry over Fingerprints Is Not Unique to Maine," Associated Press, February 21, 2000.

58. Quoted in John C. Teves, "Tenure Teachers Tough to Fire in State," *Bakersfield Californian,* May 13, 1996.

59. Stephen E. Gorrie, "We Educators Know What Is Best," *MTA Today,* February 8, 1999.

60. Deb Kollars, "Better Teaching Vowed in City High Schools," *Sacramento Bee,* February 6, 2000.
61. *Time,* February 14, 2000.
62. Debra J. Saunders, "Those Who Can't, Sue," *The Weekly Standard,* March 4, 1996.
63. Jay Mathews, "A Math Teacher's Lessons in Division," *Washington Post,* May 21, 1997.
64. Quoted in *The Education Intelligence Agency Communiqué,* November 22, 1999.
65. Quoted in Robert Jablon, "Dress Code Wears on Nerves of Some L.A. Teachers," Associated Press, May 12, 2002.
66. "Grounded Teacher," *Wall Street Journal,* June 9, 1999.
67. Associated Press, "Teachers Demand Pay for Two-Minute Extra Work," May 14, 1997.
68. Quoted in Associated Press, "Teachers Fight, Students Lose," February 3, 2000.
69. Barbara Behrendt, "Drama Volunteer Upsets Teachers' Union," *St. Petersburg Times,* August 28, 1999.
70. Jorge Sanchez, "She's Not Playing Teacher, She Is One," *St. Petersburg Times,* September 2, 1999.
71. Ann Bradley, "Volunteer Teacher Leads to Conflict with Vermont Union," *Education Week,* December 1, 1999.
72. Quoted in Sherry Posnick-Goodwin, "Fremont Agreement Controls Growth of Reserves," *California Educator,* October 1997.
73. Lynette Holloway, "Tied by Red Tape, School Heads Use Diplomacy to Get Anything Done," *New York Times,* November 4, 1998.
74. James E. Wilkerson, "Teachers Won't Roll over in Thorpe Pastry Tiff," *Allentown Morning Call,* December 3, 1998.
75. Lynette Holloway, "New York Teachers Union Blocks Replacements at School for the Deaf," *New York Times,* July 2, 2000.
76. Quoted in Justin Blum, "School Schedule Change Derailed," *Washington Post,* June 13, 2000.
77. Quoted in Jan Barry, "Ringwood Teachers Union Assails Pay Ruling," *Bergen (New Jersey) Record,* July 16, 1999.
78. Mhari Doyle, "Olathe School District Wants Court's Guidance," *Kansas City Star,* June 7, 2000.
79. Carol Innerst, "Schools of Education Seen Failing," *Washington Times,* May 8, 1998.
80. John Leo, "Dumbing Down Teachers," *U.S. News & World Report,* August 3, 1998.
81. Heather MacDonald, "Why Johnny's Teacher Can't Teach, *City Journal,* Spring 1998; www.city-journal.org/html/8_2_al.html.
82. Drew H. Gitomer, Andrew S. Latham, and Robert Ziomek, *The Academic Quality of Prospective Teachers: The Impact of Admissions and Licensure Testing* (Princeton, N.J.: Educational Testing Service, 1999), p. 20.

83. Gary Palmer, "The Vast Big Mule Conspiracy," Alabama Policy Institute, January 15, 2002; www.alabamafamily.org/gp_latest4.htm.

84. Edwin Vieira Jr., "Are Public Sector Unions Special Interest Political Parties?" *DePaul Law Review,* Vol. 27 (1978), p. 293.

85. *The Education Intelligence Agency Communiqué,* March 8, 1998.

86. Karen Archia, "ESP Amendment Approved, *NCAE Info,* April 12, 1999.

87. *The Education Intelligence Agency Communiqué,* April 6, 1998.

88. "UniServ Goal Is Simple: Service to You, the Member," *NSEA Voice,* August 1998, p. 35.

89. *The Education Intelligence Agency Communiqué,* November 16, 1998.

90. "A Quarter Century of Service," *NEA Today,* October 1995, p. 35.

91. "WEASO Members Promoted to WEA Management," *Just Rewards,* January 2000.

92. *The Education Intelligence Agency Communiqué,* June 7, 1999.

93. Ann Bradley, "Old NEA Staff Could Impede New Unionism," *Education Week,* October 8, 1997.

94. Richard Phalon, "Empire Builders," *Forbes,* February 22, 1988.

95. E-mail from David Denholm, June 5, 2002.

96. Janet Novak, "Strength from Its Grey Roots," *Forbes,* November 25, 1991.

97. Peter Brimelow and Leslie Spencer, "Comeuppance," *Forbes,* February 13, 1995; includes some reproduced PTA documents relating to Proposition 174.

98. Charlene K. Haar, *The Politics of the PTA* (New Brunswick, N.J.: Transaction Publishers, 2003), p. 88.

99. Quoted in Nancy E. Roman, "Teacher Unions Fight to Save Power," *Washington Times,* April 19, 1999.

100. Pamela Riley with Rosemary Fusano, LaRae Munk, and Ruben Peterson, *Contract for Failure: The Impact of Teacher Union Contracts on the Quality of California Schools* (San Francisco, Calif.: Pacific Research Institute, 2002), p. 4.

101. Leo Troy, *The New Unionism in the New Society: Public Sector Unions in the Redistributive State* (Washington, D.C.: George Mason University Press, 1994).

102. Quoted in Dave Benjamin, "Board to Parents: Prepare for Union's Work Stoppage," *The News Transcript,* October 11, 2000.

103. Quoted in Riley et al., *Contract for Failure,* p. 48; e-mail, May 21, 2002.

104. Peter Brimelow, "Bottomless Pit," *Forbes,* November 3, 1997.

105. Quoted in Ann Bradley, "Teachers' Contract Deters Achievement, Study Says," *Education Week,* October 1, 1997.

106. Riley et al., *Contract for Failure,* Executive Summary, p. 2.

107. Posted on the Evergreen Teachers Association web page at www.hometown.aol.com/callacruz/evergreenteachers/logon/title.html.

108. Quoted in Melissa L. Jones, "Teacher's Demand Denied," *Arizona Republic,* June 2, 1998.

109. Reported in *New York School Board,* August 17, 1998.

110. Lynette Tanaka, editorial, *NEA Today,* May 1996, p. 31.

111. Robert King, "Teacher Union Resisting Bonuses," *St. Petersburg Times,* October 20, 1999.

112. Warren Henderson, "WEA Wins Big in CWU Salary Dispute, Other Cases Likely," *WEA Action,* March 2000.

113. Quoted in *The Education Intelligence Agency Communiqué,* December 21, 1998.

114. Quoted in Robin Farmer, "$5,000 Bonus Urged for New Teachers," *Richmond Times-Dispatch,* December 15, 1998.

115. Quoted in Bart Jansen, "Teacher Bonus Bill Earns House OK," Associated Press, April 1, 1999.

116. Quoted in *The Education Intelligence Agency Communiqué,* February 22, 1999.

117. Howard Libit, "Survey Says Yearly Bonus for Teachers Should Flunk," *Baltimore Sun,* March 1, 1999.

118. Beth Daley, "Education Foundation Criticizes City Hiring," *Boston Globe,* March 27, 2000.

119. Richard Lee Colvin, "Battle Likely over Teacher Seniority in L.A.," *Los Angeles Times,* March 28, 2000.

120. Quoted in Becky Stover, "Teachers Win on Pay but Will Lose 11 Jobs," *Cedar Rapids Gazette,* May 1, 1998.

121. Bob Klose, "Sonoma Teachers' Contract Could Force More Cutbacks," *Santa Rosa Press Democrat,* March 23, 2000.

122. Todd A. DeMitchell and Richard Fossey, *The Limits of Law-Based School Reform: Vain Hopes and False Promises* (Lancaster, Pa.: Technomic, 1997), p. 191.

123. *The Education Intelligence Agency Communiqué,* August 16, 1999.

124. "Negotiating Change: Education Reform and Collective Bargaining," NEA Research Division, 1992, p. 7.

125. Ibid., p. 5.

126. George Nerren, "Collective Bargaining," Tennessee School Boards Association, August 1995.

127. Hayes Mizell, "Educators: Reform Thyselves," *Education Week,* April 5, 2000.

128. Lucy Hood, "Unions, Business Pick SASD Favorites," *San Antonio Express-News,* April 23, 2000.

129. Quoted in Associated Press, "Teachers Union Agrees to Settle Suit over Political Payments," August 21, 1999.

130. Kenneth D. Smith, "(Very) Liberal Education," *Washington Times,* February 17, 2000; and Emily Bazar, "Avoid Politics, Suit Tells Schools: Prop 26 Foes Allege Lobbying," *Sacramento Bee,* February 9, 2000.

131. Guillermo Contreras, "Rio Grande High Students Riot," *Albuquerque Journal,* September 18, 1998.

132. Joanna Frazier, "School Employees Accused of Misusing Federal Money," *Riverside (California) Press-Enterprise,* November 19, 1998.

133. Janet Bingham, "Teacher Tactics Anger Tax Foes," *Denver Post,* September 4, 1998.

134. Anand Vaishnav, "Amid Contract Talks, Boston Teachers Use Ad Blitz to Woo Public," *Boston Globe,* August 9, 2000.

135. G. Gregory Moo, *Power Grab: How the National Education Association Is Betraying Our Children* (Washington, D.C.: Regnery, 1999), p. 124.

136. John Chadwick, "Union's Role Cited in Budget Approval," *Bergen (New Jersey) Record,* April 20, 2000.

137. Mike Wowk, "Voucher Group Alerts Vendors," *Detroit News,* September 8, 2000.

138. Mildred Muzzy Bettinger, "Corona-Norco Teachers Back 2 of 3 Winners," *CTA Action,* December 1995.

139. Ann Bradley, "Teachers' Contract Deters Achievement, Study Says," *Education Week,* October 1, 1997.

140. Diann Myer, letter to the editor, *U.S. News & World Report,* March 20, 2000.

141. Wayne Johnson, "Make No Mistake About It," *California Educator,* June 2000.

142. Associated Press, "Governor Opens Financial Books to Teachers Union Officials," February 12, 1997.

143. Quoted in Norman Draper, "Despite State Funding Increases, School Districts Keep Cutting," *Minneapolis Star Tribune,* March 6, 2000.

144. Quoted in Debra O'Connor, "Teachers' Pay Hikes Under Fire," *St. Paul Pioneer Press,* January 25, 2000.

145. Robert Whereatt, "Auditor Criticizes School District for Paying Staff Bonuses," *Minneapolis Star Tribune,* July 29, 1999.

146. Quoted in Scott Cooper, "School Districts May Face Another Funding Crisis," *Tulsa World,* May 26, 2000.

147. Quoted in Diane Brooks, "Some Districts Ignore Directives to Raise Pay Only for Newer Teachers," *Seattle Times,* September 22, 1999.

148. Dana DiFilippo, "Teacher Union Wants to Recruit for CPS," *Cincinnati Enquirer,* September 2, 1999.

149. "A New 'Company Store,' " *Las Vegas Review Journal,* August 28, 1997.

150. *The Education Intelligence Agency Communiqué,* November 29, 1999.

151. PoliticalMoneyLine posts the NEA Federal Election Commission reports at www.tray.com/cgi-win/x pacpg.exe?DoFn=C0000325100.

152. "PAC Activity Increases in 2000 Election Cycle," Federal Election Commission press release, May 31, 2001; www.fec.gov/press/053101pacfund/053101pacfund.html.

153. The text of Landmark's complaints is posted at www.landmarklegal.org/complaints.cfm?category_id=3.

154. E-mail from Mark Tapscott, May 28, 2002. See also Mark Tapscott, "What Are the Teacher Unions Hiding . . ." January 21, 2002; www.townhall.com/columnists/marktapscott/mt20020121.shtml.

155. WEA Bargaining Team memo to Board of Directors and UniServ Council presidents dated October 11, 1995.

156. National Education Association, "Strategic Plan and Budget, Fiscal Years: 2000–2002," p. 31.

157. Quoted in *The Education Intelligence Agency Communiqué,* September 26, 1997.

158. Quoted in Tom Howard, "Union Workers Picket Union," *Billings Gazette,* April 3, 1998.

159. Joe Williams, "Staff of Teachers Union to Protest Stalled Contract," *Milwaukee Journal Sentinel,* November 17, 1998.

160. Associated Press, "MEA Staff Files Unfair Labor Charges," September 5, 1996.

161. "PSEA Staff Members File Labor Practice Suit," *Harrisburg Patriot,* August 10, 1999.

162. "Striking the Teachers," *Wall Street Journal,* February 14, 2000.

163. Brian Thevenot and Chris Gray, "Schools CEO's Daughter in Private School," *New Orleans Times-Picayune,* September 15, 2000.

164. "The Role of Government in Education," by Milton Friedman, in *Economics and the Public Interest,* ed. Robert A. Solo (Rutgers, N.J.: Rutgers University Press, 1955). Full text online at www.schoolchoices.org/roo/fried1.htm.

165. Bob Chase, "A 'Devil's Deal,' " *Washington Post,* September 14, 1997.

166. Posted on the web page of the Pennsylvania State Education Association. See also www.psea.org/voice/article.cfm?artID=221

167. Michigan Education Association president Lu Battaglieri, quoted in *The Education Intelligence Agency Communiqué,* August 30, 1999.

168. California Teachers Association president Del Weber to the CTA State Council, June 5, 1993.

169. NEA president Bob Chase, speaking to the union's Representative Assembly in Orlando, Florida, July 3, 1999.

170. *NEA Focus,* October 14, 1997, citing a Chase speech to the National Urban League and the Congress of National Black Churches.

171. California Teachers Association executive director Ralph J. Flynn to the CTA State Council, June 5, 1993.

172. Andrew J. Coulson, *Market Education: The Unknown History* (New Brunswick, N.J.: Transaction Publishers, 1999), p. 227.

173. "The Professoriat: The Second Oldest Profession," *Weekly Standard,* November 20, 2000.

174. John Ryor, "The Voucher Issue," Florida Teaching Profession–NEA web page, January 1999.

175. Keith Geiger, address to the 1995 NEA Representative Assembly, Minneapolis, July 3, 1995.

176. Matthew Miller, "Bold Experiment to Fix City Schools," *Atlantic Monthly,* July 1999.

177. Matthew Berry, "School Choice for All Ages," *Washington Times,* July 28, 2000.

178. Letters to the Editor, *Commentary,* June 2000.

179. NEA press release, December 10, 1998.

180. Reg Weaver, address to the National Association for the Advancement of Colored People convention, New York City, July 13, 1999.

181. Cited in Miller, "Bold Experiment."

182. Quoted in *The Education Intelligence Agency Communiqué,* May 3, 1999.

183. Howard Fuller, speech to the Second Annual Symposium on Educational Options for African Americans, Milwaukee, March 2, 2000.

184. Justin Blum, "Special-Ed Bus Audit Cites Waste," *Washington Post,* November 22, 2000.

185. "Back Talk," *NEA Today,* September 1999.

186. Address to the National Education Association Representative Assembly, July 4, 1994.

187. *NEA Now!* May 1997.

188. Miller, "A Bold Experiment to Fix City Schools," *Atlantic,* July 1999.

189. Matthew J. Brouillette, "School Employee Unions Oppose School Choice to Protect Their Turf," *Viewpoint on Public Issues,* Mackinac Center for Public Policy, July 5, 1999.

190. Andrew Young, "Let Parents Choose Their Kids' Schools," *Los Angeles Times,* April 29, 1999.

191. "Easy Choice," *New Republic,* September 11, 2000.

192. Tim Chavez, "Vouchers Offer Hope to Parents, Much-Needed Competition to Public Schools," *Nashville Tennessean,* September 12, 2000.

193. Dana Milbank, "Schoolyard Tussle," *New Republic,* December 14, 1998.

194. Christopher W. Hammond, "The Effects of Town Tuitioning in Vermont and Maine," *School Choice Issues in Depth,* Vol. 1, No. 1 (Indianapolis, Ind.: Milton and Rose D. Friedman Foundation, n.d.)

195. "Catholic School Must Hold Talks with Union, Court Rules," *Education Week,* June 18, 1997.

196. Quoted in David Gibson, "Teachers Demonstrate," *Bergen (New Jersey) Record,* August 26, 1999.

197. Quoted in *The Education Intelligence Agency Communiqué,* March 29, 1999.

198. Mike Antonucci, "Who's an Extremist?" *Wall Street Journal,* May 20, 1997.

199. Quoted in Shirin Parsavand, "Conservatives Angered by Area Survey of 'Right,' " *Schenectady Gazette,* May 21, 1997.

200. NEA Center for the Advancement of Public Education, "The Radical Right," *In Brief,* November 1996.

201. Thomas Toch, "Why Teachers Don't Teach," *U.S. News & World Report,* February 26, 1996.

202. "Overview and Introduction to the Extreme Right: A State's Approach," *NEA: Radical Right,* undated.

203. Ann Bradley, "Training Sessions Target Religious Right at the Grassroots," *Education Week,* October 18, 1995.

204. Lois Tinson, "The Open Doors," *California Educator,* September 1996.

205. Wayne Johnson, "Make No Mistake About It," *California Educator,* September 1999.

206. NEA Center for the Advancement of Public Education, "The Radical Right."

207. Ibid.

208. "Overview and Introduction," *NEA: Radical Right.*

209. "Region 2 Leaders' Conference Exposes Misuse of Charter Act," *CTA Action,* November 1995.

210. Edmonds Education Association, "Future Search: The Role of Association Advocacy in the 21st Century," Summary Report, June 16, 1995.

211. Quoted in Ann Bradley, "Training Sessions Target Religious Right at the Grassroots," *Education Week,* October 18, 1995.

212. Poppy DeMarco Dennis, "Winning Elections: Organizing Tips from San Diego," Community Coalition Network, 1994.

213. National Council for Higher Education, *NCHE Update,* December 1997.

214. Steve Lemken, "Editor's Corner," *NEA Now!* January 1998.

215. "NEA President Hails Defeat of Proposition 226," *MTA Today,* June 16, 1998.

216. Daniel Pipes, *Conspiracy: How the Paranoid Style Flourishes and Where It Comes From* (New York: The Free Press, 1997), p. 22.

217. National Education Association, "The Real Story Behind 'Paycheck Protection'—The Hidden Link Between Anti-Worker and Anti-Public Education Initiatives: An Anatomy of the Far Right," October 1, 1998, p. 62.

218. Ibid. p. 20.

219. *The Education Intelligence Agency Communiqué,* April 22, 1998.

220. Mike Antonucci, "It's Elementary for NEA to Hire Watson," *Investor's Business Daily,* May 14, 1998.

221. Robert Greene, "NEA Targets Union Dues Proposals," Associated Press, October 1, 1998.

222. Quoted in Michael W. Lynch, "Paranoid Report," *Reason,* December 1998.

223. *The Education Intelligence Agency Communiqué,* December 7, 1998.

224. "*Morning News* Wins Awards from Teachers Group," *Dallas Morning News,* April 13, 2000.

225. Steven Greenhouse, "Two Largest Teachers Unions Announce Preliminary Merger," *New York Times,* January 27, 1998.

226. Rich Gibson, "NEA-AFT-AFL-CIO? Not Just No, But HELL NO!" *Z Magazine,* July 1998.

227. Anjetta McQueen, "Union, Teachers Closer on Agreement," Associated Press, July 5, 2000.

228. November 19, 1999, Gallup Poll posted, not surprisingly, on the California nurses' web site www.calnurse.org/cna/new2/glp111899.html.

229. *Do You See What I'm Saying? Using Message to Reconnect with the Public* (NEA Publications, 1997), p. 7.

230. Ibid. p. 11.

231. Ibid. p. 12.

232. Ibid. p. 29.

233. Ibid. p. 19.

234. Ibid. p. 27.

235. "Handling Media and Public Attention," from *Criminal Abuse of Students by School Employees,* handbook posted on WEA web site prior to February 27, 1999.

236. Keith Geiger, letter to the editor, *U.S. News & World Report,* March 9, 1996.

237. David Berliner, speaking before the NEA Representative Assembly in New Orleans, July 4, 1994.

238. John Stossel, "Public Schools in Bad Shape," *20/20,* ABC News, November 12, 1999.

239. *Sharpener,* February 11, 1998.

240. David Gergen, "Chasing Better Schools," *U.S. News & World Report,* December 8, 1997.

241. Ann Bradley, "New Union Boss," *Education Week,* June 23, 1999.

242. Jodi Wilgoren, "Doesn't She Look Familiar? Why, It's Sandra Feldman," *New York Times,* July 8, 2000.

243. Ann Bradley, "Fighting All My Life," *Education Week,* October 1, 1997.
244. Katherine Kapos, "After Tough Legislative Fight, President of UEA Carries On," *Salt Lake Tribune,* May 15, 2000.
245. Matthew Bowers, "Teacher Brings Personal Touch to New VEA Post," *The Virginian-Pilot,* August 1, 2000.
246. The Kamber Group, "An Institution at Risk: An External Communications Review of the National Education Association," January 14, 1997, p. ii.
247. Ibid.
248. Ibid., p. iii.
249. Ibid., p. 33.
250. *The Education Intelligence Agency Communiqué,* October 26, 1998.
251. Mary Mogan Edwards, "School Unions Slam Report by Task Force," *Columbus Dispatch,* April 25, 1997.
252. Roger Alford, "Audit Suggests Cost-Cutting at Columbus Schools," *Columbus Dispatch,* September 10, 1998.
253. Speech to the Conference on Peer Assistance and Review, Columbus, Ohio, May 17, 1998.
254. Tamar Lewin, "An Issue of Teachers Who Fail to Teach," *New York Times,* August 5, 1997.
255. *The Education Intelligence Agency Communiqué,* March 1, 1999.
256. *Peer Assistance and Peer Review: An AFT/NEA Handbook,* September 1998, p. A3.
257. Susan Staub, letter to the editor, *Education Week,* November 11, 1997.
258. Mike Antonucci, "Teacher Peer Review Claims Don't Add Up," Alexis de Tocqueville Institution, December 19, 1997.
259. California Teachers Association, *Bargaining Issues #4,* October 27, 1999.
260. Wayne Johnson, *California Educator,* December 1999.
261. All material in this chapter on NEA charter schools is from Mike Antonucci, "Loving Charter Schools—to Death," Alexis de Tocqueville Institution, May 25, 1999.
262. David Hill, "Labor Pains," *Teacher Magazine,* February 1998.
263. Quoted in Melissa L. Jones, "AEA Charter School Won't Open," *Arizona Republic,* July 10, 1999.
264. "SDTA to Create Charter School," *CTA Action,* June/July 1996.
265. Quoted in Gordon Bonin, "Charter Schools Discussed in Augusta," *Bangor News,* January 6, 2000.
266. *NEA Today,* November 1999.
267. *NEANY Advocate,* September 1999.
268. Sandra Peterson, "Let's Put the Brake on Charters," posted on the Education Minnesota web site.
269. Quoted in Douglas Frantz and Catherine Collins, "Nothing to Celebrate," *Teacher Magazine,* October 1999.
270. Bob Peterson and Michael Charney, "Rethinking Union Strategy a Year After the Failed Merger," *Education Week,* September 8, 1999.
271. Posting on National Education Association, "New Unionism," listserv, June 25, 1999.

272. See for example "Some Schools Working to Limit Homework Burden Facing Students and Their Parents," WABC-TV, New York, December 8, 2000; www.abclocal.go.com/wabc/features/WABC_ourschools_homework.html; "Homework Helpers," NEA Today Online, January 1998, www.nea.org/neatoday/9801/homework.html; "Homework Dreaded—By Parents," by Valerie Strauss, *Washington Post,* March 12, 2002

273. Quoted in Peter Brimelow, "Too Much Homework?" *Forbes,* December 25, 2000.

274. "Recess Is 'In Recess' As Schools Cut Child's Play," *Education Reporter,* October 2001; www.eagleforum.org/educate/2001/oct01/recess.shtml.

275. David W. Kirkpatrick, "Teacher Unions and Collective Bargaining—in Retrospect," *Government Union Review,* Fall 1993; www.schoolreport.com/schoolreport/articles/teacherunionsandcollectivebargaining_9_93.htm.

276. Quoted in Dana DiFilippo, "School Board Accused of Caving," *Cincinnati Enquirer,* January 28, 2000.

277. "Teacher Reality Check, Please," *Chicago Tribune,* July 7, 2000.

278. "Without Merit," *Wall Street Journal,* July 10, 2000.

279. Author Julia E. Koppich, quoted by Jeff Archer, "NEA Delegates Take Hard Line Against Pay for Performance," *Education Week,* July 12, 2000.

280. Ibid.

281. "Teachers Against Reform," *Washington Post,* July 7, 2000.

282. Andrew Rotherham, "Don't Worry, Performance Pay Is Coming," *Chicago Tribune,* July 11, 2000.

283. "NEA Says No to Merit Pay," *New Dem Daily,* July 7, 2000.

284. Quoted in Ann Bradley, "Merger Camps Making Push in Home Stretch," *Education Week,* June 10, 1998.

285. Sam Pizzigati, "The Merger Fails—What Next for Education Unions?" *WorkingUSA,* November–December 1998.

286. Richard Lee Colvin, "Battle Likely over Teacher Seniority in L.A.," *Los Angeles Times,* March 28, 2000.

287. "Negotiating Change," p. 25.

288. Lois Tinson, "This Is Our Chance to Interact," *CTA Action,* September 1995.

289. Ken Ward, "Disunity in the Union," *Las Vegas Review-Journal,* October 28, 1999.

290. *The Education Intelligence Agency Communiqué,* May 13, 2002.

291. Myron Lieberman, *Public Education: An Autopsy* (Cambridge, Mass.: Harvard University Press, 1993) p. 315.

292. Denise Rockwell Woods, speech to the NEA Representative Assembly, July 3, 1994.

293. Dick Morris, *Behind the Oval Office: Winning the Presidency in the Nineties* (New York: Random House, 1997), p. 272.

294. Caroline Minter Hoxby, "Rising Tide," *Education Next,* Winter 2001; www.educationnext.org/20014/68.html.

295. Henry F. Cotton, "Educational Free Agency," *Education Week,* March 24, 1999.

296. E-mail from J. E. Stone, May 18, 2002. See also J. E. Stone, "Value-Added

Assessment: An Accountability Revolution," in Marci Kansoroom and Chester E. Finn, eds., *Better Teachers, Better Schools,* (Washington, D.C.: Thomas B. Fordham Foundation, 1999).

297. Milton Chappell, "Seeking a New Foundation: Legislative and Practical Alternatives to the Current Monopoly Bargaining Model Will Enhance the Viability of Independent Teacher Groups," *Government Union Review,* Vol. 16, No. 3 (Summer 1995).

298. Associated Press, "Despite Law Ending Tenure, Few Teachers Being Replaced," March 15, 2000.

299. Quoted in Jen Sansbury, "Teachers Push Tenure at Local Level," *Atlanta Journal-Constitution,* March 15, 2000.

300. Peter Brimelow, "Europe's Real Problem," *Forbes,* April 2, 2001.

301. Estimate by Edwin S. Rubenstein, assumes minimum wage for 14.9 million fourteen- to seventeen-year-olds currently enrolled in public and private schools.

302. For the interconnections between the organizations seeking accreditation authority over teachers, see "Policy Brief: The Best Teachers: Getting Them, Keeping Them" (Alexandria, Va.: The Foundation Endowment, Spring/ Summer 2001).

303. Quoted in Rebecca Winters, "How to Lure Teachers," *Time,* November 6, 2000.

304. "New Teachers Make Good," *Boston Herald,* January 2, 2001.

305. Ronald A. Wolk, "Alternative Answers," *Teacher Magazine,* January 2001.

306. Vicky Schreiber Dill and Delia Stafford-Johnson, "The Data Is In: What Works in Alternative Teacher Certification Program Design," LoneStar Foundation, January 10, 2001. www.educationnews.org/data_is_in.htm

307. E-mails from Michael Podgursky, April 17, 2002, and April 30, 2002. See also Professor Podgursky's web page, http://web.missouri.edu/~econ4mp/ welcome.htm.

308. Quoted in Anne Ryman, "Frugal Districts Buck Tradition," *Arizona Republic,* June 14, 2000.

309. Quoted in Brian Harmon, "Contracting Jobs to Save Schools $2 Million," *Detroit News,* June 13, 2000.

310. Matt Surman, "Office Temp Service Wants to Recruit Substitute Teachers," *Los Angeles Times,* March 14, 2000.

311. Associated Press, "Public Schools Hiring Privateers to Teach the Slowest," April 19, 1999.

312. Jay Mathews, "Privatizing Title I," *School Administrator,* May 2000.

313. See William W. Cutler III, *Parents and Schools: The 150-Year Struggle for Control in American Education* (Chicago: University of Chicago Press, 2000).

INDEX